colour atlas of
vertebrate anatomy

colour atlas of
vertebrate anatomy

an integrated text and dissection guide

Gillian M King MA DPhil
University Museum and St Hilda's College Oxford

David RN Custance MA PhD MI Biol
Westminster School London

Blackwell Scientific Publications Oxford London Edinburgh Boston Melbourne
Bolsover Press London New York
1982

Distributed in all countries except the USA, Canada and
Japan by Blackwell Scientific Publications Ltd.

Distributed in the USA and Canada by:
Gower Medical Publishing Ltd., Middlesex House,
34–42 Cleveland St., London W1P 5FB, England

Distributed in Japan by:
Nishimura Co. Ltd., 1-754-39, Asahimachi-dori,
Niigata-Shi 951, Japan

ISBN 0-9507676-0-3 (Bolsover Press)
         0-632-01007-X (Blackwell Scientific Publications) .

British Library Cataloguing in Publication Data:
King, G.M.
     Colour atlas of vertebrate anatomy
     1. Vertebrate – Anatomy
     I. Title II. Custance, D.R.N.
     596′.04   QL805

     ISBN 0-9507676-0-3

Project Editor   Marinella M. Nicolson

Design and Illustration   Phil Jones
                           Jeremy J.D. Cort
                           Teresa Foster

Photographic Supervisor   Rosemary Allen

Printed in Hong Kong by Mandarin Offset International
Ltd.

Preface

The purpose of this book is to provide an introduction to comparative vertebrate anatomy for biology undergraduates. The information is presented in the form of colour photographs of step-by-step dissection stages integrated with a text on comparative anatomy. Dissection plays an important part in understanding the anatomy of an animal and this book has been designed to make full use of the wealth of information made available through dissection. The accompanying text aims to outline the evolutionary and functional aspects of the anatomy revealed in the photographs and an additional text gives clear instructions on the execution of the dissections.

The animals dissected in this book have been chosen as representative examples of each of the six classes of vertebrates and in most cases they can be used as a guide to dissection of other vertebrates in the same class. Each of the six chapters deals with one animal and opens with information on the evolutionary history of the class to which it belongs. The comparative anatomy of the vertebrate brain is considered in the final chapter.

Acknowledgements

The authors wish to thank the many people who helped in the preparation of this book. In particular, thanks are due to Prof. Frank Cox and Prof. Barry Cox of King's College London, for their enthusiasm and continued support of the project. We are indebted not only to them but also to Dr. A. Milner (Birkbeck College, London) and Dr. T. S. Kemp (University Museum, Oxford) who both read parts of the manuscript. Any inaccuracies remaining are, of course, our own responsibility. We would also like to thank the cheerful and hardworking production team at Bolsover Press whose encouragement sustained us on several occasions.

G.M. King
D.R.N. Custance

Slide Atlas of Vertebrate Anatomy and Dissection
The slide atlas, which is based on the material in this
book, has been specially designed to provide a high
quality, practical aid to teachers. It is presented as a
number of volumes in which printed material, containing
colour photographs, labelled and captioned drawings
and diagrams, is bound together with wallets holding
35mm slides of all the illustrations in the book.

The 'Slide Atlas of Vertebrate Anatomy and Dissection'
comprises the following six volumes:
Volume 1: Dogfish and Skate (67 slides)
Volume 2: Codling (23 slides)
Volume 3: Frog (29 slides)
Volume 4: Lizard (22 slides)
Volume 5: Pigeon (27 slides)
Volume 6: Rat (35 slides) and Vertebrate Brain (4 slides)

The 'Slide Atlas of Vertebrate Anatomy and Dissection'
is available from:
Bolsover Press,
Middlesex House,
34-42 Cleveland St.
London W1 P 5FB

Contents

Vertebrate phylogeny

The grades of organisation within the vertebrates over geological time (which are illustrated here by blocks of colour) do not necessarily represent natural groups, but they do give an approximation to the evolutionary pathway taken by the vertebrates.

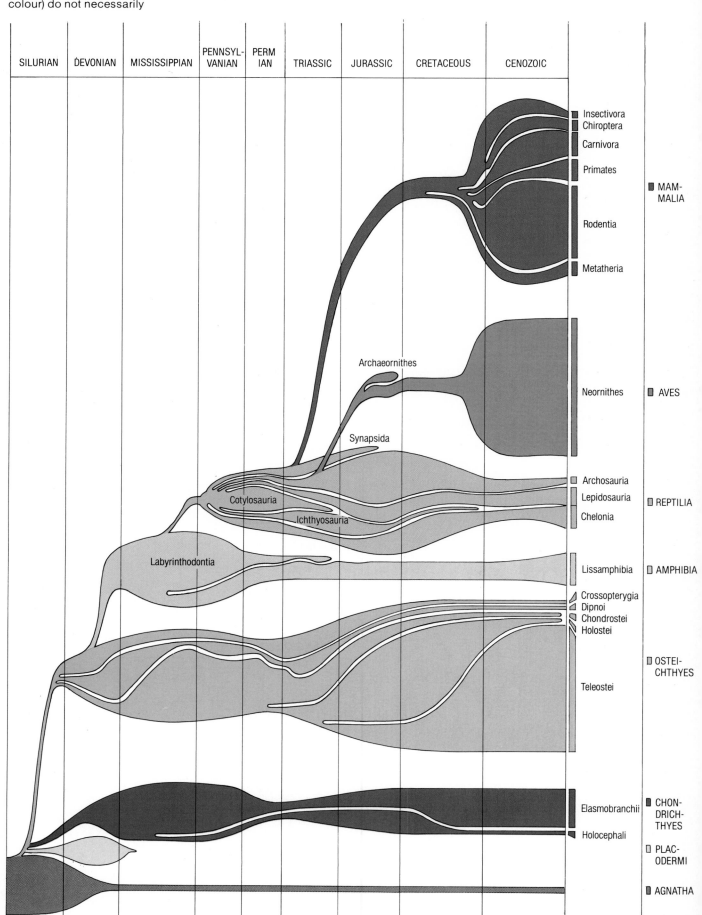

Introduction to dissection technique

In order to produce a good dissection, it is necessary:

- to understand the techniques of dissection and to dissect carefully
- to have available an adequate range of dissection instruments in good condition
- to have an adequate understanding of the basic anatomy of the animal being dissected

The following instruments are the minimum needed, and preferably should be of stainless steel or nickel plated.

1. A pair of blunt forceps, with tips 2-3 mm across.
2. A pair of fine forceps with guide pins, and tips no more than 1 mm across.
3. A pair of large scissors, with blades 4.5 cm long.
4. A pair of small scissors, with blades about 2.5 cm long
5. A handle for disposable scalpel blades, a packet of blades with a straight edge and sharp point, and a packet of blades with a convex edge, all to fit the handle.
6. A blunt probe or 'seeker', either straight or bent.
7. A pair of mounted needles.
8. Something to keep the instruments in, preferably a canvas roll with loops into which they fit.

Much of the skill of dissection is common sense. Before you start a dissection make sure that you have adequate illumination, and that there is enough space for you to rest the weight of your arms on the table whilst dissecting. Also, use a new sharp scalpel blade for each dissection.

If you experiment with ways of making a cut, you will find it much easier to cut in some directions than in others. It is much easier to cut away from yourself or to make a scalpel cut along a line pointing obliquely to your left. Therefore, whenever necessary, turn the dish, or board, so that you can cut in these directions.

When dissecting, begin in an area where there is little danger of damaging the structures you wish to display. Gradually extend your area of dissection outwards from this point. Always cut upwards with your scalpel into the overlying tissues. Never cut down towards the structures. If you do, you will be more likely to damage the organs before you see them. Remember that blood vessels and nerves normally run in connective tissue between blocks of muscle. Dissection is therefore most sensibly carried out by separating the muscles, and cutting through a block of muscle only after it has been fully separated from the surrounding tissue. On completing a stage of dissection, trim back any ragged edges of the tissues you have cut. Pieces of black card can be placed behind nerves and blood vessels in order to display them.

Most systems in most animals are bilaterally symmetrical. It is therefore sensible to attempt one side first. If you make mistakes, carefully note what has happened and then use the knowledge you have gained to make a better dissection on the other side. Use a notebook in which to record reminders of the difficult phases and danger points of the dissection.

Your notebook containing the drawings of your dissections is important as a record of what you, as a scientist, have discovered and observed. Adequate materials and care are the first essentials of a good drawing. Use a reasonably sharp pencil and don't use glossy or lined paper.

The drawing of your dissection should be large enough for the smallest object in it to be clearly and accurately drawn. If one region has smaller, more detailed structures than the remainder, it may be useful to make an additional drawing of this region, noting its relationship to the drawing of the whole dissection.

Techniques which make your drawing easier to understand should be used, for example pencil shading and the use of colour.

Anatomical directions

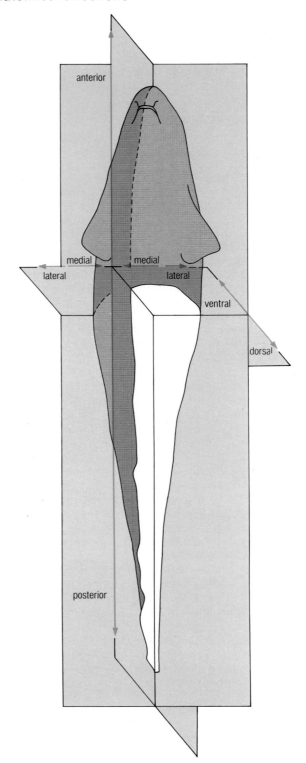

Introduction to vertebrate anatomy

In the following chapters we shall be studying the anatomy of the vertebrates in some detail. However, before we do this, it is important to appreciate that all vertebrates have many features in common and, unlike the invertebrates, their basic anatomy is strikingly consistent throughout the five main groups (fish, amphibians, reptiles, birds and mammals). The following are the features common to most vertebrates:

1. A notochord in the embryo, which usually degenerates in the adult.
2. Gill slits (at least in the embryo).
3. A hollow dorsal nerve cord.
4. A post-anal tail (which is secondarily lost in various forms. e.g. apes and Man).
5. Segmentation of the trunk.
6. A closed circulation in which blood leaves the heart and moves posteriorly in the dorsal blood vessel, returning in a ventral blood vessel. This is opposite to the direction of circulation in the majority of invertebrates.
7. A large degree of cephalisation.
8. A vertebral column, ribs and skull. The possession of cartilage and usually bone.
9. Paired limbs (which may be secondarily lost).
10. Kidneys derived from the embryonic mesoderm.

Vertebrate anatomy is clearly very different from that of the invertebrates. How then, did these vertebrate features evolve? This question has stimulated considerable debate, a full account of which would take us out of the scope of this book. However, it is worth considering briefly the relationship of the vertebrates to their closest living invertebrate relatives, the tunicates and amphioxus. The vertebrates, tunicates and amphioxus all belong to the phylum Chordata, which is often divided into four sub-phyla. These are the Vertebrata (vertebrates), Cephalochordata (amphioxus), Urochordata (tunicates, or sea squirts) and the Hemichordata (acorn worms), although some authorities would remove Hemichordata from the chordates. They all share some of the features listed above, and it is these shared features which are clues to the invertebrate origins of the vertebrates.

At a first glance, most tunicates bear no resemblance to the vertebrates because the adults are barrel-shaped, filter feeders with only two external structures – an inhalent opening at the top and an exhalent opening at the side. The only vertebrate feature which they possess is found internally – the highly developed pharyngeal gill apparatus (fig. I). Thus it seems unlikely that the tunicates were ancestral to the vertebrates. However, some tunicates (the Ascidiacea) have a free-swimming tadpole-like larval form which possesses several vertebrate characteristics (fig. II). The tail is a swimming organ, with a notochord, on either side of which muscle cells are found. The notochord, like the vertebral column in fish, acts as an incompressible elastic rod which prevents the body shortening when the muscles contract. Dorsal to the notochord is a hollow nerve tube which shows the rudiments of cephalisation – it is swollen at the anterior end and contains two sense organs.

The sessile, filter feeding tunicates are quite different from what is considered to be the ancestral vertebrate form. Vertebrates are highly mobile animals, and, consequently, it was thought that the ancestral vertebrate (fig. III) was a

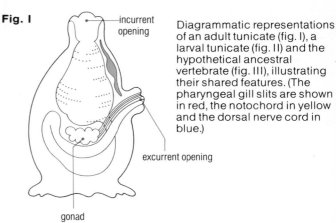

Fig. I

incurrent opening

excurrent opening

gonad

Fig. II

brain

excurrent opening

incurrent opening   heart

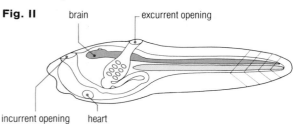

Diagrammatic representations of an adult tunicate (fig. I), a larval tunicate (fig. II) and the hypothetical ancestral vertebrate (fig. III), illustrating their shared features. (The pharyngeal gill slits are shown in red, the notochord in yellow and the dorsal nerve cord in blue.)

Fig. III

skull   vertebrae   dorsal blood vessel   kidney

brain

gonad

mouth

anus

heart

ventral blood vessel

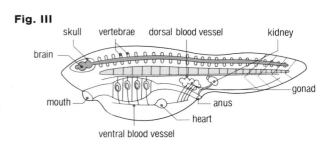

small, actively swimming animal which became larger and more complex and finally gave rise to the earliest fishes. However, the closest living invertebrate relatives of the vertebrates are inactive, often sessile, filter feeders. Where, then, did the vertebrates come from? Two evolutionary pathways have been postulated. If the chordate ancestor of the vertebrates was active and free-swimming, the tunicates must represent a side-branch of vertebrate evolution. The free-swimming ancestor would have adapted to a sessile filter feeding existence which would have involved the progressive loss of those features necessary for an active life:

Free-swimming chordate ancestor

increasing activity and size

decreasing activity

vertebrate

sessile adult tunicate

larva

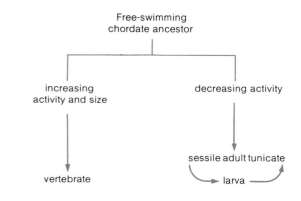

Alternatively, the ancestor may have resembled an adult tunicate which had an active larval stage. Neoteny, the process by which larval features are retained in the adult, would have given rise to an animal with a notochord and segmental muscle blocks forming a post-anal tail, the structures necessary for fish-like locomotion. Sensory structures at the anterior end are a pre-requisite of an active, bilaterally symmetrical animal. The consequent

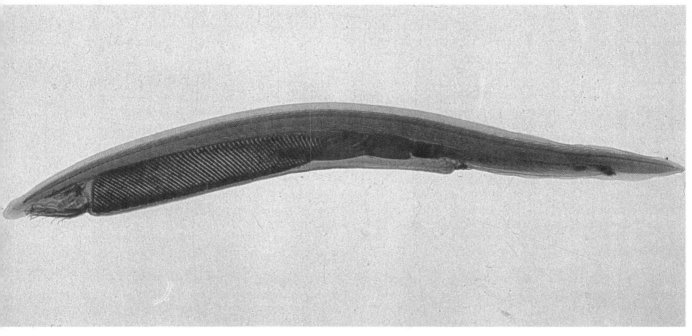

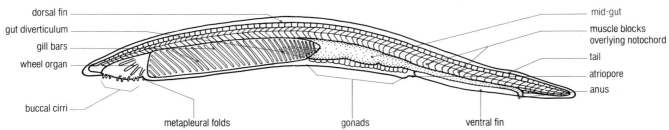

dorsal fin — mid-gut

gut diverticulum — muscle blocks
overlying notochord

gill bars — tail

wheel organ — atriopore

— anus

buccal cirri —

metapleural folds — gonads — ventral fin

Fig. IV A stained, mounted
specimen of amphioxus, x 15.

swelling of the nerve cord for processing sensory information would be the first stage of brain development and cephalisation. The animal would probably be a filter feeder with well-developed pharyngeal gill slits. The description above fits that of the expected ancestral vertebrate very closely:

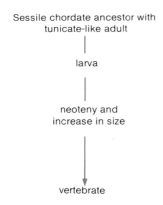

Sessile chordate ancestor with
tunicate-like adult

↓

larva

↓

neoteny and
increase in size

↓

vertebrate

The body plan of amphioxus (fig. IV) is very similar to that shown in fig. III. It resembles a fish in its shape and locomotion. It has a post-anal tail with a notochord and segmental muscle blocks on each side of the body. There is a dorsal hollow nerve cord and a circulatory system characteristic of the vertebrates. Its pharynx contains many gill slits which are strengthened by cartilage-like material. The features it shares with the vertebrates have led many to believe that amphioxus is the nearest living invertebrate relative of the vertebrates.

However, amphioxus is not considered to be a vertebrate for several reasons. It has neither paired fins nor limbs, and lacks the vertebrae, ribs and skull typical of the

vertebrate skeleton. In addition, cephalisation is very poorly developed. There are some other features of amphioxus which would not be expected in an early vertebrate. The excretory structures, the solenocytes, are of ectodermal origin, unlike those of vertebrates which are of mesodermal origin. The notochord, unlike that of a vertebrate, extends to the extreme tip of the animal's front end. In fact even its locomotion and feeding, when examined closely, are atypical of vertebrates. Its feeding system is ciliary powered and not muscle powered. Amphioxus does not exhibit the mobility and active food-finding behaviour expected in vertebrates despite its notochord and serially arranged myotomes. It spends most of the time buried in sand.

Some workers believe that such specialisations prevent amphioxus from being placed on the direct evolutionary line to the vertebrates. They consider amphioxus to be a specialised and modified descendant of the kind of animal that was ancestral to the vertebrates – a descendant that took to burrowing. Other workers see amphioxus as an ancestral vertebrate form, arguing that an increase in body size and a greater degree of activity would result in vertebrate features such as cephalisation, muscle powered filter feeding and the vertebrate kidney.

The most popular view is that amphioxus is not a vertebrate but that it is a specialized descendant of the chordate ancestor of the vertebrates. However, it is useful to look closely at amphioxus because it possesses a body plan which approximates to that of the expected ancestral vertebrate. The concept of an ancestral vertebrate plan is an essential part of the study of comparative anatomy and frequent references to it will be made in the following chapters.

The features of amphioxus can be clearly seen in a stained mounted specimen (see fig. IV). The following features should be noted: streamlining of the body; the V-shaped muscle blocks; the dorsal and ventral fins; and, running forward on either side of the body, the metapleural folds. A chamber called the oral hood is found anterior to the metapleural folds. Deep within this chamber is the wheel organ and the mouth. Water enters the oral hood in a current generated by the cilia on the gill bars. It leaves through the gill slits in the pharynx, which open into the atrium and then to the outside through a pore called the atriopore. The wheel organ is an adaptation to filter feeding. It consists of ciliated grooves which catch particles of food that fall out of the main current of water. In the pharynx, more particles are trapped by mucus strings. The system is typical of filter feeding mechanisms. It employs cilia, mucus, and involves both intracellular and extracellular digestion.

One of the organs in the pharynx (fig. V), responsible for producing mucus, is the endostyle. It has been found that radioactive iodine is concentrated by certain cells of the endostyle. A similar situation is found in the larval stage of the lamprey which is also a filter feeder with an endostyle. At metamorphosis specific cells within the endostyle give rise to thyroid tissue, which would suggest that this organ is a homologue of the thyroid tissue in vertebrates.

The gills do not take part in respiration; their only function is to provide a filter feeding structure. Oxygen is mostly absorbed through the body wall.

The notochord, and the hollow nerve cord lying dorsal to it should be noted. There is no expanded brain. Dorsal and ventral nerve roots leave the nerve cord on either side of the body. Unlike those in most vertebrates, the roots remain separate. The ventral roots run to the myotomes, while the dorsal roots run between the myotomes, carrying sensory and motor fibres to the non-segmental muscles. The dorsal and ventral roots therefore alternate in position, (see p. 1.21)

A transverse section through the pharynx (fig. V) shows the coelomic spaces. These are found lateral to the gill bars, ventral to the endostyle, lateral to the gonads and around the mid-gut caecum. The gill coelomic spaces contain the solenocytes (or flame cells).

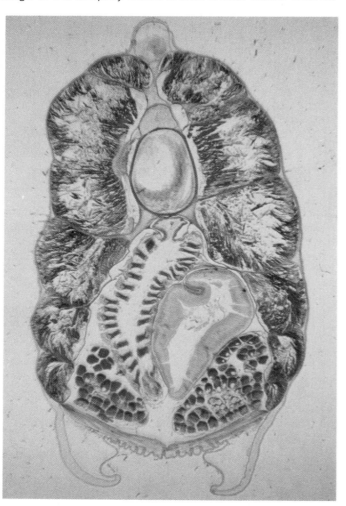

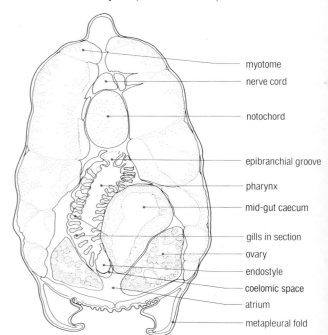

myotome
nerve cord
notochord
epibranchial groove
pharynx
mid-gut caecum
gills in section
ovary
endostyle
coelomic space
atrium
metapleural fold

Fig. V A transverse section of a specimen of amphioxus, x 30.

1 The Dogfish

Chondrichthyes
Elasmobranchii
Selachii
Scyliorhinus canicula

The Skate

Chondrichthyes
Elasmobranchii
Batoidea
Raia clavata

Introduction

The dogfish and skate belong to the class Chondrichthyes, the cartilaginous fish. Although the dogfish is a highly specialised animal its anatomy resembles the hypothetical ancestral condition more closely than that of the skate and most other vertebrates. Consequently, this chapter will use the dogfish to illustrate both the hypothetical ancestral vertebrate condition and chondrichthyean characteristics. An additional dissection of the cranial nerves in the skate is shown in figs. 1.61 – 1.67. This is because the relationship between the brain and cranial nerves is most easily illustrated in this animal.

Chondrichthyans are characterised by an internal skeleton of cartilage. Although the cartilage may contain calcium carbonate to strengthen it, it never contains true bone. They lack an air bladder, which the osteichthyans possess (described later). Fertilisation is internal in all cartilaginous fish; the internal edge of the pelvic fin is modified in the male to form a clasper, which is a special organ for transmitting sperm from male to female. A spiral valve is present in the intestine which is absent from most of the higher bony fish. These features are described in greater detail as they are revealed in the dissection later.

The dogfish is a shark. It belongs to one of the two large groups of cartilaginous fish, the subclass Elasmobranchii, which includes sharks, skates and rays. Most sharks are streamlined pelagic predators. Skates and rays are dorsoventrally flattened for a bottom-dwelling existence. The other large group, the Holocephali, includes the bizarre rabbit-fish, or chimaeras, which have characteristic long whip-like tails, large eyes, a rabbit-like snout and pavement-like tooth-plates which are used to crush hard food such as molluscs.

The dogfish is a 'modern' shark. It is thought that, during evolution, sharks have passed through three organisational levels, culminating in the 'modern' shark. The first sharks are found in Middle Devonian deposits. They were pelagic predators, on the whole, and were adapted to tearing and seizing of prey. The jaws were long and quite firmly attached to the braincase. The body was rather stiff and the symmetrical tail was used for propulsion of the body, but did not produce much lift to counteract the tendency of the body to sink. The fins were also rather stiff so that the body was not particularly manoeuvrable.

The second organisational level again contained pelagic predators. The tail was asymmetrical and, together with more mobile pectoral fins, helped to counteract the tendency of the shark to sink. In addition, there was a radiation of bottom-feeders with crushing dentitions.

The third, or 'modern', level of sharks began in the Jurassic. Here, the vertebral column is strengthened in order to act as a firm base for muscle attachment and as a shock absorber. The jaws are shortened to produce a bigger bite force; and the snout is extended, presumably to accommodate the elaborate olfactory apparatus. This results in the characteristic ventral mouth. The upper jaw is attached much more loosely to the braincase through the hyomandibular bone, and protrusion of the jaws is possible (see p. 1.33). The 'modern' dentition permits shearing and sawing of food, but has been adapted in various species, to sucking, grasping, crushing, gouging and filtering. Dogfish are 'modern' sharks and are therefore placed in the order Selachii. The dogfish family contains some of the smaller, off-shore sharks. They are streamlined and adapted to efficient swimming and predatory feeding.

1.1

Skeleton

The chondrichthyan skeleton, unlike that of other vertebrates, contains no bone. All the individual elements are made of cartilage. This raises a question about the evolutionary history of the cartilaginous skeleton. Is it primitive and ancestral to the bony skeleton; or is it a secondary state, in that chondrichthyeans once had bone, which has since been lost? We know that the earliest vertebrates already possessed bone and that fossils of bony fish are found somewhat earlier in the fossil record than those of cartilaginous fish. This would suggest that the ancestors of cartilaginous fish were bony. However, there are workers who point out that cartilage does not fossilise well and it is therefore unlikely that a cartilaginous ancestor would be found in the fossil record. Therefore, the absence of chondrichthyan fossils earlier than osteichthyan ones is negative evidence. The problem is compounded by the lack of knowledge about the ancestors of both bony and cartilaginous fish.

The skeleton can be divided into the axial skeleton (vertebral column and ribs) and the appendicular skeleton (limbs, or fins, and the girdles attaching them to the vertebral column). The vertebral column consists of many individual vertebrae in both bony and cartilaginous vertebrates. Each vertebra is composed of a spool-shaped centrum which, in dogfish and most bony fish, is concave at both ends (amphicoelous), and a dorsal projection surrounding the nerve cord, the neural arch.

In cartilaginous fish extra elements are present between the neural arches, filling in the gaps and surrounding the nerve cord in a continuous sheath of cartilage (see fig. 1.2). The individual vertebrae are not particularly firmly attached to their neighbours. There are, for example, no accessory articulating surfaces as seen in land animals. This is because in water the vertebral column does not need to bear the weight of the animal. Instead it must resist the change in length that tends to occur when the fish's muscle blocks contract. In this context it performs the same function as the notochord in amphioxus.

Little of the musculature is attached directly to the vertebral column. Successive muscle blocks are separated by sheets of connective tissue called myocommata and it is to these that the muscles are

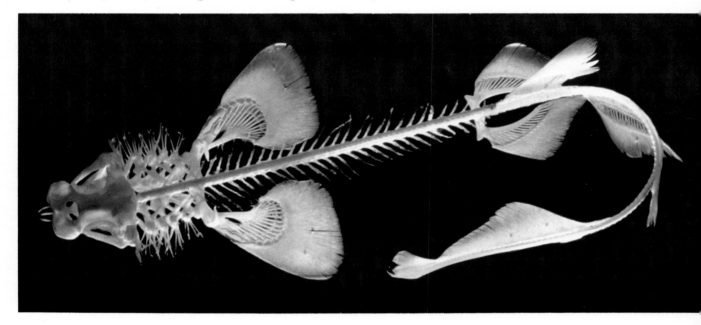

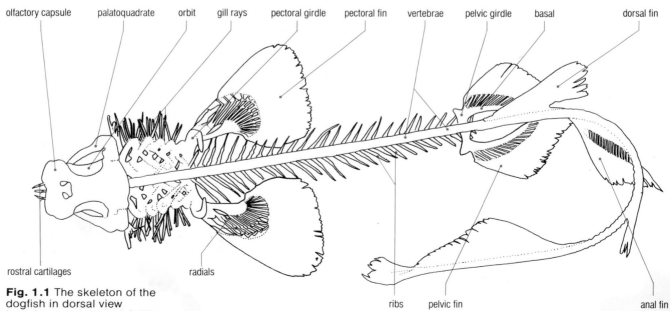

olfactory capsule · palatoquadrate · orbit · gill rays · pectoral girdle · pectoral fin · vertebrae · pelvic girdle · basal · dorsal fin

rostral cartilages · radials

ribs · pelvic fin · anal fin

Fig. 1.1 The skeleton of the dogfish in dorsal view (specimen courtesy of Griffin and George Ltd).

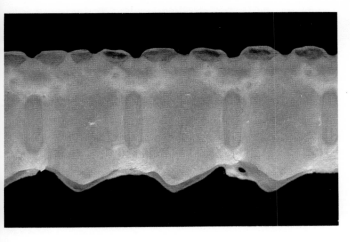

Fig. 1.2 Dogfish vertebrae in left lateral view

foramen for dorsal nerve root
foramen for ventral nerve root
intercalary plate
supradorsal cartilage

attached. Ribs occur in the myocommata and these are attached to the vertebral column, forming the necessary mechanical link between it and the musculature. Each muscle segment is divided into ventral and dorsal halves by a connective tissue septum running right along the body. Ventral ribs are found where the myocommata reach the wall of the coelom ventrally. Towards the tail of the fish the ventral ribs of each side become closer to each other until they eventually fuse to form the V-shaped haemal arch. This is the only regional variation seen in the vertebrae. In cartilaginous fish only short ribs, probably of the ventral series, are present. Dorsal ribs are found in bony fish, as seen later (see fig. 2.3).

The paired fins articulate with the fin girdles. The pectoral girdle is attached to the vertebral column by muscles and the pelvic girdle is embedded in the ventral body wall.

The movement of the tail is the main source of propulsion in most fish. In order to create a greater surface area to move against the water, the tail is broadened out into a fan shape by many dermal fin-rays which articulate with the neural and haemal arches of the tail vertebrae. Elasmobranchs have an asymmetrical (heterocercal) tail where the end of the vertebral column tilts upwards and the major part of the tail membrane is below the column (see fig. 1.3). The asymmetrical tail produces lift which is necessary to prevent the fish sinking. The pectoral fins also produce lift and, consequently, their form approximates to that of an aerofoil. This is quite different from the bony fish, as seen in the codling later (p. 2.4).

Early vertebrates were covered extensively with dermal bone, and the dermal denticles are thought to be the last remnants of this covering. They consist of a bone-like base containing a complex pulp cavity, covered by a mass of dentine and capped by a thin layer of enamel-like material (see fig. 1.4).

Fig. 1.4 Transverse section through the skin of a dogfish showing a placoid scale, x 50.

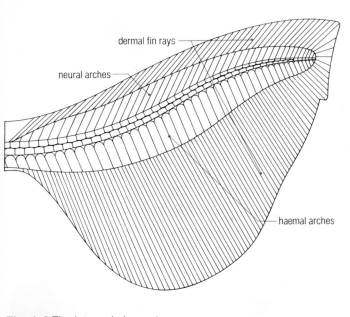

dermal fin rays
neural arches
haemal arches

Fig. 1.3 The internal elements of the elasmobranch tail.

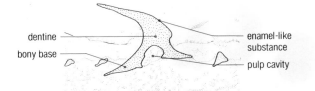

dentine
bony base
enamel-like substance
pulp cavity

Abdominal cavity

The abdominal organs lie in a cavity called the coelom. In an embryo the coelom develops from splits in the mesodermal tissue, which is one of the three embryonic layers. The mesoderm extends down the flanks of the animal's body either side of the midline. Dorsally, the mesoderm is segmented into somites which will eventually produce the segmental skeletal muscle (myotomes), kidneys and gonads. Ventrally, the mesoderm is not segmented. It is termed lateral plate mesoderm and it is here that the coelom forms. The tissue either side of the coelom will produce various structures: that nearest the axis of the body will produce the outer covering of the digestive tract; the mesoderm nearer the periphery of the body will produce non-segmental muscle such as that associated with the gut, throat and jaws.

The earliest vertebrates were probably filter feeders. This method of feeding does not require a stomach since it utilises a continuous stream of particulate food. Elasmobranchs feed on much larger pieces of food which are not broken down much in the mouth. A stomach, therefore, serves as a storage place and also initiates mechanical and enzymatic digestion.

In all vertebrates, the liver is an important metabolic and storage site. Some glycogen is stored in the elasmobranch liver but the majority of the stored material is oil. Some forms of this oil can contain up to 90% of a hydrocarbon called squalene which has a low specific gravity of 0.86. When it is stored in large quantities it lowers the overall density of the shark. In order to achieve neutral buoyancy the correct amount of squalene must always be present. This is done by carefully regulating the metabolism of fat compounds in association with that of carbohydrates and proteins. How this regulation is controlled is not understood.

The gall bladder is responsible for storing bile which reduces fats to a small particle size. A carnivorous diet would contain significant quantities of fat and, consequently, carnivores like the dogfish usually have well-developed gall bladders (see fig. 1.9).

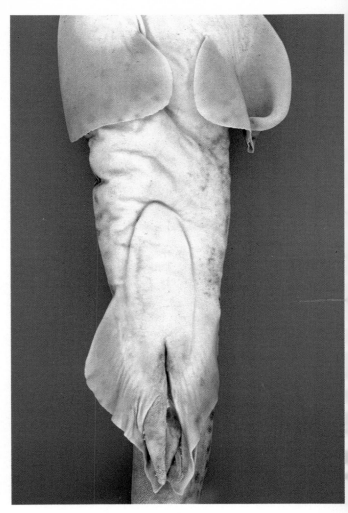

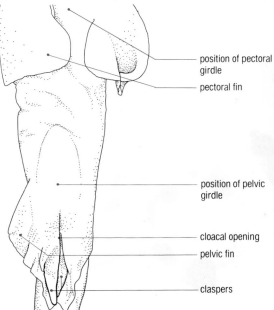

position of pectoral girdle

pectoral fin

position of pelvic girdle

cloacal opening

pelvic fin

claspers

Fig. 1.5 Ventral abdominal view – animal prepared for dissection

● Peg out the dogfish, ventral surface uppermost.

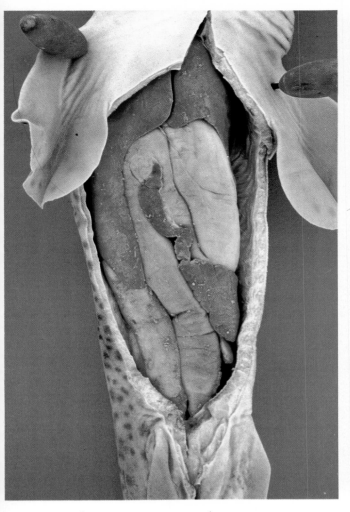

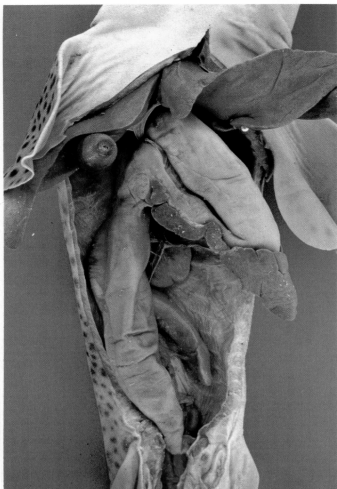

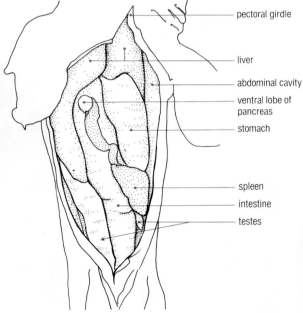

pectoral girdle

liver

abdominal cavity

ventral lobe of pancreas

stomach

spleen

intestine

testes

liver

hepatic portal vein

posterior intestinal vein

right testis

anterior mesenteric artery

intestine

rectum

rectal gland

cut pelvic girdle

cardiac region of stomach

ventral lobe of pancreas

pyloric region of stomach

lienogastric vein

spleen

dorsal lobe of pancreas

left testis

cloaca

Fig. 1.6 Abdominal cavity – 1st dissection stage

● Open the abdomen by making a median incision along the ventral surface from the cloaca to the pectoral girdle. Cut through the pelvic girdle to expose the cloaca. Take care not to damage the underlying gut and liver.

● Cut back the body wall on each side to reveal the gut, liver, spleen and testes.

Fig. 1.7 Abdominal cavity – 2nd dissection stage

● Expose the hepatic portal vein by drawing the liver lobes forward. Take care not to damage these delicate structures.

● Gently separate the cardiac and pyloric regions of the stomach.

● Displace the intestine to the animal's right side to reveal the pancreas. Take care not to damage the underlying testes.

1.5

Abdominal veins

We can gain some idea of the early vertebrate organisation of the venous system from fig. 1.8. There appear to be three basic systems.

1. The hepatic portal and hepatic veins.
2. The cardinal veins, dorsal to the coelom. These carry blood from the head and the dorsal part of the body to the heart.
3. The abdominal veins which drain the ventral part of the body.

In the lung-bearing vertebrate, a fourth system, the pulmonary circulation, must be added.

The prominent hepatic portal vein can be seen in fig. 1.9, running from the intestine to the liver. This vein carries newly absorbed nutrients to the liver for detoxification or storage. Its presence means that an additional capillary bed is introduced into the blood circulation which serves the digestive system. This leads to a reduction in the pressure of the blood, but this disadvantage is more than compensated for by the important monitoring activities of the liver. The hepatic vein is a median vein, which empties into the sinus venosus of the heart. It undergoes modification in lungfish and in all tetrapods.

The cardinal veins can be divided into a posterior pair and an anterior pair. The posterior pair runs forward along the trunk either side of the aorta towards the heart. The anterior pair runs backwards from the head to meet the posterior cardinals. From this junction, a common cardinal vein runs to the sinus venosus of the heart. This pattern is found in the dogfish and other elasmobranchs, but it is modified in all other jawed vertebrates.

A feature of the elasmobranch circulation, not thought to represent the ancestral condition, is the renal portal vein. Blood from the tail and posterior body does not flow straight to the heart in the posterior cardinal but is diverted via the renal portal vein into an additional network of capillaries around the kidney. New vessels take the blood away from the kidney back into the posterior cardinal and to the heart. The reason for this diversion is not understood.

Paired abdominal veins are present in elasmobranchs. They drain blood from the lower part of the trunk musculature, and from the pelvic and pectoral fins. The inferior jugular sinus, found in the ventral part of the head end of the animal, performs the same function as the abdominal vein.

The intestine (fig. 1.10) contains a spiral valve not found in most bony fish. It is thought that the valve slows down the passage of food and provides a bigger surface area for digestion. In a predaceous animal feeding intermittently on large items, this system would ensure that maximum nutrients are obtained from the food and that the nutrient flow into the blood stream is even.

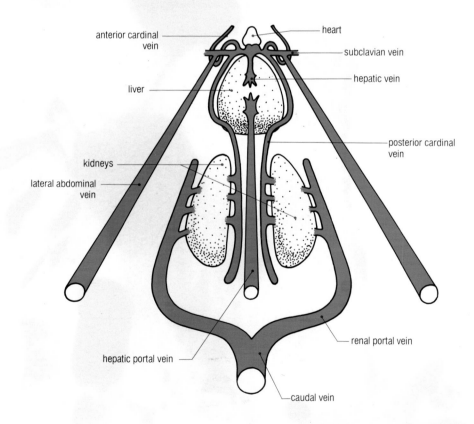

Fig. 1.8 The major veins of a dogfish in ventral view.

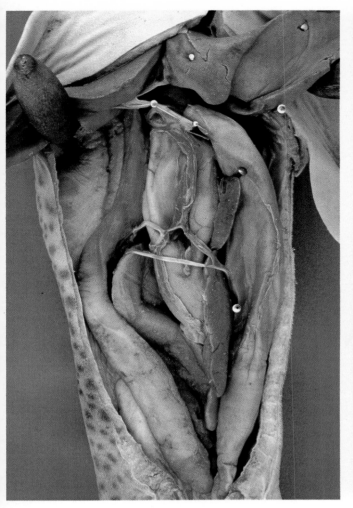

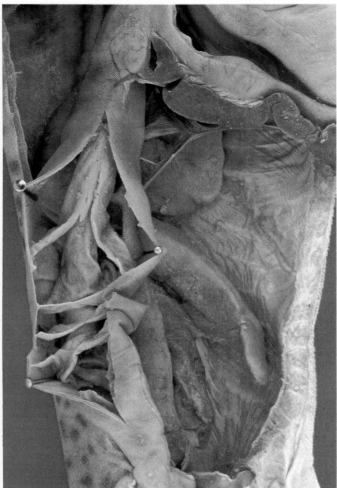

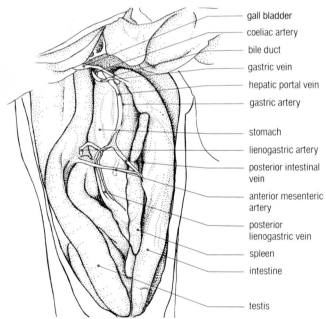

	gall bladder
	coeliac artery
	bile duct
	gastric vein
	hepatic portal vein
	gastric artery
	stomach
	lienogastric artery
	posterior intestinal vein
	anterior mesenteric artery
	posterior lienogastric vein
	spleen
	intestine
	testis

	ventral lobe of pancreas
	intestine
	pyloric region of stomach
	spleen
	hepatic portal vein
	lienogastric vein
	posterior intestinal vein
	anterior mesenteric artery
	dorsal lobe of pancreas
	intestinal folds of spiral valve
	rectum

**Fig. 1.9 Abdominal veins –
1st dissection stage**

● Expose the mesentery on the dorsal surface of the intestine by turning the stomach and intestine over to the animal's left side.

● Clear the mesentery from its attachment to the intestine in order to show the hepatic portal vein and its branches, and the coeliac, anterior mesenteric and lienogastric arteries.

**Fig. 1.10 Abdominal veins –
2nd dissection stage**

● Turn the stomach and intestine back to their original position. Slit the intestine ventrally along its length, from the rectum towards the pancreas, to show the spiral valve.

● Wash out the contents of the intestine and pin out the walls of the valve to show the intestinal folds.

Male urinogenital system

The urinogenital system of the dogfish retains some features of the postulated ancestral vertebrate plan. This plan can best be deduced by looking at the development of the system in a vertebrate embryo. Here one can see the interaction of the kidneys and gonads which arise in the embryo from the segmented mesoderm.

It is thought that in the ancestral vertebrate each segment of the mesoderm produced one nephric unit, or nephron. This would result in a row of nephrons, segmentally arranged down the side of the body. In the embryo the development of the nephrons begins at the head end and continues posteriorly, so that the oldest nephrons are those found anteriorly. The nephrons cannot open directly to the

Fig. 1.11 Diagrams of the anterior part of the trunk of an embryo (skin removed) to show the development of the kidney tubules and archinephric duct. a, b and c are successive stages.

exterior since they are obstructed by blocks of myotomal muscle. A longitudinal duct forms, connecting all the nephrons and emptying into the cloaca. This is the archinephric duct, sometimes referred to as the Wolffian duct (see fig. 1.11). Such an arrangement might have occurred in the ancestral vertebrate but it is found in very few living vertebrates. Instead, the oldest (anterior) part of the row of nephrons degenerates. Nephrons in the more posterior part of the row proliferate so that there may be more than one per segment. This has happened in the elasmobranchs. In fact, the kidney tubules are concentrated only in the most posterior part of the row. The reason for this seems to be that the testis has become associated with the anterior part of the row (fig. 1.12). It has taken over the tubules to transport sperm to the archinephric duct (or vas deferens) and, thence, out of the body. The excretory part of the kidney is drained partly by the archinephric duct and partly by a new structure, the urinary duct. In females, the ovary never becomes associated with the nephrons in this way. It develops a new duct, the oviduct, to transport eggs, and the anterior end of the row degenerates completely.

The elasmobranch kidney consists of many kidney tubules which bear well-developed renal corpuscles and extensive convoluted tubules.

The renal corpuscle consists of the glomerulus (a knot of arterial capillaries) and the Bowman's capsule. The blood passes through the glomerulus at a fairly high pressure, and ions and small molecules, like water and glucose, are filtered out of the glomerular blood and collected in the Bowman's capsule. From here they pass into the kidney tubule. There is a rough correlation between the size of the renal corpuscle and the amount of filtrate produced. The well-developed corpuscles of the elasmobranch produce a large amount of filtrate and therefore dispose of a lot of water. This situation would be expected in an animal in which the body tissues are hypertonic to their environment. However, elasmobranch body tissues are hypotonic to the environment and therefore one would expect the renal corpuscles to be small and produce little filtrate. In fact, elasmobranchs do not lose water passively to the environment because the total osmotic pressure of the blood is higher than that of the surrounding water. This is due to the retention of large quantities of urea which is concentrated from the urine by the kidney tubule.

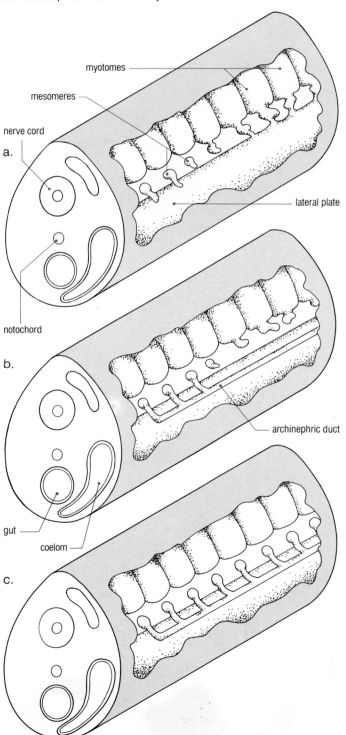

a.

myotomes

mesomeres

nerve cord

lateral plate

notochord

b.

archinephric duct

gut

coelom

c.

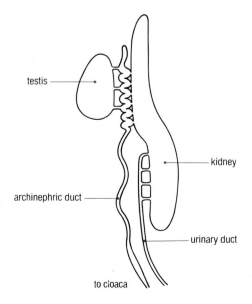

testis

kidney

archinephric duct

urinary duct

to cloaca

Fig. 1.12 A diagram of the male elasmobranch urinogenital system.

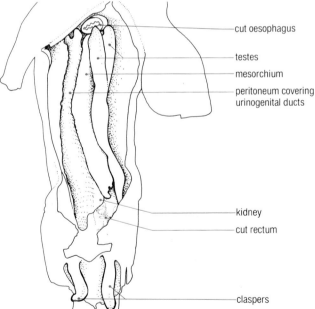

cut oesophagus

testes

mesorchium

peritoneum covering
urinogenital ducts

kidney

cut rectum

claspers

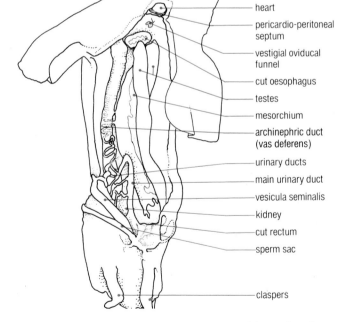

heart

pericardio-peritoneal
septum

vestigial oviducal
funnel

cut oesophagus

testes

mesorchium

archinephric duct
(vas deferens)

urinary ducts

main urinary duct

vesicula seminalis

kidney

cut rectum

sperm sac

claspers

**Fig. 1.13 Male urinogenital
system – 1st dissection
stage**

● Remove the intestine by
cutting posteriorly through the
rectum close to the rectal
gland, and anteriorly through
the oesophagus. Cut the
mesentery, taking care not to
damage the delicate
mesorchium holding the
testes in place. This will free
the gut so that it can be
removed.

● Draw the liver lobes forward
so that they can be removed
by cutting through their
anterior attachments.

● Expose the peritoneum,
which covers the urinogenital
ducts and kidney, by pulling
the right testis over to the
animal's left side.

**Fig. 1.14 Male urinogenital
system – 2nd dissection
stage**

● Carefully strip the
peritoneum from the surface
of the urinogenital ducts.

● Cut the anterior wall of the
abdominal cavity away, along
with the posterior and ventral
surfaces of the pericardium.

● Expose the vesicula
seminalis and the sperm sac

lying on top of the main urinary
duct, by removing the
peritoneum, posteriorly.

● Gently separate the sperm
sac and vesicula seminalis
and displace to the animal's
right side.

● Displace the main urinary
duct and its branches to the
left, and trace the connection
of the reproductive and
urinary systems to the
urinogenital sinus.

Female urinogenital system

In the female dogfish, unlike the male, the gonads do not become associated with the nephrons. The ovary develops a new duct, the oviduct, to transport eggs and the anterior end of the row degenerates completely (fig. 1.15).

Eggs at various stages of development are found in the ovary of a mature female. Fully developed eggs at ovulation may measure 2cm in diameter and contain a large amount of yolk. After ovulation, the eggs enter the oviduct where they acquire a thin, horny shell secreted by the shell gland (nidamental gland).

The mode of development of the embryos varies in different elasmobranchs. The egg may lose contact with the mother and pass to the exterior, surrounded by its horny egg-case. The enclosed embryo is nourished by yolk and the young hatch as free-swimming miniature adults. This happens in the dogfish and the egg-capsules are the familiar 'mermaid's purses' which can be found stranded on beaches (see fig. 1.16). Alternatively, the shell may be thin, membranous and delicate. In this case the egg remains in the swollen lower end of the uterus, the ovisac, and soon loses its temporary shell. However, it still feeds on its yolk supply and so is nutritionally independent of the mother. This kind of development occurs in the nurse shark. In other sharks, the shell gland is much reduced and the embryo is retained within the uterus and nourished by the mother. An umbilical cord develops at the tip of which is the yolk sac. The latter branches to form a 'yolk-sac placenta' in direct contact with the walls of the uterus from which it receives its nutrients. This kind of development is seen in *Mustelus laevis*.

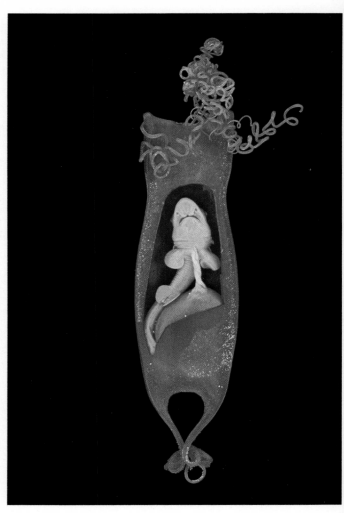

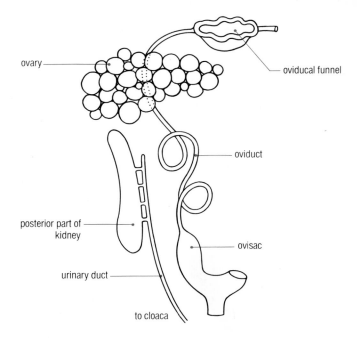

Fig. 1.15 A diagram of the female elasmobranch urinogenital system.

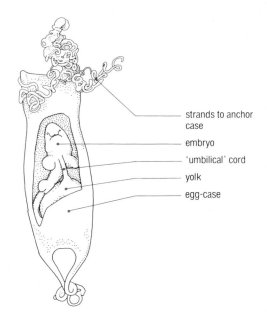

Fig. 1.16 Egg capsule of the dogfish dissected to show the developing embryo.

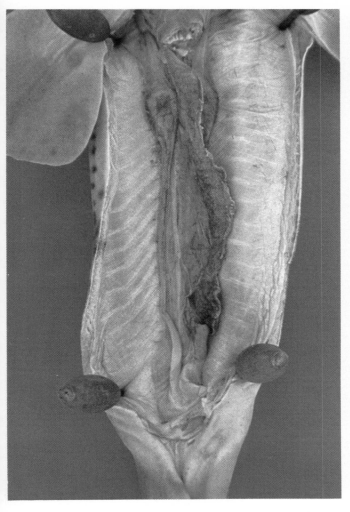

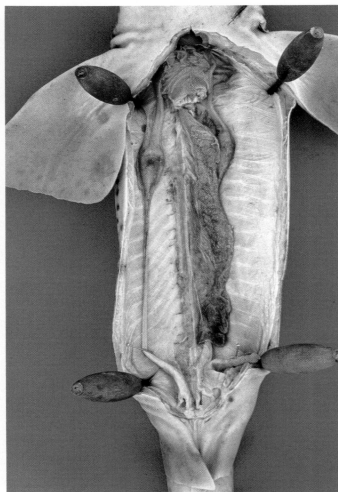

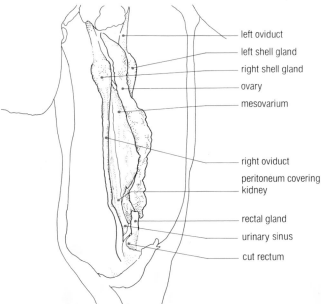

left oviduct

left shell gland

right shell gland

ovary

mesovarium

right oviduct

peritoneum covering kidney

rectal gland

urinary sinus

cut rectum

heart

oviducal funnel

left oviduct

left shell gland

right shell gland

posterior cardinal sinus

dorsal aorta

right oviduct

ovary

kidney

urinary ducts

urinary sinus

cut edges of urinary sinus

Fig. 1.17 Female urinogenital system – 1st. dissection stage

● Remove the intestine and liver lobes as described in fig. 1.13.

● Displace the ovary across the left side of the abdominal cavity in order to reveal the underlying peritoneum covering the urinary sinus and the kidney on the right side. Note the granular appearance of the ovary due to the inclusion of eggs.

Fig. 1.18 Female urinogenital system – 2nd. dissection stage

● Cut away the anterior end of the abdominal cavity in order to display the oviducal funnels.

● Carefully remove the peritoneum from the surface of the kidney to show the urinary ducts and the urinary sinus, which is opened to trace its path to the cloaca. Take care not to damage the posterior cardinal sinus when removing the peritoneum covering the kidney.

● Displace the right oviduct and shell gland laterally.

Branchial musculature

Water is drawn over the gills using both suction and force pumping (see fig. 1.19). This system can be compared with that of the teleost described later. Changes in the pressure of the oro-branchial cavity (mouth and pharynx) and the para-branchial (gill) cavity are brought about by volume changes. This is achieved by the action of the head-and throat muscles. The mouth is opened and the gill slits closed while the volume of the oro-branchial and para-branchial cavities is increased. Water is sucked in. This is a passive action which occurs as a result of relaxation of the superficial constrictor muscles and elastic recoil of the gill arch skeleton. The superficial constrictor muscles are a band of muscles which run around the head region dorsally, laterally and ventrally. When they contract they reduce the volume of the oro-branchial cavity thus increasing the pressure and forcing water out into the para-branchial cavities. Contraction of the septal constrictor muscles in the gills (fig. 1.23) increases the water pressure in the para-branchial cavities thus forcing water out through the primary gill lamellae; the mouth must be closed in order to accomplish this.

It was once thought that the ventral branchial muscles such as the coraco-hyal and coraco-mandibular (figs. 1.22 and 1.25) were important in respiratory movements. However this does not seem to be the case; these muscles are only used in very rapid ventilation, or when biting. They pull the lower jaw and ventral part of the branchial skeleton downwards and backwards.

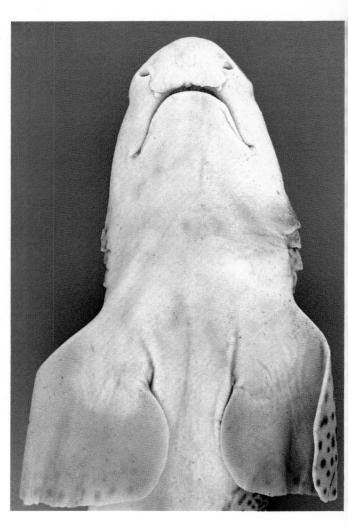

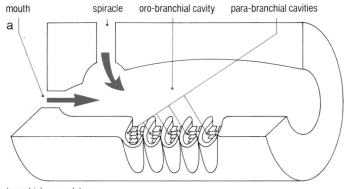

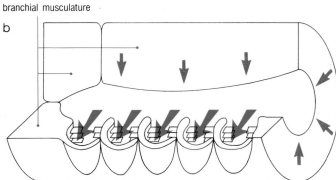

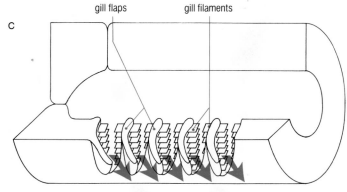

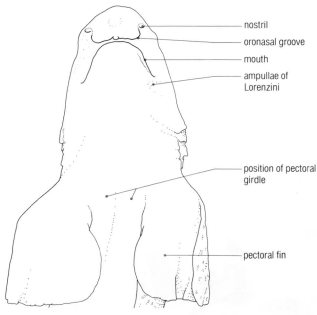

Fig. 1.20 Ventral cranial view – animal prepared for dissection

◀ **Fig. 1.19** A diagram showing the respiratory movements of the dogfish. In (a) the mouth and spiracle are open. There is a reduction in pressure in the oro-branchial cavity and water is drawn in. In (b) the volume of the oro-branchial cavity is reduced, whilst the mouth and spiracle are closed thus forcing water into the para-branchial cavities. In (c) the water pressure in the para-branchial cavities is greater than that external to the fish and, consequently, water is forced out through the gills. The blue arrows represent the direction of water flow. The red arrows represent the direction of muscle action.

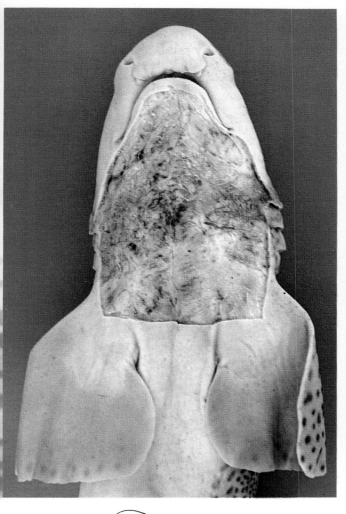

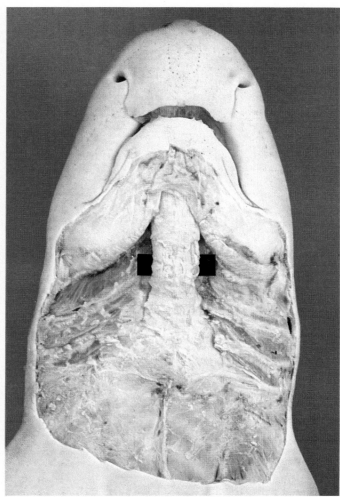

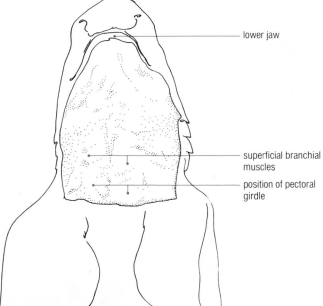

lower jaw

superficial branchial muscles

position of pectoral girdle

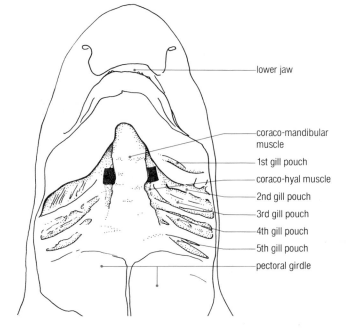

lower jaw

coraco-mandibular muscle

1st gill pouch

coraco-hyal muscle

2nd gill pouch

3rd gill pouch

4th gill pouch

5th gill pouch

pectoral girdle

Fig. 1.21 Branchial musculature – 1st dissection stage

● Make a shallow median incision through the ventral surface of the skin from the pectoral girdle to the centre of the lower jaw. Take care not to damage the underlying muscle.

● Deflect the skin laterally and remove it from each side.

The branchial muscles will now be exposed.

Fig. 1.22 Branchial musculature – 2nd dissection stage

● Make a shallow median incision along the ventral surface of the superficial branchial muscle.

● Deflect this muscle laterally and remove it to expose the coraco-mandibular and coraco-hyal muscles running between the lower jaw and the pectoral girdle. Take care not

to damage the connective tissue covering the floor of the gill pouches.

● Separate the coraco-mandibular muscle, along its length, from the coraco-hyal muscles. A slip of black paper has been inserted between the muscle layers.

1.13

There are five gill slits and a specialised opening, the spiracle, on each side of the dogfish head. In the dissection diagrams the gill slits have been numbered 1 to 5 from anterior to posterior (the spiracle has not been included in this numbering). It must be remembered that this does not imply that gill slit number 1 is homologous with the gill slit associated with segment 1 of a hypothetical ancestral vertebrate. We know that this is not the case. We are using the numbers purely for convenience. The gills themselves (figs. 1.23 and 1.24), are found in these gill slits. Between each opening is a cartilaginous structure, the gill bar or septum, which bears two gill surfaces. The gill bar and its filaments are termed a holobranch. The ceratobranchial cartilage supports the gill and branchial rays may extend from this cartilage and run between the filaments; the latter are attached to the gill septum along most of its length.

The spiracle is a special gill opening which lies between the mandibular and hyoid arches. In fast-swimming sharks it may be very reduced or absent but in bottom-dwelling skates it is a large and important opening, through which water is drawn into the pharynx. In the dogfish, only a small gill structure, the pseudobranch, is associated with the spiracle (fig. 1.37). This does not receive deoxygenated blood via an afferent branchial artery; instead, it is supplied with oxygenated blood from one of the other efferent arteries behind it.

Fig. 1.23 Transverse section of a dogfish gill arch, x 7.

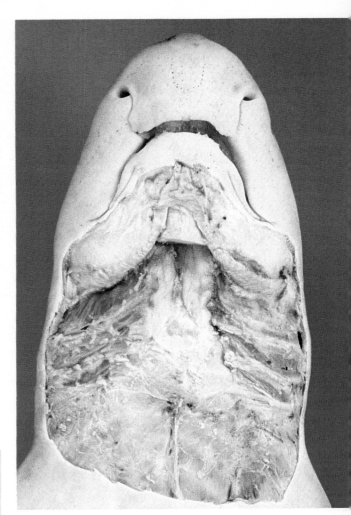

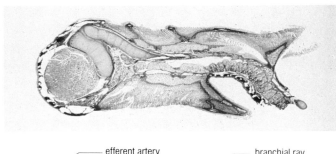

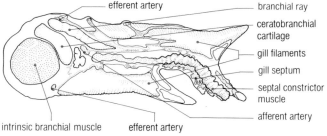

efferent artery
branchial ray
ceratobranchial cartilage
gill filaments
gill septum
septal constrictor muscle
afferent artery
intrinsic branchial muscle
efferent artery

Fig. 1.24 A diagrammatic representation of a dogfish gill arch illustrating the relationship between the gill septum and the gill filaments which bear the gill lamellae.

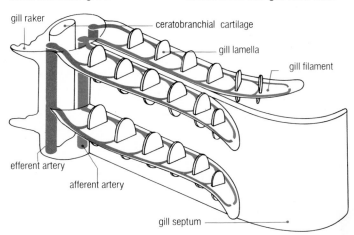

gill raker
ceratobranchial cartilage
gill lamella
gill filament
efferent artery
afferent artery
gill septum

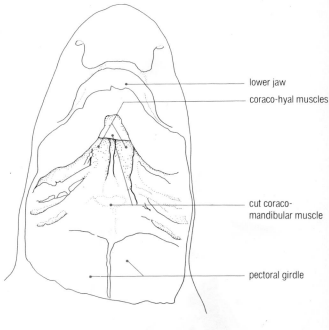

lower jaw
coraco-hyal muscles
cut coraco-mandibular muscle
pectoral girdle

Fig. 1.25 Branchial musculature – 3rd dissection stage

● Cut the coraco-mandibular muscle at its posterior attachment to the pectoral girdle. Turn the cut surface forwards so that the muscle can be cut close to its insertion between the mandibles. Removal of this muscle exposes the two coraco-hyal muscles lying underneath.

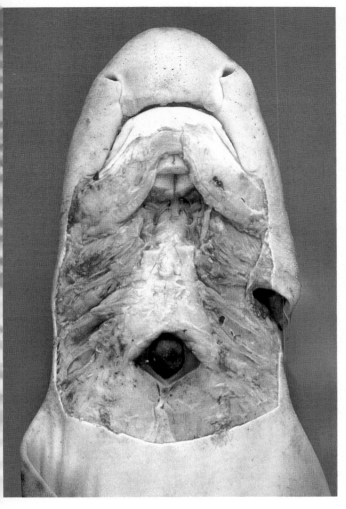

Heart and aortic arches

The cardiovascular system of the dogfish retains certain features expected in the ancestral condition (as seen already in fig. 1.8). The main elements of the system are the heart, the ventral aorta, the dorsal aorta, the venous system and the afferent and efferent branchial arteries (see fig. 1.32). The afferent branchial arteries carry deoxygenated blood from the ventral aorta to the gills. Here, an incoming stream of water provides oxygen. The oxygenated blood is carried away by the efferent branchial arteries to the epibranchial arteries which join the dorsal aorta. The body is supplied by the dorsal aorta and the venous system returns the blood to the heart.

The gills in the dogfish are used for respiration, unlike those of amphioxus which are used for filter feeding. The circulation is a simple one-way circuit. The heart is not divided into right and left halves and there is no double circulation to keep oxygenated and deoxygenated blood separate. Blood pressure in the system is fairly low since the blood does not return to the heart once it has passed through the capillary network in the gills. It is unlikely that this presents a problem since the fish is supported by water and its cardiovascular system does not need to work against gravity. A low-pressure blood stream also transports metabolites relatively slowly. However, this is probably not inhibitive since the fish has a fairly low metabolic rate. This type of system would be unsuitable for a terrestrial existence and consequently it is modified in the tetrapods.

The dogfish heart (fig. 1.27) is a simple tube connecting four consecutive chambers. The sinus venosus and the atrium are thin-walled distensible sacs. These chambers collect blood, ensuring that there is a constant supply of blood for the ventricle to pump. The ventricle provides the main contractile force of the heart and therefore it is very muscular. The conus arteriosus is a narrow thin-walled chamber which constrains the flow of blood as it passes out of the heart and is supplied with valves to prevent backflow. This chamber may help to make the otherwise intermittent flow of blood more regular.

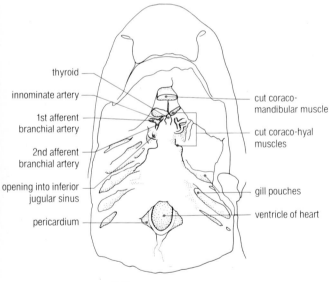

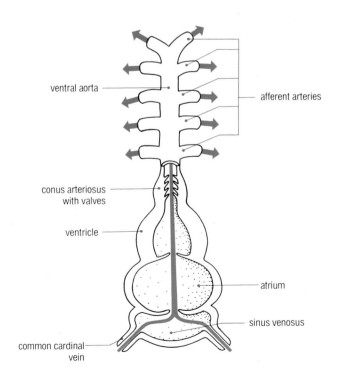

Fig. 1.26 Afferent branchial arteries – 1st dissection stage

● From this point, a specimen with latex-injected blood vessels is used. The pericardium has been opened ventrally and the ventricle has been injected with blue latex which passes into the ventral aorta and the afferent branchial arteries. Red latex has been injected into the dorsal aorta and efferent branchial arteries.

● Gently separate the two coraco-hyal muscles from the underlying tissues and cut free at the pectoral girdle and mandibles. Take care not to damage the thyroid and the innominate arteries which are found just under these muscles at their anterior end.

Fig. 1.27 A simplified diagram of the dogfish heart to show the four chambers and the direction of blood flow.

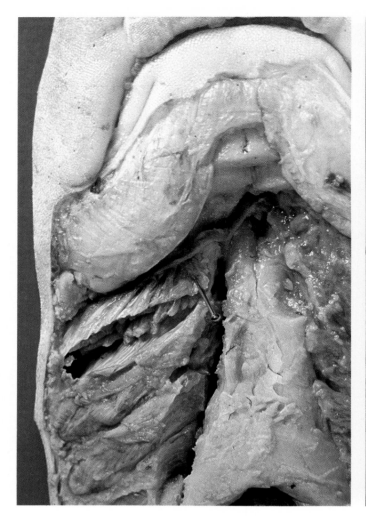

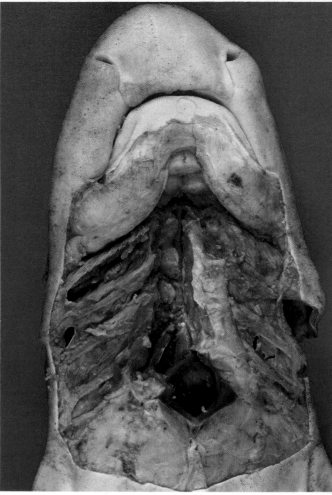

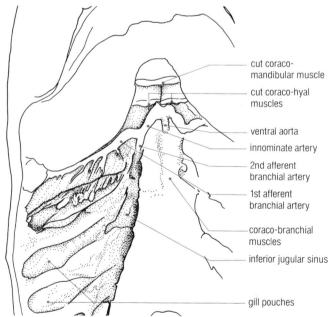

cut coraco-mandibular muscle
cut coraco-hyal muscles
ventral aorta
innominate artery
2nd afferent branchial artery
1st afferent branchial artery
coraco-branchial muscles
inferior jugular sinus
gill pouches

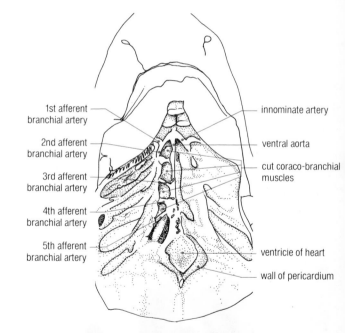

1st afferent branchial artery
2nd afferent branchial artery
3rd afferent branchial artery
4th afferent branchial artery
5th afferent branchial artery
innominate artery
ventral aorta
cut coraco-branchial muscles
ventricle of heart
wall of pericardium

Fig. 1.28 Afferent branchial arteries – 2nd dissection stage

● Carefully remove the thyroid gland.

● Clear the innominate artery on each side to expose its division into the first and second afferent branchial arteries.

● Find the right inferior jugular sinus by passing a

seeker through its anterior opening near the base of the second afferent branchial artery.

● Open the sinus by cutting through the ventral floor. Take care not to damage the underlying branchial arteries 3, 4 and 5, which emerge laterally between the coraco-branchial muscles.

Fig. 1.29 Afferent branchial arteries – 3rd dissection stage

● Gently separate the five coraco-branchial muscles on the right side from their partners on the left.

● Cut each muscle close to its base attachment to the basibranchial cartilage in the ventral floor of the pharynx. Take care not to damage the ventral aorta which runs along

the mid-line from the pericardium to its anterior division into the two innominate arteries.

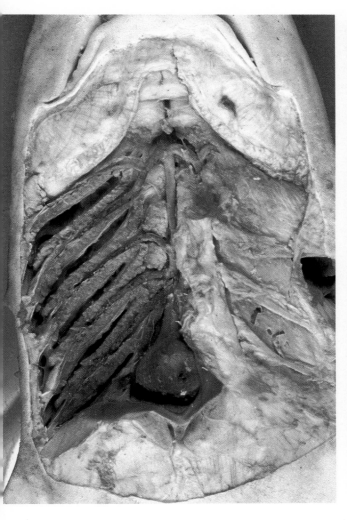

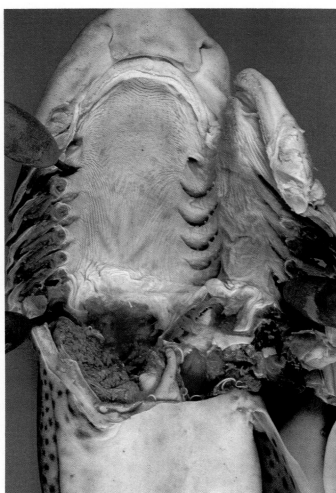

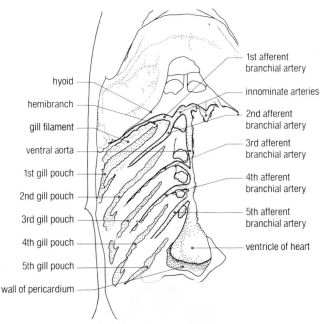

Fig. 1.30 labels:
- hyoid
- hemibranch
- gill filament
- ventral aorta
- 1st gill pouch
- 2nd gill pouch
- 3rd gill pouch
- 4th gill pouch
- 5th gill pouch
- wall of pericardium
- 1st afferent branchial artery
- innominate arteries
- 2nd afferent branchial artery
- 3rd afferent branchial artery
- 4th afferent branchial artery
- 5th afferent branchial artery
- ventricle of heart

Fig. 1.31 labels:
- upper pharynx covered in mucous membrane
- cut angle of jaw
- spiracle
- internal gill clefts
- pectoral girdle

Fig. 1.30 Afferent branchial arteries – 4th dissection stage

● Trace the right innominate artery to its division into the first two afferent arteries.

● The first afferent lies close to the hyoid; carefully cut away its connective tissue. Trace the second afferent along its gill arch; expose it by deflecting each set of gill lamellae laterally.

● Free the arteries by cutting the arterioles which project distally into the gill lamellae. Trim back the lamellae to the level of the dissected arteries.

● Dissect and free the remaining branchial arteries.

● Cut away the ventral floor of the pericardium to show the connection between the ventral aorta and the conus arteriosus of the heart.

Fig. 1.31 Efferent branchial arteries – 1st dissection stage

● Cut through the angle of the jaw on the right side and continue this cut medially along the side of the pharynx. Take care not to damage the roof and the floor of the pharynx.

● Continue the cut backwards to a point just behind the pectoral girdle.

● Make a cut across the ventral abdominal body wall so that the lower half of the pharynx and pectoral girdle can be hinged back on the animal's left side.

1.17

The efferent arteries transport oxygenated blood from the gills to the dorsal aorta via the epibranchial arteries (fig. 1.32). The anatomy of the efferent system differs from that of the afferent system in the following way. The efferent branchial arteries form a loop around each gill; the anterior side is termed pre-trematic and the posterior side, post-trematic. This loop carries oxygenated blood into the epibranchial arteries, which in turn join the dorsal aorta. The afferent vessels are fairly straight, unbranched arteries which run between the gills.

As stated before, the spiracle is not supplied with an afferent artery, only with an efferent, the hyoidean artery. This arises from the pre-trematic branch of the first efferent artery. The carotid arteries also arise from this pre-trematic branch. They form a distinctive loop joining the dorsal aorta.

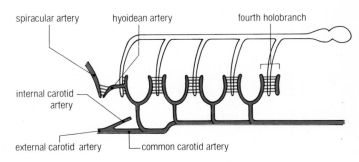

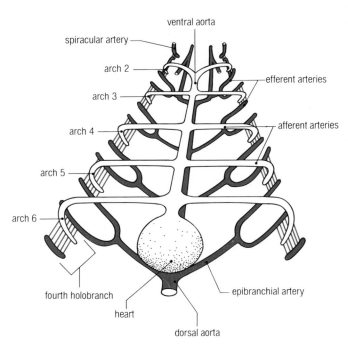

Fig. 1.32 The aortic arches of an elasmobranch. In both drawings the ventral surface is uppermost, and the top drawing shows a left lateral view. These diagrams illustrate the relationship between the afferent, efferent and epibranchial arteries and the dorsal and ventral aortae.

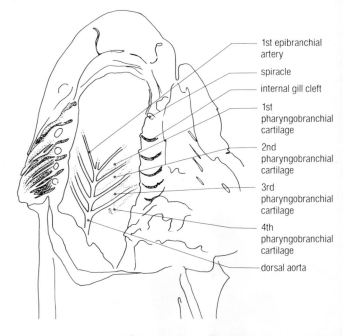

Fig. 1.33 Efferent branchial arteries – 2nd dissection stage

● Make a shallow median incision in the mucous membrane covering the roof of the pharynx. Take great care not to damage any of the underlying epibranchial arteries which lie close to the surface of the roof of the pharynx.

● Carefully deflect each half of this membrane laterally, and then remove it by cutting along the lateral borders.

1.18

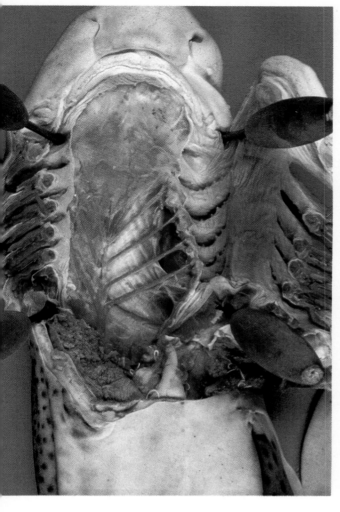

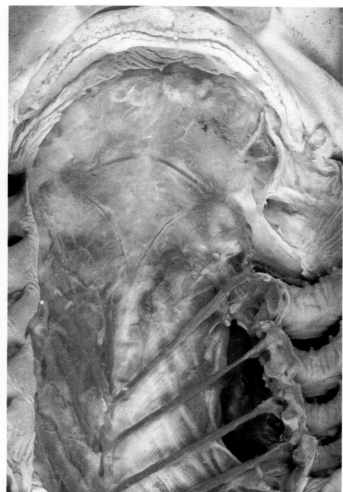

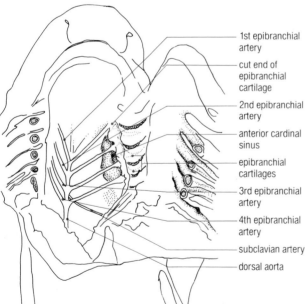

1st epibranchial artery

cut end of epibranchial cartilage

2nd epibranchial artery

anterior cardinal sinus

epibranchial cartilages

3rd epibranchial artery

4th epibranchial artery

subclavian artery

dorsal aorta

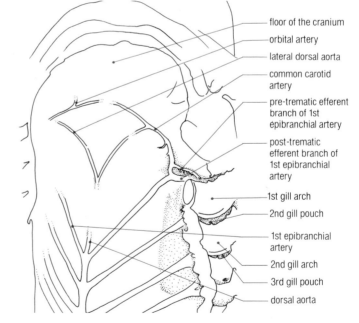

floor of the cranium

orbital artery

lateral dorsal aorta

common carotid artery

pre-trematic efferent branch of 1st epibranchial artery

post-trematic efferent branch of 1st epibranchial artery

1st gill arch

2nd gill pouch

1st epibranchial artery

2nd gill arch

3rd gill pouch

dorsal aorta

Fig. 1.34 Efferent branchial arteries – 3rd dissection stage

● Dissect away the four left pharyngobranchial cartilages from the surrounding connective tissue and cut close to their connection with the epibranchial cartilages in the gill arches. Take particular care when removing the first pharyngobranchial cartilage not to damage the first epibranchial artery which is closely attached to its anterior border.

● Clear the four left epibranchial arteries to show their connection between the dorsal aorta and the gill pouches.

● Cut away the wall of the oesophagus and the surrounding connective tissue posteriorly, to show the dorsal aorta and the left subclavian artery.

Fig. 1.35 Efferent branchial arteries – 4th dissection stage

● Trace the first epibranchial artery under the edge of the epibranchial cartilage of the second gill arch. This will show its division into pre-trematic and post-trematic efferent arteries serving the first gill pouch.

● Gently scrape the connective tissue away from the surface of the cranial cartilage. This demonstrates the course of the common carotid arteries which run in the cartilage and form a loop with the dorsal aorta and the first efferent branchial arteries.

The fifth gill arch is not supplied by its own efferent. There is a pre-trematic artery which empties into the post-trematic branch of the fourth epibranchial artery (fig. 1.36).

From the completed dissection of the branchial arteries, note the loop formed by the carotid artery, the dorsal aorta and the first epibranchial artery (fig. 1.37). Contrast the organisation of the efferent and afferent arteries with that of the teleost later on.

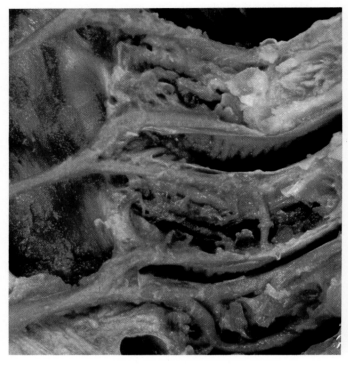

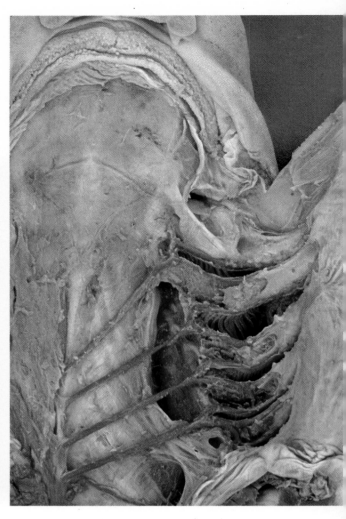

Fig. 1.36 A gill arch dissected to show the fourth afferent branchial artery, and the loop joining the third epibranchial artery and the pre-trematic branch of the fourth epibranchial artery. The efferent artery serving the fifth gill arch can also be seen.

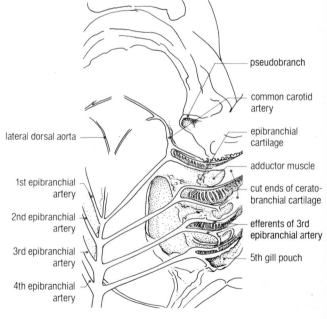

Fig. 1.37 Efferent branchial arteries – 5th dissection stage

● Trace the remaining three epibranchial arteries under their respective epibranchial cartilages to show their connection with the pre-trematic and post-trematic efferent branchial arteries, serving gill pouches 2–5.

● Make an incision along the mucous membrane above the cartilage in each gill arch.

● Now deflect the mucous membranes laterally to show the efferent arteries running along the borders of the gill pouches.

● Carefully cut away the epibranchial and cerato-branchial cartilages to show the efferent arteries more clearly. The fifth gill arch is served by a pre-trematic efferent artery only, and this carries blood into the post-trematic branch of the fourth epibranchial artery.

Cranial nerves

The organisation of the cranial nerves is often used to illustrate the theory that the vertebrate head, like the body, was fully segmented in the ancestral condition. During evolution, specific requirements made on the head have modified the ancestral organisation, even in the lower vertebrates. Again, a developing embryo gives the best approximation to ancestral conditions.

It seems that early in vertebrate evolution, the internal skeletal system and the muscular system developed simultaneously. The organisation of these systems still exists in fish in broadly the same form. The musculature is derived from the mesoderm of the embryo and is metameric. Each myotome needs to be innervated, therefore the nervous tissue also takes on a segmental appearance (see fig. 1.38). Further innervation is required for the lateral plate musculature (associated with the visceral organs) and the sense organs. Consequently, the dorsal nerve cord must give off fibres, in or between each segment, to the segmental muscles (somatic motor) and the non-segmental muscles (visceral motor) and sensory fibres receiving stimuli from the internal organs (visceral sensory) and the skin and skeletal muscles (somatic sensory). These various fibres leave the dorsal nerve cord as nerve tracts, or roots, which may be ventrally or dorsally placed. The dorsal root leaves the nerve cord intersegmentally. It is probable that in the ancestral vertebrate, somatic motor fibres left in the ventral root and all other fibres in the dorsal root. However, this pattern is modified in lower vertebrates so that some of the visceral motor fibres also exit from the ventral root. Also, the two roots join a short way from the nerve cord, to divide later on when they reach the various organs that they supply. This arrangement of dorsal and ventral roots is found in the spinal nerves but the arrangement of the cranial nerve roots is more complicated. However, it is still possible to work out whether the nerves concerned are ventral or dorsal roots and what kind of fibres they contain. This is done in the hope of demonstrating that the arrangement of the cranial nerves is only a modified form of the arrangement of the spinal nerves. If the cranial nerves also had a segmental background, this would indicate that the head was once fully segmented.

We can distinguish between ventral and dorsal roots by finding out whether they carry motor or sensory fibres. These fibres may be distinguished by the position of their cell bodies. Those of the motor fibres are located in the nerve cord or brainstem; whereas the cell bodies of sensory nerve fibres are located outside the cord, forming ganglia. The ventral roots only carry motor fibres so we do not expect to see ganglia associated with them. However, the dorsal roots carry sensory fibres as well as motor fibres and ganglia are present.

Some of the cranial nerves do not seem to fall into the dorsal ventral categorisation. This is because the specialised sensory structures of the head have no counterparts along the spinal column.

For easy reference the cranial nerves are numbered in the order in which they leave the brainstem. Nerve I, the olfactory nerve, leaves the brain most anteriorly in the majority of vertebrates, and nerve XII, the hypoglossal, most posteriorly.

To complicate interpretation of the cranial nerves further, the muscles of the head are not generally segmentally derived muscles. You will remember that in the embryo, segmental muscle arises from the mesoderm and non-segmental muscle (of the gut and gill arches) develops from the lateral plate mesoderm. Consequently, the majority of the muscles that you can see in the dogfish head, including the jaw muscles, have a non-segmental origin. This causes problems when trying to relate the cranial nerves to the segment that they innervate. The exceptions to this are the small eye-moving muscles which are derived from the once segmental myotome muscles. They have obviously become very modified during evolution; but it is possible to trace the cranial nerves (III, IV and VI) which innervate these muscles and, as expected, they are ventral roots.

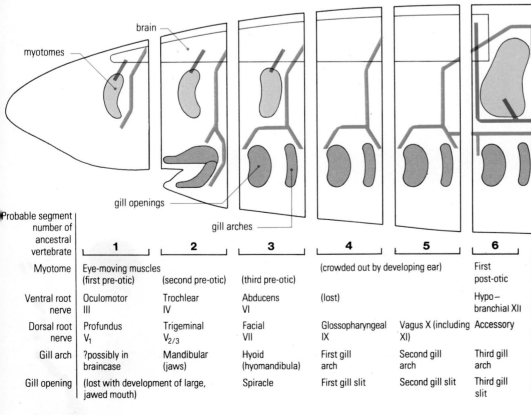

Probable segment number of ancestral vertebrate	1	2	3	4	5	6
Myotome	Eye-moving muscles (first pre-otic)	(second pre-otic)	(third pre-otic)	(crowded out by developing ear)		First post-otic
Ventral root nerve	Oculomotor III	Trochlear IV	Abducens VI	(lost)		Hypo-branchial XII
Dorsal root nerve	Profundus V_1	Trigeminal $V_{2/3}$	Facial VII	Glossopharyngeal IX	Vagus X (including XI)	Accessory
Gill arch	?possibly in braincase	Mandibular (jaws)	Hyoid (hyomandibula)	First gill arch	Second gill arch	Third gill arch
Gill opening	(lost with development of large, jawed mouth)		Spiracle	First gill slit	Second gill slit	Third gill slit

Fig. 1.38 Diagram to represent the segmental nature of the head of the ancestral vertebrate. The cranial nerves are divided into ventral roots (shown in red line), and dorsal roots (shown in blue line). Note the segmentally arranged gill openings, gill arches and myotomes which, together with the cranial nerves, are listed in the table directly underneath the segment that they occupy.

1.21

**Fig. 1.39 Cranial nerves –
1st dissection stage**

● Dissect the fish from the dorsal surface.

● If the animal has already been used for a dissection of the efferent branchial arteries, then the cranial nerves must be exposed on the side which has not been cut in hinging back the lower jaw.

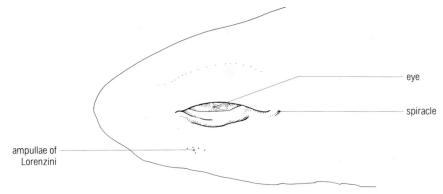

eye

spiracle

ampullae of
Lorenzini

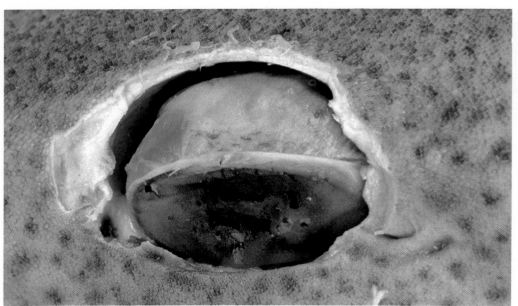

**Fig. 1.40 Cranial nerves –
2nd dissection stage**

● Remove the eyelid.

● Draw the top of the eyeball out of the orbit in order to expose the superior rectus and the superior oblique muscles which are attached to the posterior surface at the top of the eyeball.

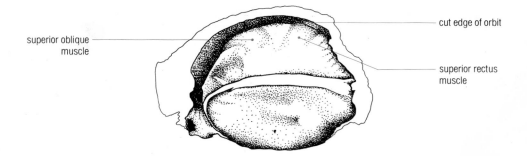

cut edge of orbit

superior oblique
muscle

superior rectus
muscle

1.22

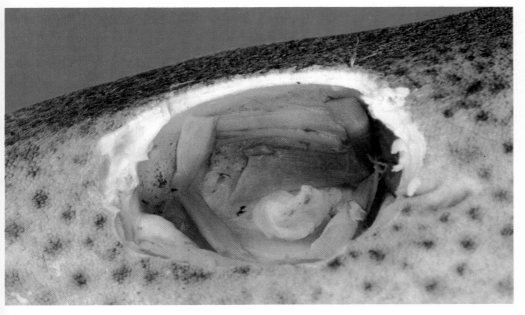

**Fig. 1.41 Cranial nerves –
3rd dissection stage**

● Cut the superior rectus and superior oblique muscles close to the surface of the eye and free the eyeball from its attachment to the orbit.

● Pull the eyeball outwards and find the connections of the anterior, posterior and inferior rectus muscles.

● Cut these muscles as close as possible to the surface of the eye.

● Cut the inferior oblique muscle in a similar way.

● Now free the eyeball from its remaining connection, the optic nerve (II), and remove it from the orbit. Take care not to damage the oculomotor nerve (III) or the branches of nerves V and VII which cross the floor of the orbit.

● Carefully wash out the orbit and locate nerves II, III, IV, V and VII, and their branches.

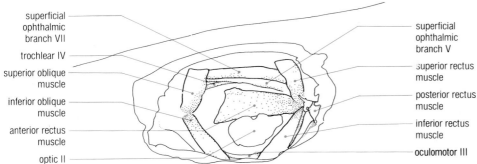

superficial ophthalmic branch VII
trochlear IV
superior oblique muscle
inferior oblique muscle
anterior rectus muscle
optic II

superficial ophthalmic branch V
superior rectus muscle
posterior rectus muscle
inferior rectus muscle
oculomotor III

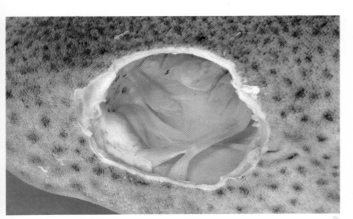

The optic nerve (II) carries sensory fibres from the retina in the eye (fig. 1.41). You will remember that sensory fibres have their ganglia outside the nerve cord, or brainstem. Those of the optic nerve are actually located in the retina. Nerve II falls into the category of special nerves since it supplies a specialised head structure. Other nerves which fall into this group are: the olfactory nerve (I); the auditory nerve (VIII); the glossopharyngeal nerve (IX); and the vagus nerve (X). The last two supply the lateral line system (p. 1.29).

Nerve I, as expected, supplies the olfactory structures. In the dogfish, these are a pair of pouches on the under surface of the snout. As water flows through the pouch it is monitored on a series of ridges found on the bottom of the pouch. These ridges are covered by an epithelium containing the olfactory receptor cells. They differ from other vertebrate receptor cells by communicating directly with the brain; they send out long fibres which enter the olfactory bulb of the brain (fig. 1.55). Minute quantities of chemical substances can be detected by the olfactory epithelium and, in sharks, this sense is particularly well developed.

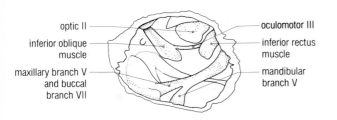

optic II
inferior oblique muscle
maxillary branch V and buccal branch VII

oculomotor III
inferior rectus muscle
mandibular branch V

Fig. 1.42 A view of the ventral surface of the orbit of the eye. The dorsal surface is seen in fig. 1.41.

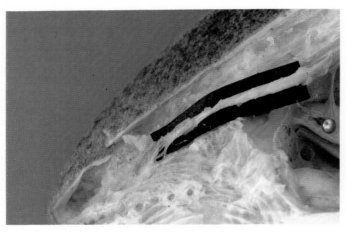

superficial ophthalmic branch V and VII

ampullae of Lorenzini

trochlear IV

superior oblique muscle

anterior branches superficial ophthalmic branch V and VII

Fig. 1.43 Black paper has been placed underneath the superficial ophthalmic nerve to highlight its course and its anterior branches.

The superficial ophthalmic nerve contains fibres of both nerves V and VII (fig. 1.43). Somatic sensory fibres supply the sense organs in the skin of the snout and another part of the nerve supplies the lateral line system (lateralis branch). Consequently, the superficial ophthalmic nerve also falls into the category of special nerves. We shall see other 'mixed' nerves like this, in particular, the trigeminal, the facial, the glossopharyngeal and the vagus nerves.

The trochlear nerve (IV) is one of the nerves which innervates the eye-moving muscles. It carries somatic motor fibres; and, as expected, it is a ventral root.

Nerve V, the trigeminal, is a large nerve with three main branches (see fig. 1.45). It brings in sensory stimuli from the head and it also innervates the jaw muscles. It therefore contains somatic sensory fibres and visceral motor fibres. The motor fibres are visceral because they innervate non-segmental muscle.

The trigeminal nerve was probably originally associated with an anterior gill slit which was lost as the mouth extended backwards in early vertebrates (see p.1.21). The three main branches are: the profundus (V_1) which receives stimuli from the skin of the snout; the maxillary branch which innervates the upper jaw (V_2); and the mandibular branch which supplies the lower jaw (V_3). The trigeminal nerve is a dorsal root.

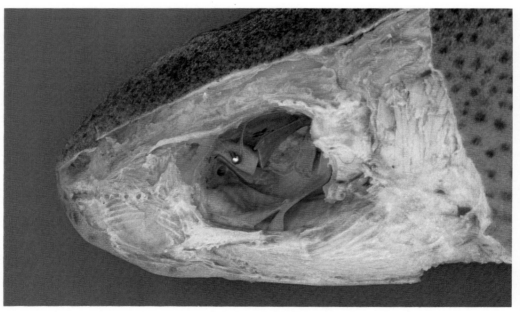

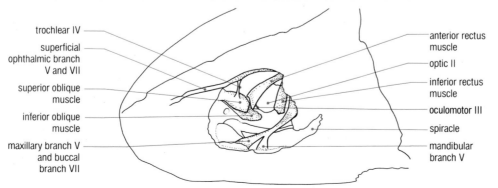

trochlear IV

superficial ophthalmic branch V and VII

superior oblique muscle

inferior oblique muscle

maxillary branch V and buccal branch VII

anterior rectus muscle

optic II

inferior rectus muscle

oculomotor III

spiracle

mandibular branch V

Fig. 1.44 Cranial nerves – 4th dissection stage

● To clear the skin from one half of the head, make a median dorsal incision and deflect the skin laterally to the level of the lower jaw and back as far as the first gill slit. Take great care to remove only the skin, particularly in the region just anterior to the dorsal edge of the orbit where the superficial ophthalmic branches of nerves V and VII emerge. Care must also be taken in the region near the spiracle where the post-spiracular branch of the facial VII crosses the surface of the lateral muscle.

● Find the superficial ophthalmic nerve which runs forwards from the dorsal anterior edge of the orbit.

● Carefully cut away the dorsal edge of the orbit to free the proximal end of the nerve.

● Pin down the superior oblique muscle to show the trochlear nerve (IV).

● Dissect the superficial ophthalmic nerve clear from the snout as far as its anterior branches. The course of the nerve is highlighted in fig. 1.43 by slipping black paper underneath it.

Fig. 1.45 Cranial nerves – 5th dissection stage

● Trace the mandibular and maxillary branches of nerve V across the floor of the orbit.

● Trace the nerves into the muscle of the jaw by dissecting away the overlying connective tissue.

● Follow the maxillary branch of nerve V ventrally to show the division into the mandibular branch of nerve V and the buccal branch of nerve VII. The course of the nerve is highlighted by placing black paper under its branches.

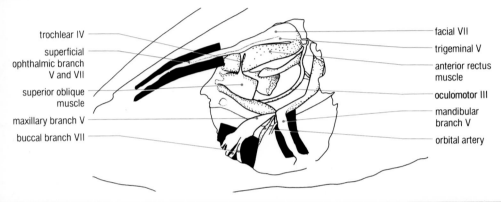

trochlear IV
superficial ophthalmic branch V and VII
superior oblique muscle
maxillary branch V
buccal branch VII

facial VII
trigeminal V
anterior rectus muscle
oculomotor III
mandibular branch V
orbital artery

Fig. 1.46 Cranial nerves – 6th dissection stage

● The facial nerve (VII) has many branches, one being the hyomandibular branch which further divides into pre-spiracular and post-spiracular branches. Find the hyoidean and mandibular branches of the post-spiracular branch which emerges from just behind the spiracle. Trace these ventrally and posteriorly towards the mandible and hyoid.

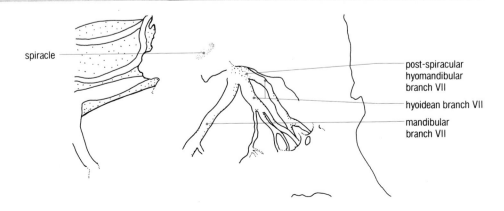

spiracle

post-spiracular hyomandibular branch VII
hyoidean branch VII
mandibular branch VII

Nerve VII is termed the facial nerve because it supplies the muscles of the face in mammals. It is partly a sensory nerve. Originally, this nerve was associated with the spiracular gill slit as the hyomandibular nerve which has pre-spiracular branches (fig. 1.47) and post-spiracular branches (fig. 1.48). The main post-spiracular branch is the hyoidean nerve which innervates the muscles of the hyoid arch and also contains some visceral sensory fibres. The mandibular nerve is another post-spiracular branch. Pre-spiracular branches contain only visceral sensory fibres. Consequently, nerve VII is a dorsal root.

Fig. 1.47 Cranial nerves – 7th dissection stage

● Find the origin of the facial nerve at the back of the orbit where it emerges with nerve V from the cranium.

● Locate and dissect clear the delicate pre-spiracular branch, which serves the pre-trematic muscle of the spiracle.

● Cut the muscle and cartilage of the posterior edge of the orbit above the spiracle, and trace the post-spiracular branch from its origin in the orbit to where it divides into the mandibular and hyoidean branches behind the spiracle.

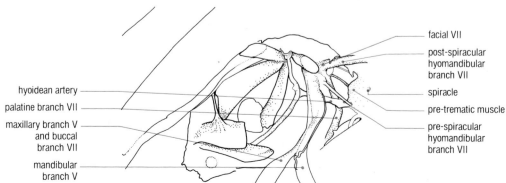

hyoidean artery

palatine branch VII

maxillary branch V and buccal branch VII

mandibular branch V

facial VII

post-spiracular hyomandibular branch VII

spiracle

pre-trematic muscle

pre-spiracular hyomandibular branch VII

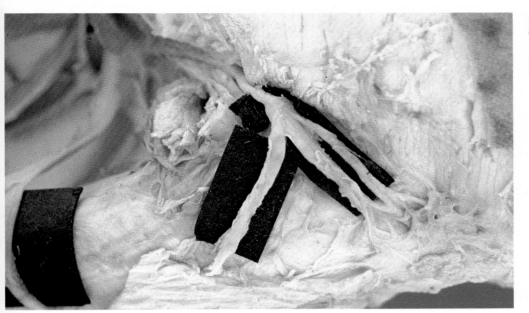

**Fig. 1.48 Cranial nerves –
8th dissection stage**

● Insert black paper under the
mandibular and hyoidean
branches of nerve VII.

spiracle

post-spiracular
hyomandibular
branch VII

hyoidean branch VII

mandibular
branch VII

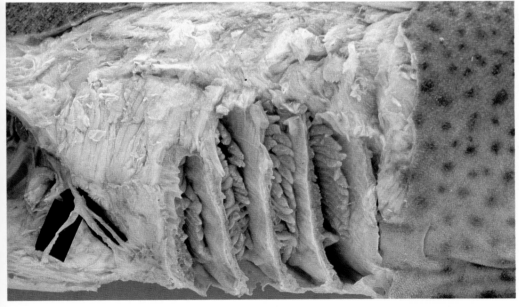

**Fig. 1.49 Cranial nerves –
9th dissection stage**

● Cut away the skin posteriorly
to expose the side of the fish
as far back as the pectoral
girdle.

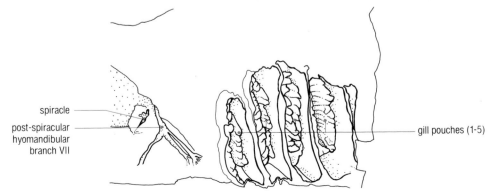

spiracle

post-spiracular
hyomandibular
branch VII

gill pouches (1-5)

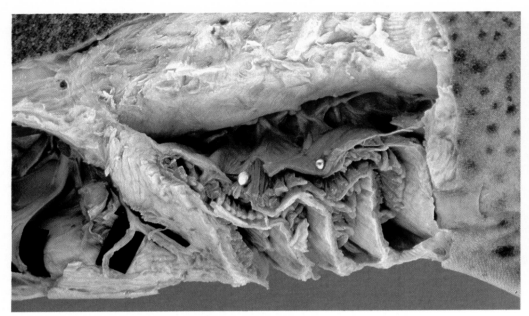

Fig. 1.50 Cranial nerves – 10th dissection stage

● Make a slit dorsally through the back of the third gill pouch, and find the anterior cardinal sinus. This large cavity runs from behind the orbit along the side of the fish to a position just in front of the girdle. Take care not to cut into the muscle on the dorsal surface of the sinus and damage the vagus nerve (X).

● Open the sinus by making a cut through the dorsolateral part of the roof, along its length. This exposes the branchial branches of the vagus nerve running across the floor of the sinus to the gills.

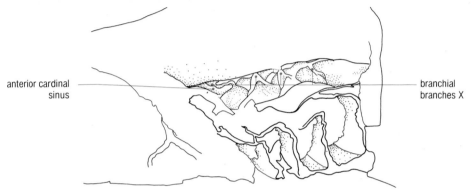

anterior cardinal sinus

branchial branches X

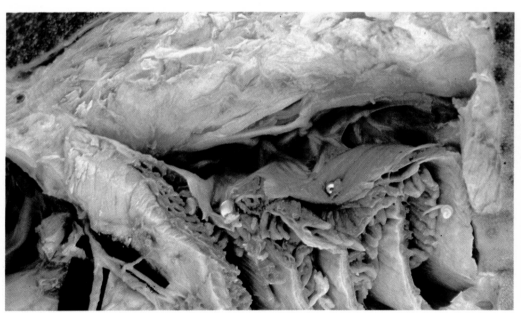

Fig. 1.51 Cranial nerves – 11th dissection stage

● Find the main trunk of the vagus nerve (X) at the back of the anterior cardinal sinus under a thin layer of connective tissue.

● Carefully remove this tissue to find where the lateral line branch of the vagus separates from the branchial/visceral branch.

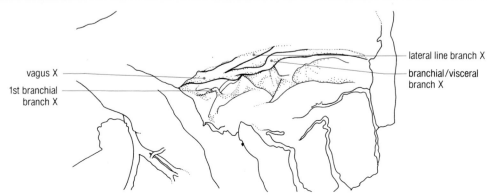

vagus X

1st branchial branch X

lateral line branch X

branchial/visceral branch X

The vagus nerve (X) is a large nerve which contains both motor and sensory fibres, and supplies various visceral organs and the lateral line (fig. 1.51). A series of branches from the vagus runs to all the gill slits (except the first and the spiracle) innervating the pharynx and gill muscles (fig. 1.52). The main branch of the vagus continues posteriorly as the abdominal branch which relays sensations from the visceral organs to the brain. The vagus, therefore, can be considered a dorsal root because it carries somatic sensory and visceral fibres. However, it also falls into the category of special nerves since it supplies the lateral line system.

The lateral line system is responsible for detecting disturbances in the water around the fish. If an object vibrates in water, firstly, it will displace water as it vibrates, and secondly, it will set up sound waves. Of these two effects, the first quickly dies down while the second can be detected some distance from the original vibrating object. These are called near-field and far-field effects respectively. The lateral line organs respond to near-field effects. Each lateral line organ, or neuromast, consists of a collection of cells, each of which bears a tuft of cilia. One particular cilium is longer than the rest and is called the kinocilium. A disturbance in the water may lead to a difference in pressure existing between different neuromast organs. The resulting flow of water will deflect the kinocilium, thus causing a nervous discharge, giving information about the movements of prey or predators.

The fish ear consists of only those structures which are called the 'inner ear' in mammals. There are no sound-conducting elements or external ear structures. The function of the ear in cartilaginous fish, and the probable original function of the inner ear in vertebrates, is monitoring equilibrium, not detecting sound. The cells in the inner ear responsible for detecting changes in body position are very like the neuromast cells of the lateral line. In fact, it is possible that the vertebrate ear evolved from a patch of neuromast cells which sunk below the surface in the head region.

The inner ear consists of two large sac-like structures and a smaller sac, which are all connected by three semicircular canals. Each sac contains an area of sensory cells, a macula. The cilia of these cells are embedded in a gelatinous structure, the cupula, which often bears a mass of calcium carbonate crystals, the otolith. Otoliths are denser than the surrounding fluid and so tend to sink due to gravity. If the head tilts or if the fish experiences linear acceleration, the movement of the cupula and otolith will relay this information via the auditory nerve to the brain. It is possible that these sensory cells in sharks also respond to low frequency sound-vibrations.

In each semicircular canal more neuromasts are found, again with the cilia buried in cupulae but without otoliths. The canals are fluid-filled. If the fish is subjected to angular acceleration, the movement of the fluid inside the canal tends to lag behind the movement of the canal itself. The cupula of the sensory cells projects into the fluid and travels with the fluid as it moves. However, the sensory hairs are embedded in the canal wall and therefore travel with its velocity. The difference in the velocities tends to bend the cupula and the hair cells, so setting up a nervous discharge. Two of the canals are oriented vertically in the head at right angles to each other, and the other canal is horizontal. Therefore, deflections in three planes can be detected.

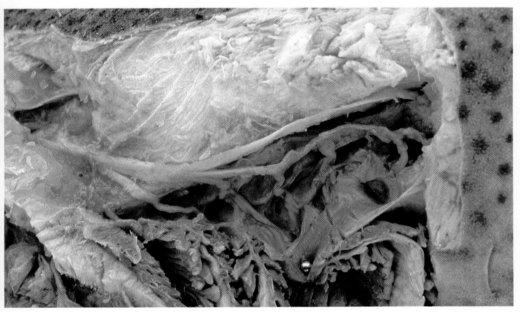

Fig. 1.52 Cranial nerves – 12th dissection stage

● Trace the lateral line branch of the vagus posteriorly and dissect it clear.

● Trace the three posterior branchial branches to gill pouches 3-5, where they divide into pre-trematic and post-trematic fibres. The main trunk of the vagus continues posteriorly along the anterior cardinal sinus to form the visceral branch.

● Trace the main trunk of the vagus anteriorly, through the muscle at the back of the head into the cranium. In order to do this, it is necessary to slice away this muscle and the cartilage of the cranium to show the nerve and its connection with the medulla oblongata. This will inevitably result in the removal of the auditory capsule, its nerve and the semicircular canals.

● Find the origin of the first branchial branch of the vagus nerve. This will have been exposed during the dissection step above. Trace this nerve distally to the second gill pouch.

medulla oblongata

position of auditory capsule and semi-circular canals

glossopharyngeal IX

lateral line branch X

visceral branch X

branchial branches (1-4) X

2nd gill pouch

The glossopharyngeal nerve (IX) is quite small and innervates most of the tongue and pharynx (fig. 1.53). It is associated with the first gill slit. In most vertebrates, nerve IX carries visceral sensory and visceral motor fibres, and it therefore falls into the dorsal root category. It innervates part of the lateral line system as well; so, like the vagus nerve, it also belongs in the special nerve group.

Brain

It is thought that primitively the vertebrate brain was a region of the dorsal nerve cord elaborated in order to deal with stimuli from the sensory organs of the head, and to produce local reflexes in the head and throat region. During the evolution of the vertebrates the brain has taken on a co-ordinating function in assessing and organising information from other parts of the body.

In a developing embryo as soon as the neural tube (which will later give rise to the nerve cord) is complete, the brain expands to form three vesicles. These are the forebrain, midbrain and hindbrain. Later, the brain divides further. From the forebrain the telencephalon is produced. In higher vertebrates this gives rise to the cerebral hemispheres. The forebrain also produces the diencephalon which will give rise later to the thalamus and hypothalamus. The hindbrain divides to form the regions which will become the cerebellum and medulla in the adult (see fig. 1.54).

The thalamus is a relay centre sending information to the cerebrum. It is thought to be responsible for the level of awareness of pleasure and pain. The hypothalamus integrates and co-ordinates autonomic functions such as water balance and temperature regulation. Its ventral

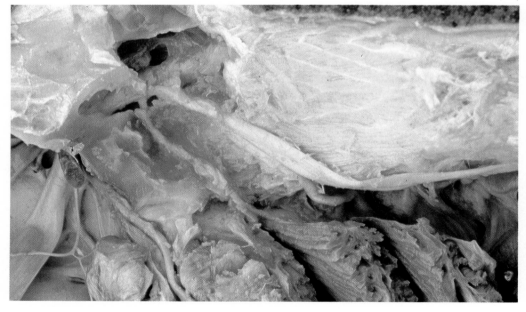

Fig. 1.53 Cranial nerves – 13th dissection stage

● Carefully carry on slicing the cranium forwards into the region anterior to the entry of the vagus nerve. This exposes the entry of the glosso-pharyngeal nerve (IX) which serves the first gill pouch.

● Trace this nerve distally to show its pre-trematic and post-trematic branches.

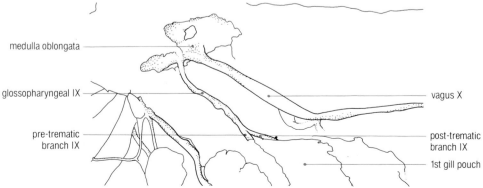

medulla oblongata

glossopharyngeal IX

pre-trematic branch IX

vagus X

post-trematic branch IX

1st gill pouch

surface bears the hypophysis which is an endocrine gland. The cerebellum controls motor co-ordination and maintenance of equilibrium. It provides unconscious timing and control of muscles. The cerebrum contains the olfactory and somatic sensory areas, and the pallium which is thought to be responsible for the control of schooling, aggressive and reproductive behaviour, as well as learning.

In sharks and dogfish the olfactory lobes are large and the optic lobes are prominent (fig. 1.55). The cerebellum is also large in the more active species.

This may be the only opportunity that you have of seeing the brain *in situ* and in association with the cranial nerves. The other vertebrates which you will study have bony braincases and it is therefore more difficult to expose the brain without damaging it. You can compare the dogfish brain with brains of other vertebrates in chapter 7.

The choroid plexus is a thin, folded membrane, supplied with blood vessels. It produces the cerebro-spinal fluid which fills the central canal (or ventricles) of the brain. This fluid passes from the central canal through various foramina to occupy a space between the membrane adhering very closely to the brain and spinal column, and another outer membrane which is more loosely attached. There are special areas in this space where the fluid is absorbed back into the venous system. The main function of the cerebro-spinal fluid is to cushion the nervous tissue against mechanical damage.

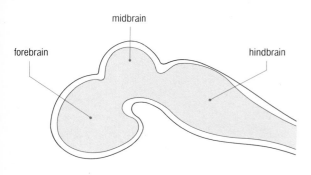

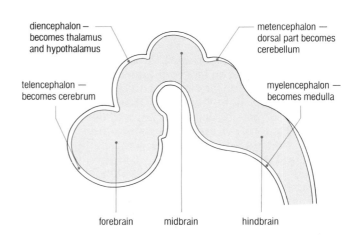

Fig. 1.54 A section of a developing mammalian brain at the primary vesicle stage (left), and at the secondary vesicle stage (right).

Fig. 1.55 Cranial nerves – 14th dissection stage

● Carefully remove the cartilaginous roof of the cranium to reveal the main regions of the brain and cranial nerve I.

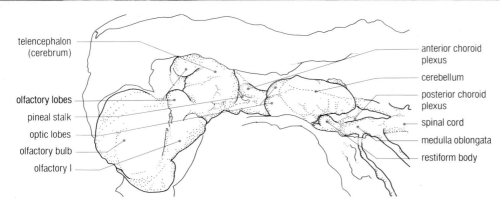

Skull

The dogfish skull, like the rest of the skeleton, is composed only of cartilage. One of the most obvious differences between this skull and that of a bony fish is the absence of the dermal bones which give the bony fish skull its appearance of complexity (fig. 2.21).

Three main cartilages make up the dogfish skull: the chondrocranium, or braincase; the palatoquadrate, or upper jaw; and the mandibular, or lower jaw cartilage (fig. 1.56). There are additional cartilages such as the hyomandibula which suspends the jaws from the chondrocranium. Small labial cartilages may be present in some elasmobranchs, in the angle of the mouth (fig. 1.57). Behind the skull are the gill arches which number five in the dogfish. These arches form supports for the gill slits with which they alternate (fig. 1.58). Each arch consists of several elements: a pharyngobranchial, epibranchial, ceratobranchial, basibranchial, and hypobranchial cartilage.

The jaws and the hyomandibula have an interesting evolutionary history. The first vertebrate fossils known, as well as the present-day lampreys and hagfish, do not have jaws. It is thought that the earliest vertebrates may have had more gill arches in the pharynx than those species living today. A current of water would have entered the mouth and passed out through the gill slits, carrying food particles and providing oxygen for the blood. It is surmised that along the evolutionary line leading to jawed fish, one gill arch became associated with the mouth (the mandibular arch) and in time came to support it as the jaws. The next gill arch back (the hyoid arch) formed an attachment between the newly formed jaws and the hard casing around the brain, providing

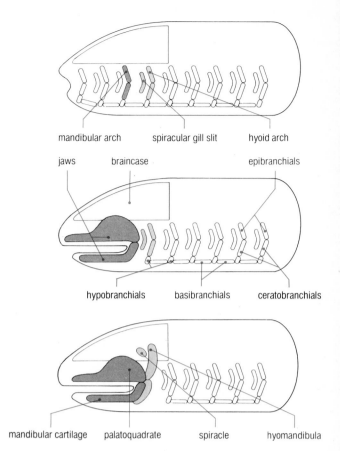

mandibular arch   spiracular gill slit   hyoid arch

jaws   braincase   epibranchials

hypobranchials   basibranchials   ceratobranchials

mandibular cartilage   palatoquadrate   spiracle   hyomandibula

Fig. 1.56 Diagram showing how vertebrate jaws might have evolved from the anterior gill arches. The fate of the first gill arch is uncertain; the second gill arch possibly formed part of the braincase, whilst the third arch formed the jaws.

Fig. 1.57 The skull of the dogfish in left lateral view (specimen courtesy of Griffin and George Ltd).

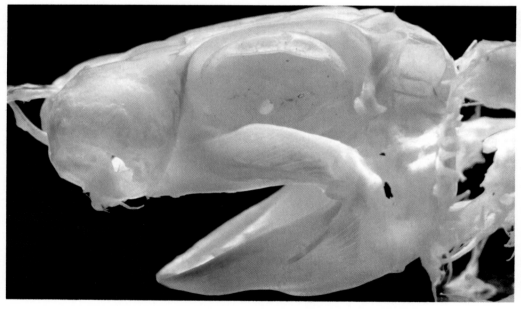

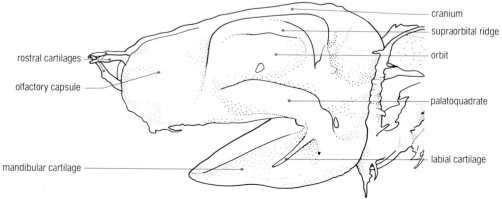

rostral cartilages

olfactory capsule

mandibular cartilage

cranium

supraorbital ridge

orbit

palatoquadrate

labial cartilage

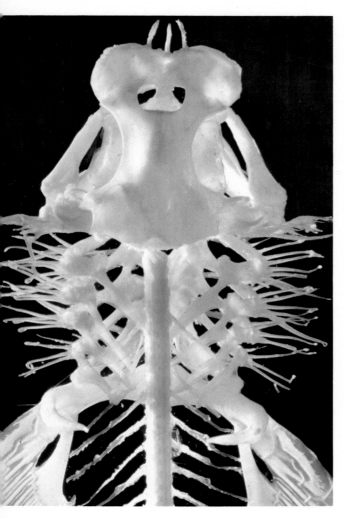

stability and support for the jaws. The main element of the hyoid arch, which came to act as a support, was the hyomandibula (see fig. 1.56). Although this element is still present in the dogfish skull, as we noted above, its role is somewhat modified. Earlier we noted that the jaws of modern sharks, including the dogfish, are mobile since the upper jaw is not fused to the chondrocranium but is only suspended from it.

The upper jaw articulates with the hyomandibula, which itself articulates with the chondrocranium. The upper jaw articulates with the lower jaw at the jaw hinge and also has orbital processes which fit into grooves on the chondrocranium. It is possible for the palatoquadrate to slide from a resting position forwards and downwards in the groove. In this position the palatoquadrate projects below the snout. In some sharks, this movement is considerable, but in the dogfish, it is quite limited. Its function might be to allow the jaws to be projected away from the delicate snout as the shark makes a grab for its prey. It also facilitates picking up food morsels from the substrate. The jaws of sharks are capable of other movements besides protrusion. As the jaws open and the upper jaw is protruded, the hyomandibula swings out laterally and anteriorly, carrying the jaw articulation with it. This increases the distance between the right and left jaw hinges, so increasing the volume of the gill chamber. The consequent reduction in pressure causes water to flow into the mouth.

In the dogfish, teeth are found on the palatoquadrate and mandibular cartilages. They are replaced as they wear out and this is a process which continues throughout life. The teeth are not all shed at the same time. Each tooth which is exposed at the surface of the jaw is connected by a band of dermis to teeth which are still within the jaw and ready to erupt. As the functional, exposed tooth gets older, it is gradually replaced by the tooth next in line within the jaw. The stimulus which causes a new tooth to erupt seems to travel along the jaw in a wave, but the details of the process are not fully understood in fishes. The result is an array of newly erupted teeth alternating with larger, more mature teeth which carry out most of the work. This ensures that at least half of the teeth in the jaws are functional at any one time, whilst the other half are in the process of maturing (see fig. 1.59).

A shark or dogfish tooth consists of an outer layer of enamel enclosing a layer of dentine which surrounds the pulp cavity. The tooth resembles the dermal denticle or placoid scale, from which it may have arisen in evolutionary history.

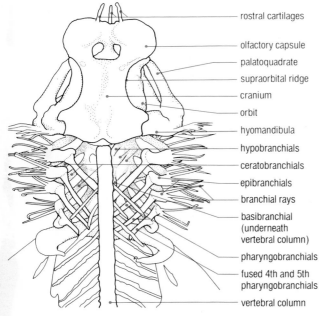

	rostral cartilages
	olfactory capsule
	palatoquadrate
	supraorbital ridge
	cranium
	orbit
	hyomandibula
	hypobranchials
	ceratobranchials
	epibranchials
	branchial rays
	basibranchial (underneath vertebral column)
	pharyngobranchials
	fused 4th and 5th pharyngobranchials
	vertebral column

Fig. 1.58 The skull and branchial skeleton of the dogfish in dorsal view (specimen courtesy of Griffin and George Ltd).

Fig. 1.59 Diagrammatic cross section of the jaw of a living shark to show the functional teeth at the surface of the jaw and the battery of teeth below the surface waiting to erupt.

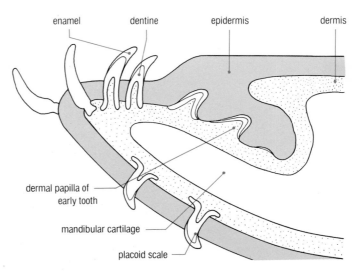

enamel   dentine   epidermis   dermis

dermal papilla of early tooth

mandibular cartilage

placoid scale

1.33

Cranial nerves of the skate

The course of the cranial nerves can be demonstrated particularly easily in the skate (figs. 1.60 – 1.67) due to its dorsoventral flattening. However, it is because of this specialisation of the skate that the dogfish has been used to illustrate the other systems; although the dogfish is also a highly specialised animal, its anatomy shares a closer resemblance with the hypothetical ancestral vertebrate form than does the skate.

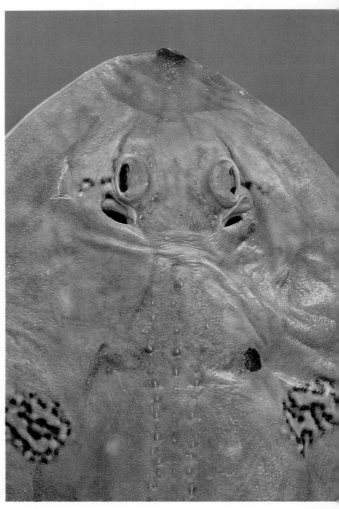

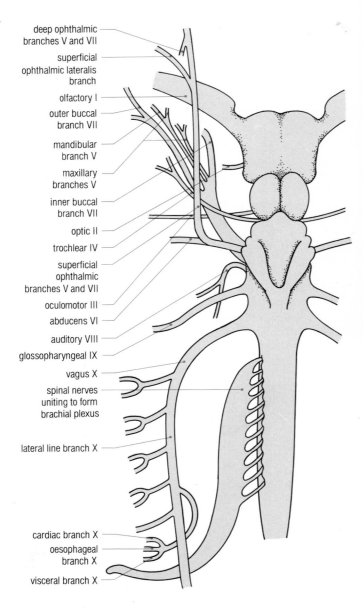

deep ophthalmic branches V and VII
superficial ophthalmic lateralis branch
olfactory I
outer buccal branch VII
mandibular branch V
maxillary branches V
inner buccal branch VII
optic II
trochlear IV
superficial ophthalmic branches V and VII
oculomotor III
abducens VI
auditory VIII
glossopharyngeal IX
vagus X
spinal nerves uniting to form brachial plexus
lateral line branch X
cardiac branch X
oesophageal branch X
visceral branch X

Fig. 1.60 A diagrammatic representation of the cranial nerves in the skate in dorsal view.

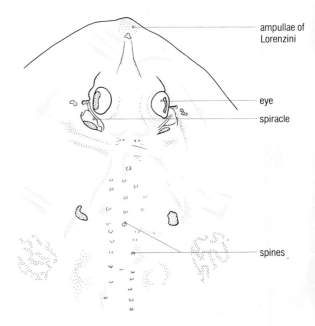

ampullae of Lorenzini
eye
spiracle
spines

Fig. 1.61 Dorsal cranial view – animal prepared for dissection.

● Peg out the skate, dorsal surface uppermost.

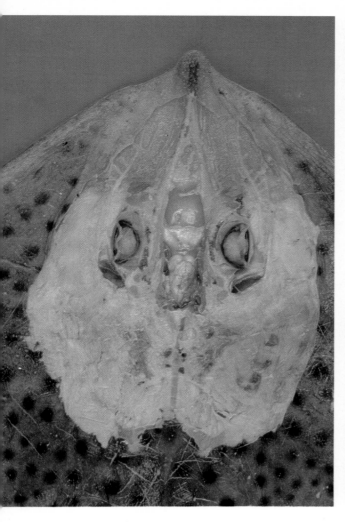

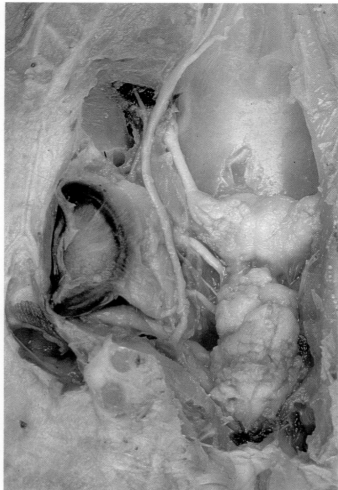

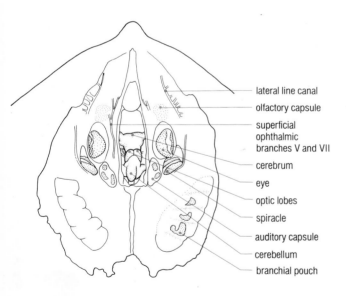

lateral line canal
olfactory capsule
superficial
ophthalmic
branches V and VII
cerebrum
eye
optic lobes
spiracle
auditory capsule
cerebellum
branchial pouch

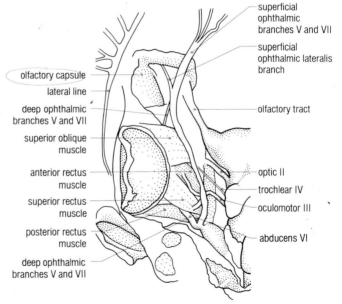

superficial
ophthalmic
branches V and VII

superficial
ophthalmic lateralis
branch

olfactory capsule
lateral line

deep ophthalmic
branches V and VII

superior oblique
muscle

anterior rectus
muscle

superior rectus
muscle

posterior rectus
muscle

deep ophthalmic
branches V and VII

olfactory tract

optic II
trochlear IV
oculomotor III

abducens VI

Fig. 1.62 Cranial nerves of the skate – 1st dissection stage.

Remove the skin from the median region of the snout taking care not to damage the superficial ophthalmic nerve and the anterior end of the lateral line system.

Extend the skin removal backwards to clear the area between and round the eyes and over the region of the gill pouches.

● Carefully cut away the roof of the cranium to expose the brain.

Fig 1.63 Cranial nerves of the skate – 2nd dissection stage.

(The second and third dissection stages are carried out on the left side.)

● Trace the superficial ophthalmic nerve from the front of the orbit forwards into the snout. Cut away the cartilage of the orbit and cranium and follow the nerve backwards to the brain; trace its lateralis and deep

ophthalmic branches in the region of the olfactory capsule.

● Clear the connective tissue from the surface of the eye to show the extrinsic eye muscles and carefully cut away the wall of the cranium to show nerves II, III and IV. Trace nerve VI into the base of the posterior rectus muscle.

● Cut away the front of the cranium to show nerve I entering the olfactory capsule.

1.35

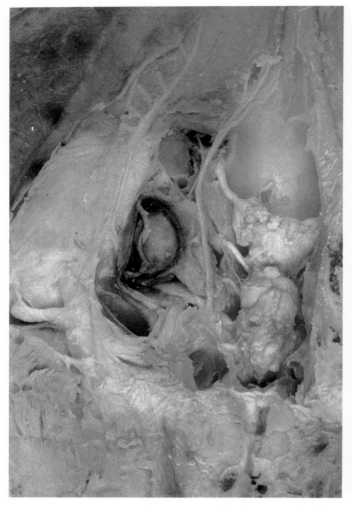

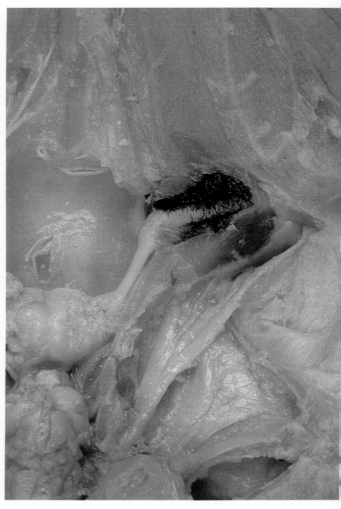

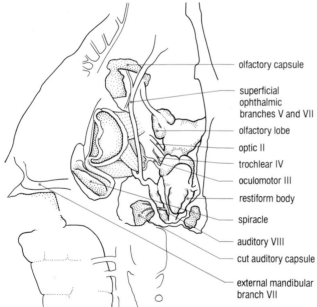

olfactory capsule

superficial
ophthalmic
branches V and VII

olfactory lobe

optic II

trochlear IV

oculomotor III

restiform body

spiracle

auditory VIII

cut auditory capsule

external mandibular
branch VII

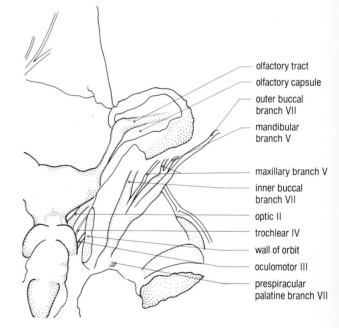

olfactory tract

olfactory capsule

outer buccal
branch VII

mandibular
branch V

maxillary branch V

inner buccal
branch VII

optic II

trochlear IV

wall of orbit

oculomotor III

prespiracular
palatine branch VII

Fig. 1.64 Cranial nerves of the skate – 3rd dissection stage.

● Carefully cut away the roof of the auditory capsule to show the entry of the auditory nerve (VIII) from the brain. Trace the branches of this nerve into the cartilaginous floor of the capsule.

● Expose the external mandibular branch of the hyomandibular nerve (VII)

where it passes in front of the branchial region behind the spiracle.

Fig. 1.65 Cranial nerves of the skate – 4th dissection stage.

(The fourth, fifth and sixth dissection stages are carried out on the right side.)

● Remove the eye by cutting through the oblique and recti muscles and nerve II.

● Observe the three main branches of nerves V and VII which cross the floor of the orbit (inner buccal VII, mandibular

and maxillary V, and outer buccal VII). Trace these nerves forwards below the olfactory capsule and backwards to their origin from the brain through the posterior wall of the orbit. Find the small prespiracular branches of palatine VII near the origin of these nerves.

● Carefully cut away the roof of the olfactory capsule to show the olfactory tract breaking up into fine olfactory nerves within the capsule.

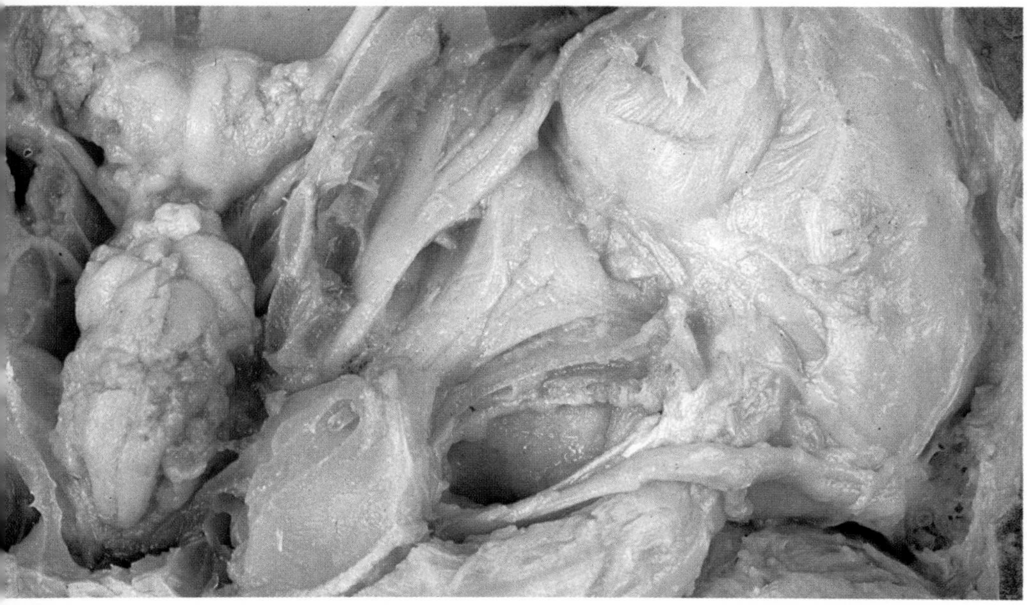

Fig. 1.66 Cranial nerves of the skate – 5th dissection stage.

● Find and expose the external mandibular branch of hyomandibular VII where it passes in front of the branchial region behind the spiracle. Trace this nerve back towards the brain, taking care not to damage it where it passes close to the skin along the posterior border of the spiracle.
● Identify and trace the chorda tympani, the hyoidean and external mandibular branches outwards from the main nerve (VII).

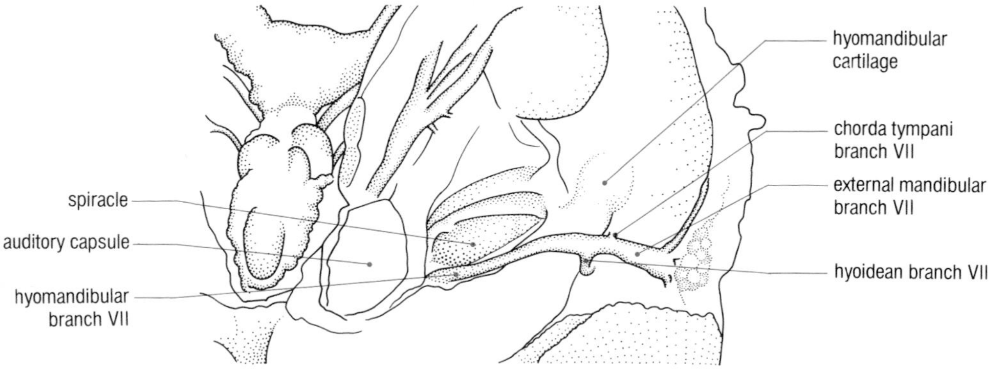

hyomandibular cartilage
chorda tympani branch VII
external mandibular branch VII
spiracle
auditory capsule
hyomandibular branch VII
hyoidean branch VII

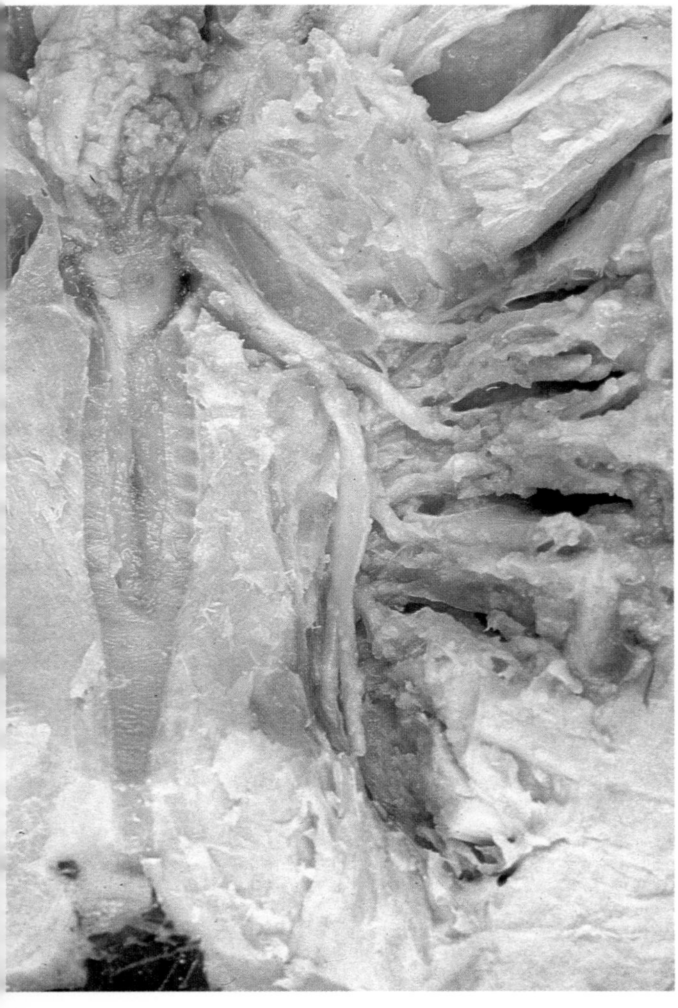

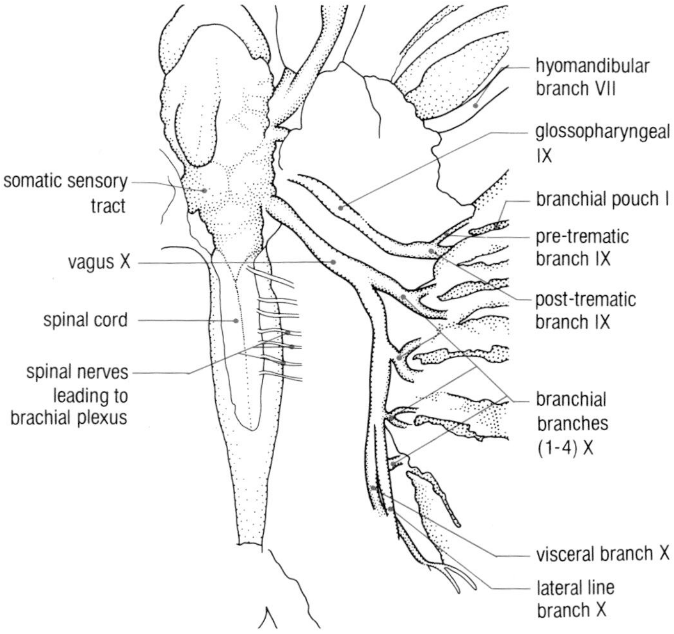

hyomandibular branch VII
glossopharyngeal IX
somatic sensory tract
branchial pouch I
pre-trematic branch IX
vagus X
post-trematic branch IX
spinal cord
spinal nerves leading to brachial plexus
branchial branches (1-4) X
visceral branch X
lateral line branch X

Fig. 1.67 Cranial nerves of the skate – 6th dissection stage.

● Cut carefully through the back of the third gill pouch to expose the anterior cardinal sinus. Observe the branchial branches of nerve X crossing the floor of the sinus. Trace these branches back to the main nerve and find where the lateral line branch arises.

● Carefully slice away the muscle and cartilage from the posterior region of the cranium to expose the first part of the spinal cord and the roots of nerves IX and X. Trace the connection between the branchial branches and the root of the vagus nerve (X).

● Cut away the cartilage of the auditory capsule to follow the course of the glossopharyngeal nerve (IX) to its pre-trematic and post-trematic branches entering the first gill pouch.

2 The Codling

Osteichthyes
Actinopterygii
Teleostei
Paracanthopterygii
Gadus callarius

Introduction

The codling belongs to the class Osteichthyes, the bony fish. We have looked at the dogfish as a representative of the cartilaginous fish and in this chapter we shall contrast its organisation with that of the codling.

The osteichthyans are characterised by a bony skeleton and the possession of a swim-bladder (or air-sac). The latter has had far-reaching consequences concerning the locomotion and body form of the bony fish, as we shall see later.

The bony fish are usually divided into three groups: the crossopterygians, now wholly extinct apart from the coelacanth, *Latimeria*; the dipnoans, or lungfish, of which just three genera exist today; and the actinopterygians, or ray-fins, of which there are over 18,000 species. The codling is a member of the teleosts which represent the most advanced level of organisation of the actinopterygians. In terms of species number, they are the most successful of all fish.

When we considered the evolution of the sharks we saw that it was possible to distinguish three organisational levels. This is also true of the evolution of the actinopterygians. Early ray-fins, or chondrosteans, were dominant in Triassic times but are now almost completely extinct. The fins were stiff and could not be folded, the tail was heterocercal and large rhomboidal scales covered the body. The jaws had a wide gape, with the lower jaw acting as a simple lever.

Towards the end of the Permian certain changes became evident in the chondrosteans. There were fewer fin-rays in the fin and the tail was less asymmetrical. The heavy scales were somewhat reduced. Such changes culminated in fish of the holostean grade, of which there are very few living members. In these fish the jaws became shorter, resulting in a bigger bite force and the cheek region became more open, allowing room for the attachment of enlarged jaw muscles. The maxilla of the upper jaw was more loosely attached to the rest of the bones of the skull and was able to swing down over the mouth.

Several groups of holosteans gave rise to the teleosts, the third and final organisational level; by the late Cretaceous these were the dominant fish. A heterocercal tail was no longer necessary to produce lift since the swim-bladder could be used to control buoyancy (see p. 2.7). Furthermore, the paired fins were freed to be used in braking and to manoeuvre the body. The scales were further reduced from the holostean condition. The premaxilla, as well as the maxilla, was only loosely attached to the rest of the skull. This meant that both bones could swing down to close in the sides of the mouth (see p. 2.14).

These changes seem to have conferred a particularly successful body plan on the teleosts so that the group has radiated widely in both fresh and marine waters. In contrast, the modern-day cartilaginous fish are confined to marine habitats. Use of the swim-bladder as a hydrostatic organ in the bony fish, and the consequent freeing of the pectoral fins (see p. 2.4) to be used in manoeuvring the body, was a very important innovation. These abilities are essential for efficient and speedy negotiation of an environment which is more confined than the open seas.

2.1

Skeleton

The principle elements making up the skeleton of the codling (fig. 2.1) and the dogfish (fig. 1.1) are similar, the main difference being the presence of bone in the codling. Before describing individual bones, it is worth considering how bone is laid down. It may arise in one of two ways. A cartilage precursor may be invaded by bone giving a so-called cartilage bone (or replacement bone). Alternatively, bone may be laid down in connective tissue, like the dermis, without a cartilage precursor. This is called dermal bone. Dermal skeletal elements tend to be flat and plate-like whereas cartilage bones are more robust.

In most fish, both bony and cartilaginous, the vertebral column does not bear the weight of the body but functions as a rod which prevents the body shortening when the fish's locomotory muscles contract. Consequently, the connections between the vertebrae need not be as strong as those seen in tetrapods. The characteristic ball-and-socket joints between tetrapod vertebrae are absent; the amphicoelous vertebrae of fish make edge-to-edge contact. Furthermore, the small extra articulations (zygapophyses) found on tetrapod vertebrae are absent in all but the largest fish, such as the tunny (fig. 2.2). In this case, presumably, they are necessary to strengthen the connections between the vertebrae. The vertebrae of bony fish differ enormously from those of cartilaginous fish. There are no associated extra elements and the neural spines, to which the axial musculature is attached, are very long.

The pectoral girdle is connected firmly to the bones at the back of the skull by the supratemporal bone. This is quite different from the situation in cartilaginous fish and land vertebrates, where the head is not connected to the pectoral girdle. The bones making up the pectoral girdle are the cleithrum (a dermal bone), the scapula and the coracoid plate (replacement bones).

The pelvic girdle is made up of replacement bone only. It is a single triangular plate, each half of which is

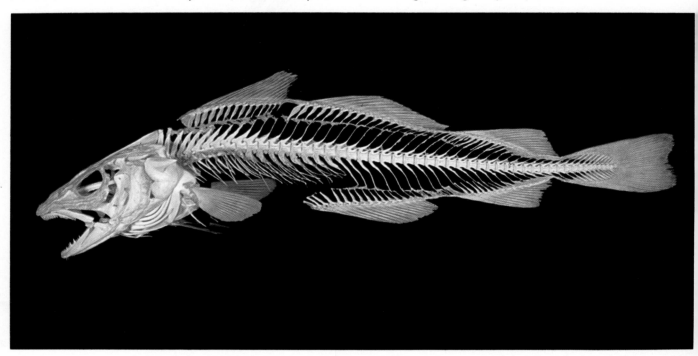

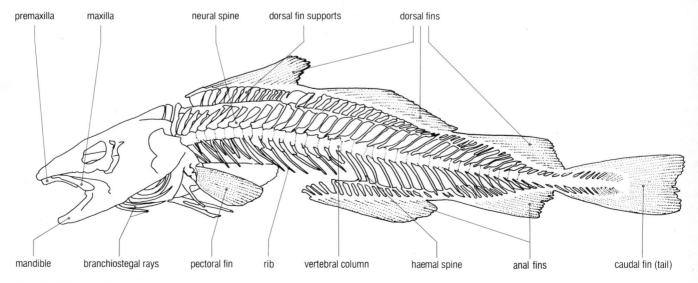

premaxilla   maxilla   neural spine   dorsal fin supports   dorsal fins

mandible   branchiostegal rays   pectoral fin   rib   vertebral column   haemal spine   anal fins   caudal fin (tail)

Fig. 2.1 The codling skeleton in left lateral view.

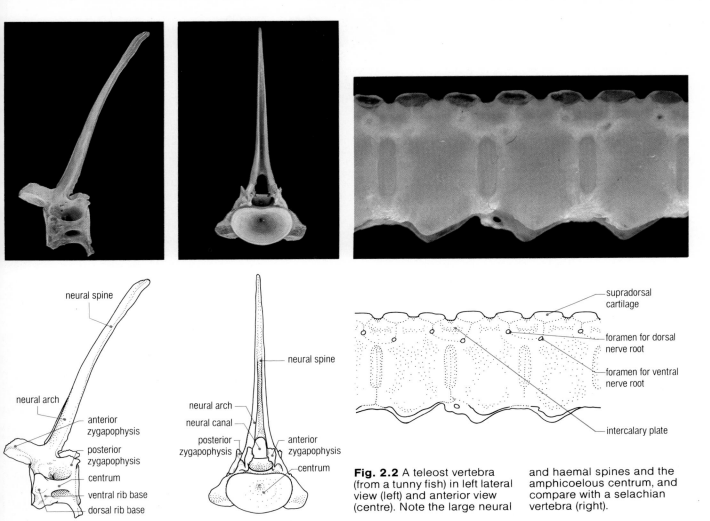

Fig. 2.2 A teleost vertebra (from a tunny fish) in left lateral view (left) and anterior view (centre). Note the large neural and haemal spines and the amphicoelous centrum, and compare with a selachian vertebra (right).

embedded in connective tissue. There is no bony connection with the vertebral column. However, a degree of stability results from the two halves of the girdle being fused to each other ventrally.

Unlike cartilaginous fish, bony fish possess both dorsal and ventral ribs (fig. 2.3).

The movement of the tail in the codling and the dogfish is the main source of propulsion during locomotion. The tail fin of the codling, unlike that of the dogfish, is externally symmetrical (homocercal). Internally, the vertebral column tilts upwards so that the tail lobe is actually entirely ventral to it. Other fins on the fish's body are used in steering and stabilising the body. They can also be used to correct occasional unwanted movements, such as the small forward reaction created as water is expelled from the gill cavity. Teleost fins are not used to produce lift and therefore they are not confined to an aerofoil form.

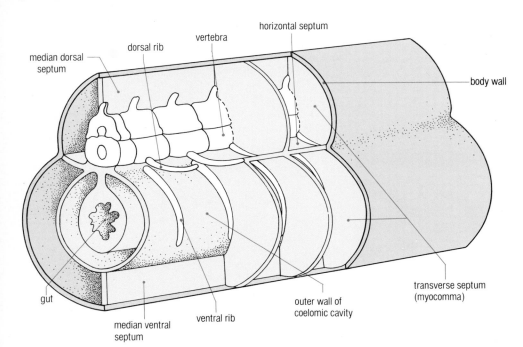

Fig. 2.3 A diagram of a section of the trunk of a bony fish showing how ribs develop in the connective tissue septa.

2.3

They are particularly suited to the fine control of locomotion since their structure confers great flexibility. Each fin consists of bony fin-rays (lepidotrichia) which are supported by rods of bone, the radials (fig. 2.4). The radials sometimes articulate with the neural or haemal arches, but often a gap exists between the radials and the arches. Each fin-ray articulates with its own radial element. Muscles run from the radials to the fin-rays and are responsible for folding and unfolding the fin, and for moving the fin-ray from side to side. Consequently, fin-rays can be moved individually and a great variety of movements of the entire fin is possible.

The scales of bony fish were very complex in the past. Early ray-finned fish bore scales which contained layers of an enamel-like substance, ganoine, and a variant of dentine called cosmine. These substances were gradually reduced as the teleost condition was approached. The scales of teleosts are quite unlike the robust dermal denticles of cartilaginous fish (fig. 2.5).

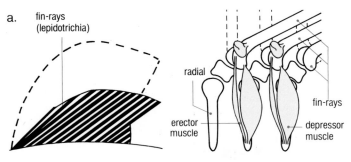

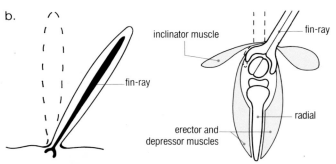

Fig. 2.4 A diagram to show the action of the muscles responsible for folding the fin, (a), and lateral movement in the fin, (b). Fin folding: on the left the dorsal fin is shown in lateral view with the fin erect (broken outline) and folded back (solid outline) under the influence of the depressor muscles; on the right, the contraction of these muscles is indicated by the fattening of their outline. Lateral movement: on the left, the dorsal fin is shown in anterior view with the fin vertical (broken outline) and rotated laterally (solid outline) under the influence of the inclinator muscles; the action of these muscles is shown on the right.

Body shape and musculature

Both the codling and the dogfish have a streamlined body which offers little resistance to movement in water (fig. 2.6). A streamlined shape is achieved when the front of the body is pointed and the greatest body width occurs not far behind the tip. The ideal body profile, which generates the least amount of drag possible, has a width equal to approximately a quarter of the length. Frictional resistance is reduced by smoothly contoured body surfaces and mucus-covered scales.

The codling is not dorsoventrally flattened at the anterior end like the dogfish, but instead is laterally compressed. Dorsoventral flattening helps to counteract the sinking tendency of the dogfish and is unnecessary in the codling which uses its air-bladder to maintain neutral buoyancy (p. 2.7). However, some pelagic teleosts which swim continuously (mackerels, tunas and swordfish), like the dogfish, do not possess a swim-bladder. Instead, the pectoral fins are streamlined and are set at an angle to the water flow so as to create lift.

The manoeuvrability of the teleosts has contributed greatly to their success. The flexible fins and hydrostatic organ have already been mentioned. Although the swim-bladder is dorsally positioned, the centre of buoyancy of the body tends to be below the centre of gravity, so the fish is unstable about its longitudinal (roll) axis. Potential instability is a prerequisite of manoeuvrability.

Lateral undulations of the body and tail provide the propulsive force in swimming. The muscle blocks of the tail region are responsible for this and can be seen through the skin. The musculature is metameric in that the muscles are serially repeated in a long sequence of body segments. Superficially they appear W or V-shaped but are more complicated than this, as shown in fig. 2.7. Each myomere is drawn out into forward and backward pointing cones. The cone of one myomere fits into the hollow of the next, so that a transverse section would show concentric rings of interlocking myomeres. This complicated pattern extends the force of contraction over more than one segment, which is necessary to produce bending of the fish's body. This pattern may also be a solution to a problem encountered when the body bends. If the muscle fibres were orientated parallel to the axis of the body, those nearest the periphery would need to contract at a greater rate than those nearest the centre. This cannot be achieved in a single muscle, and the arrangement seen in fig. 2.7 may allow all the fibres to contract at equal rates.

Fig. 2.5 A transverse section through the skin of a teleost, top, x 50. Note the scales are very thin and light in comparison with the elasmobranch placoid scales, bottom, x 50

Fig. 2.6 The codling (top) and dogfish (bottom) in left lateral view. Compare the overall shape of the body, the position and shape of the fins, the appearance of the tail, the position of the mouth and the arrangement of the gill opening(s).

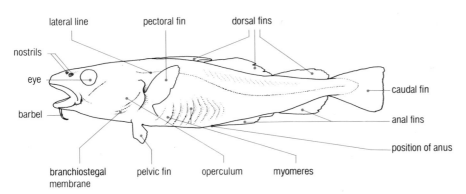

lateral line — pectoral fin — dorsal fins

nostrils

eye

barbel

branchiostegal membrane — pelvic fin — operculum — myomeres

caudal fin

anal fins

position of anus

spiracle — dorsal fins — caudal fin

eye

ventral mouth

gill openings — pectoral fin — pelvic fin

anal fin

Fig. 2.7 A diagram to show the way in which the backward and forward-pointing cones of myomeres interlock.

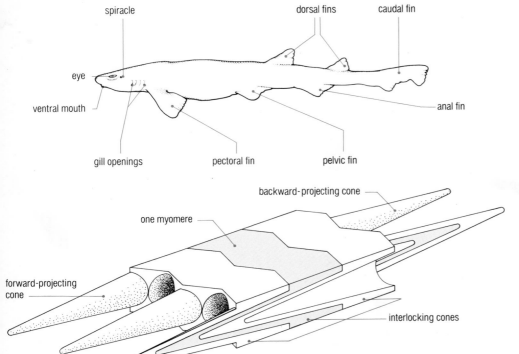

backward-projecting cone

one myomere

forward-projecting cone

interlocking cones

2.5

Body cavity

In the abdominal cavity we find the digestive system, the urinogenital system, the air-bladder, and the heart and abdominal blood vessels (both of which are described on p. 2.9).

The digestive system is not greatly different from that of the dogfish, except that the intestine has no spiral valve. Instead it is longer and may have outgrowths, the pyloric caeca (fig. 2.10), which increase the surface area for secretion of enzymes and absorption of food.

The urinogenital system is very different from the ancestral vertebrate plan. In the male the testis acquires a new duct of its own to transport sperm. In the female, the ovary acquires a duct of its own, the oviduct, while the archinephric duct drains the kidney which may be a long opisthonephros.

The air-bladder is a large transparent sac occupying the back of the abdominal cavity (fig. 2.10). In primitive teleosts, it has a connection anteriorly with the oesophagus, but not in the codling. Inclusion of an air-filled sac in the body reduces the overall density of the fish. At a certain level in the water the fish experiences an upthrust (supporting force) which balances its weight. At this level the fish is said to be neutrally buoyant. If the fish changes levels in the water, the swim-bladder is affected in the following way. If the fish descends in the water, the surrounding water pressure will increase. This reduces the volume of the swim-bladder, thereby increasing the density of the fish; it can then sink even further, or expend energy to remain at the same level. The converse happens if the fish changes to a higher level in the water. Therefore, in order to counteract volume changes in the air-bladder, the fish actively secretes and absorbs gas into and from the air-bladder. This alters its pressure and consequently its volume. Although this takes time, it does mean that the fish can remain at various levels in the water without having to expend energy. The gas is secreted by the gas gland and concentrated in the air-bladder by a network of blood vessels (rete) acting as a counter-current multiplier. A richly vascularised part of the wall, sometimes separated off as an oval organ (fig. 2.9), absorbs the gas from the air-bladder.

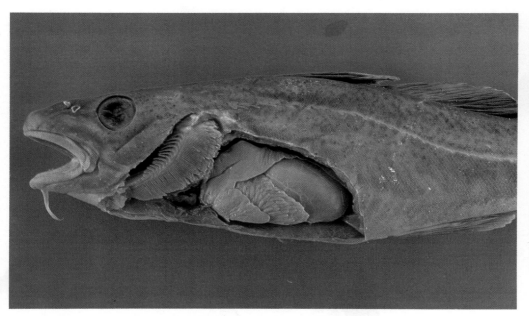

Fig. 2.8 Body cavity – 1st dissection stage

● Remove the left half of the branchiostegal membrane and its rays and the left operculum, so as to expose the whole of the gill cavity.

● Make a median ventral incision from the pelvic fins through the body wall, cutting posteriorly to the left of the anus.

● From this point, continue to cut through the body wall in a curve dorsally and then anteriorly, to a point near the top of the gill cavity. Cut through the pectoral girdle to join up with the first incision which removed the branchiostegal membrane.

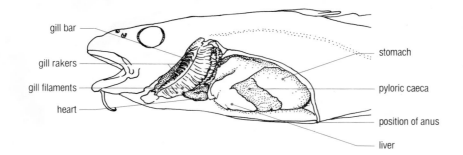

gill bar

gill rakers

gill filaments

heart

stomach

pyloric caeca

position of anus

liver

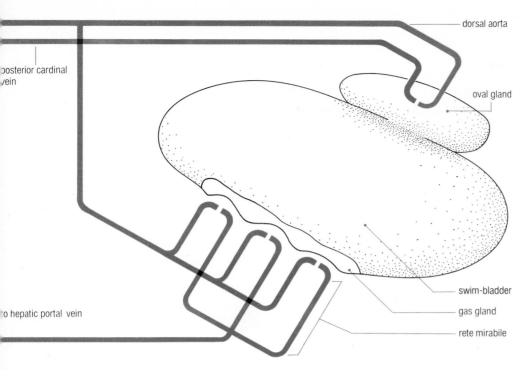

dorsal aorta

posterior cardinal vein

oval gland

to hepatic portal vein

swim-bladder

gas gland

rete mirabile

Fig. 2.9 A diagram of the teleost swim-bladder showing the rete which acts as a counter-current multiplier.

Fig. 2.10 Body cavity – 2nd dissection stage

● Using a blunt probe, find how far postero-dorsally the body cavity extends.

● Remove the remaining side wall of the body cavity to expose the posterior part of the swim-bladder.

● Cut away the large left lobe of the liver.

● Cut the membranes that hold the loop of the alimentary canal together. Unravel this so as to show its complete length.

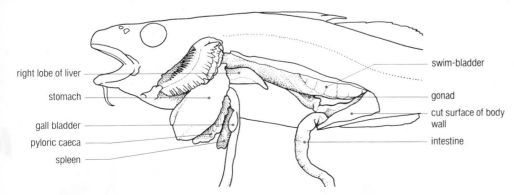

right lobe of liver

stomach

gall bladder

pyloric caeca

spleen

swim-bladder

gonad

cut surface of body wall

intestine

Gills

Opercular gills are characteristic of the codling and all bony fish; they differ from the septal gills of the elasmobranchs in that they are protected externally by the operculum, and the septa are very reduced or absent (fig. 2.11 and 2.12).

There are four gill arches and one pseudobranch on either side of the head. Each arch consists of two hemibranchs, and each hemibranch bears a row of gill filaments. The pseudobranch is thought to represent the gill arch associated with the spiracle in elasmobranchs; it is tucked away under the edge of the operculum and may have a secretory function.

On the inner margin of the gills are found gill-rakers. These stiff strainers are used to stop food particles fouling the gills.

During respiration and feeding, a continuous one-way current of water is drawn across the gills. This is achieved by changes in volume in the buccal cavity and opercular cavity. These cavities, therefore, function as pumps, and a typical cycle of movements is represented in fig. 2.13. The muscles responsible for changing the volume of the cavities are dealt with later (p. 2.10). The one-way flow of water is maintained by the use of valves. For example, the operculum, which is a flap of skin strengthened by bone, closes the chamber in which the gills are found; it prevents water flowing from the outside into the opercular cavity during ventilation of the gills. Similarly, small flaps of skin, the maxillary and mandibular valves, are found inside the mouth and prevent water flowing out of the buccal cavity.

Fig. 2.11 The gills of the dogfish (left) and teleost (right) compared. Each diagram shows a transverse section through a gill arch. Notice the arrangement of the gill septum and the gill filaments.

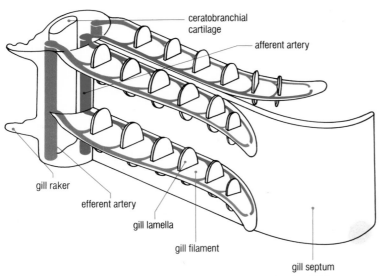

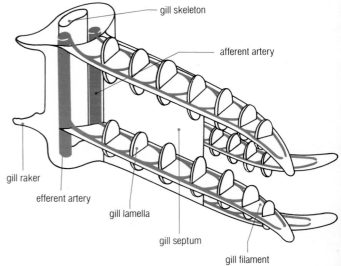

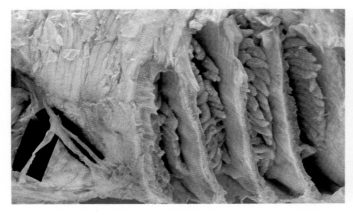

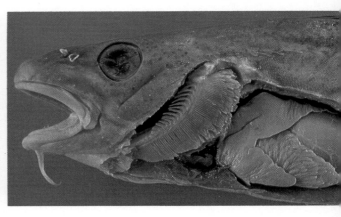

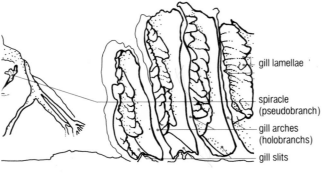

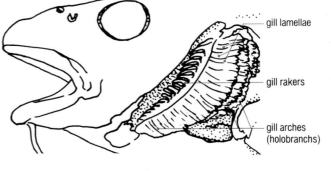

Fig. 2.12 External views of the dogfish (left) and the codling (right) dissected to show the arrangement of the gills. Note the four gill pouches opening separately to the exterior in the dogfish, and the single opercular cavity in the codling.

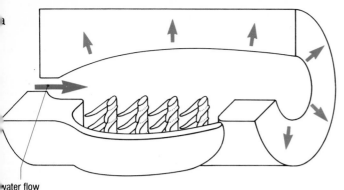

water flow

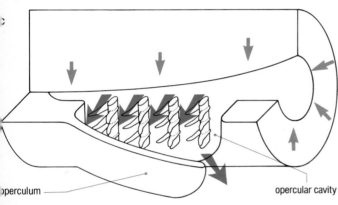

buccal cavity

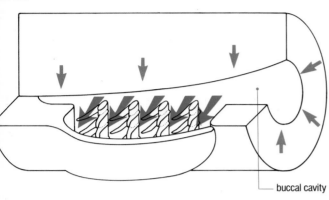

operculum

opercular cavity

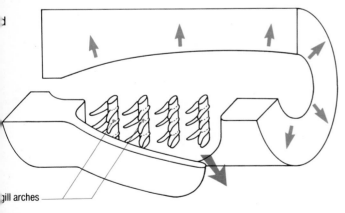

gill arches

Cardiovascular system

The cardiovascular system is very similar to that of the dogfish. The heart is built on the same plan except that the conus may be much reduced. The arrangement of the branchial arteries differs only in the absence of the spiracle in teleosts (fig. 2.14). The pseudobranch is supplied with blood from the first efferent artery. Running from the pseudobranch is the hyoidean artery, which eventually supplies the eye. Deoxygenated blood, therefore, never reaches the pseudobranch and, clearly, this structure has no respiratory function.

Unlike the situation in the dogfish there are no abdominal veins present (fig. 2.15). The veins of the pectoral fin enter the common cardinals instead. The veins of the pelvic fin drain into the renal portal system. A new vein runs from the renal portal system to enter the hepatic vein. Consequently, there are two routes which blood from the posterior part of the body may take to reach the heart: either through the renal portal and posterior cardinal, or through the new vein and the hepatic vein. This situation changes quite radically in land vertebrates.

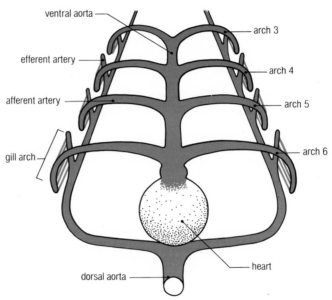

ventral aorta

efferent artery

afferent artery

gill arch

arch 3

arch 4

arch 5

arch 6

heart

dorsal aorta

Fig. 2.14 The aortic arches of a teleost in ventral view.

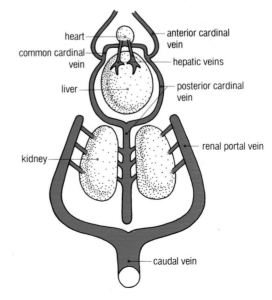

heart

common cardinal vein

liver

kidney

anterior cardinal vein

hepatic veins

posterior cardinal vein

renal portal vein

caudal vein

Fig. 2.13 A diagram illustrating the double pumping system used to ventilate the gills of teleosts. In (a) the mouth is open, the operculum is closed and water is sucked in due to a decrease in pressure in the buccal cavity. Water is forced across the gills into the opercular cavity in (b) due to an increase in pressure in the buccal cavity with the mouth closed. In (c) the mouth remains closed and the pressure in the buccal cavity continues to increase, but at a slower rate. As water fills the opercular cavity the pressure increases and the water is forced out through the operculum. The cycle is completed when the mouth opens again, in (d), and the pressure of the buccal cavity begins to drop, thus sucking in water. The pressure in the opercular cavity is still higher than that in the buccal cavity and water continues to flow out of the opercular cavity. Back-flow into the buccal cavity is prevented by the resistance of the gills.

Fig. 2.15 The major veins of a teleost in ventral view.

2.9

Jaw musculature

Volume changes in the opercular and buccal cavities are responsible for the one-way flow of water needed for feeding and respiration, as seen earlier (fig. 2.13). These changes are brought about by muscular action (fig. 2.16). The muscles involved are seen in the dissections below, (figs. 2.17, 2.18 and 2.19).

The muscles which increase the volume of the buccal cavity are the geniohyoideus, sternohyoideus, and the levator hyoidei. The first two muscles pull the lower jaw down, and the third swings the hyomandibula bone to the side, thereby creating more space in the buccal cavity. A decrease in volume is brought about by the adductor mandibulae which raises the jaw, and the adductor hyomandibulae which pulls in the hyomandibula

The volume of the opercular cavity is increased by the dilator operculi which moves the operculum laterally, and decreased by the adductor operculi which pulls the operculum back in. A complex of muscles runs between the branchiostegal rays. Contraction of certain members of this complex helps to reduce the volume of the opercular cavity, while contraction of others leads to an increase in the volume.

Clearly, some of the muscles in each of the cavities will work synergistically, thus producing the differential pressures required in the cavities to generate the one-way flow of water.

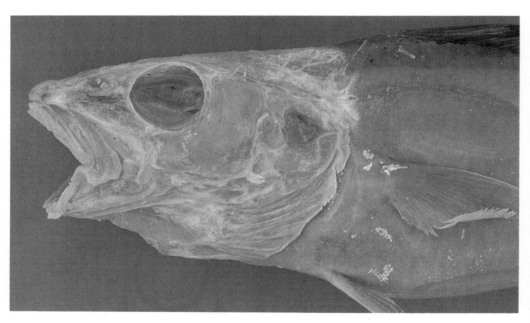

Fig. 2.16 A diagrammatic representation of the jaw muscles of a teleost. The muscles shown in blue operate the buccal cavity and those in red, the opercular cavity. The muscles responsible for decreasing the volume of a cavity are striped and those which increase the volume are shown in solid colour.

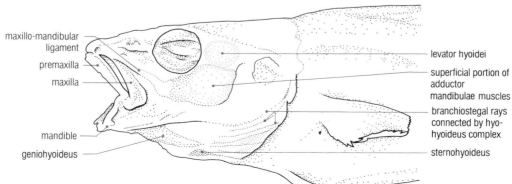

Fig. 2.17 Jaw musculature – 1st dissection stage

● Skin the ventral surface and the left side of the codling's head. Note the geniohyoideus muscle running from the lower jaw to the ventral part of the branchial skeleton and the sternohyoideus muscle running from the branchial skeleton to the shoulder girdle.

● Skin the branchiostegal rays very carefully to see the hyoideus muscle complex which runs between the branchiostegal rays.

● Remove the eyeball and the series of small bones (postorbital, suborbital, lachrymal) around the eye.

● Clear away connective tissue and note the superficial portion of the adductor mandibulae which inserts into a ligament running from the maxilla to the upper jaw (maxillo-mandibular ligament).

● Carefully clear this ligament to find these attachments. Notice the large levator hyoidei muscle just behind the orbit.

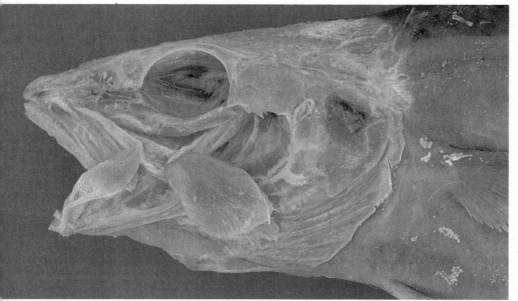

Fig. 2.18 Jaw musculature – 2nd dissection stage

● Carefully place a blunt instrument (scalpel handle or seeker) underneath the superficial portion of the adductor mandibulae and separate the muscle from the underlying tissues, freeing its dorsal and posterior edges.

● Reflect this muscle forwards and downwards to expose another, larger part of the adductor mandibulae (2). This muscle inserts by a strong tendon onto the lower jaw.

● Free the adductor mandibulae (2) at its posterior and dorsal edges and reflect it forwards. You will then see a further branch of the adductor mandibulae (3) running from the maxilla to the pterygoid.

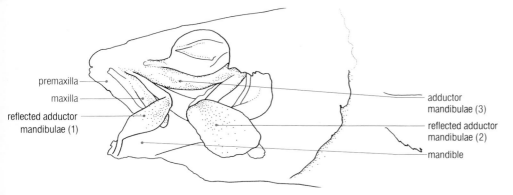

premaxilla
maxilla
reflected adductor mandibulae (1)

adductor mandibulae (3)
reflected adductor mandibulae (2)
mandible

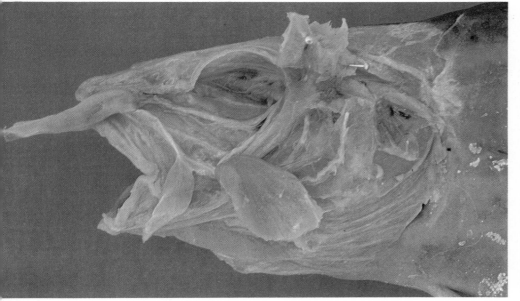

Fig. 2.19 Jaw musculature – 3rd dissection stage

● Reflect the adductor mandibulae (3) anteriorly to expose the fourth branch of the adductor mandibulae which runs from the hyomandibula to the tendon of adductor mandibulae (2).

● Find the adductor hyomandibulae which lies medial to the adductores mandibulae.

● Carefully free the ventral edge of the levator hyoidei and pin back this muscle exposing both the dilator operculi which inserts on the lateral surface of the operculum, and the adductor operculi which inserts on the inner surface. Lift the operculum upwards and forwards to see this second insertion.

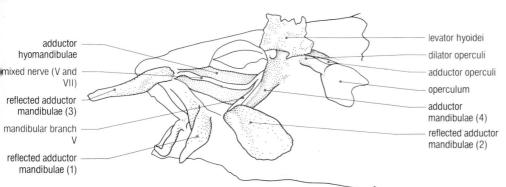

adductor hyomandibulae
mixed nerve (V and VII)
reflected adductor mandibulae (3)
mandibular branch V
reflected adductor mandibulae (1)

levator hyoidei
dilator operculi
adductor operculi
operculum
adductor mandibulae (4)
reflected adductor mandibulae (2)

Skull

The obvious difference between the skull of the codling and the skull of the dogfish is that the former is composed of bone. The bones may be cartilage bone or dermal bone.

To appreciate how cartilage and dermal bones fit together in the skull it is instructive to look again at the vertebrate embryo. We see that various separate cartilaginous structures arise in the embryonic brain-case (see fig. 2.20). These structures ultimately fuse to form the braincase and are replaced with bone in most vertebrates. Associated with the cartilages of the braincase are the cartilages of the gill arch elements. As already described, (p. 1.32), some of these form the jaw and the hyomandibular brace and are eventually replaced with bone. The composition of the skull is completed when dermal bone is laid down around these original structures. The bones of a teleost skull (fig. 2.22) are very numerous and highly variable, so it can be a very complicated task to determine whether they are cartilage or dermal in origin. The more important bones may be classified as shown in fig. 2.21.

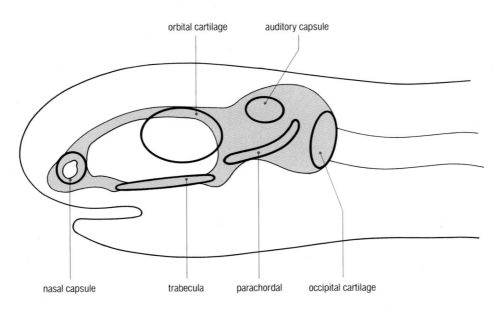

orbital cartilage   auditory capsule

nasal capsule   trabecula   parachordal   occipital cartilage

Fig. 2.20 A diagram to illustrate the main cartilaginous elements of the embryonic skull. The regions ringed by a heavy black line represent the earliest stage of development whilst the blue regions show the incorporation of these elements into the braincase at a later stage in the embryo.

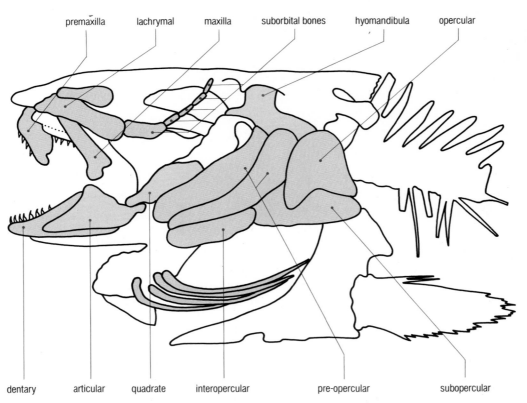

premaxilla   lachrymal   maxilla   suborbital bones   hyomandibula   opercular

dentary   articular   quadrate   interopercular   pre-opercular   subopercular

Fig. 2.21 A diagram of the teleost skull showing the principal dermal bones (blue) and cartilage bones derived from the gill arches (red).

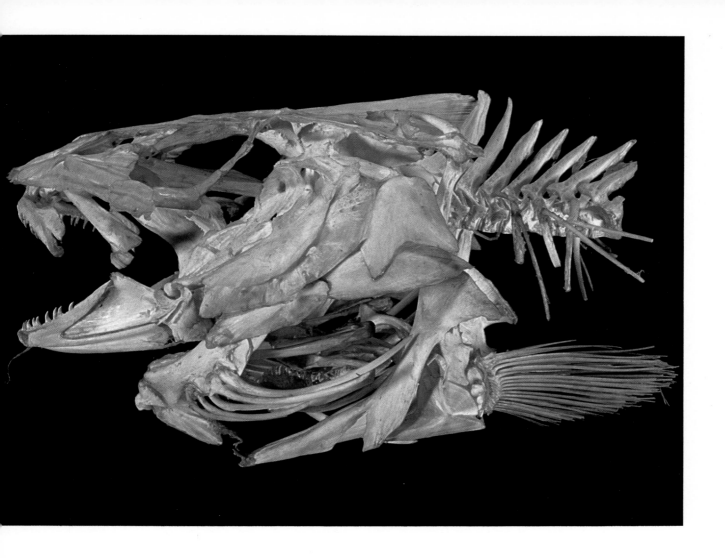

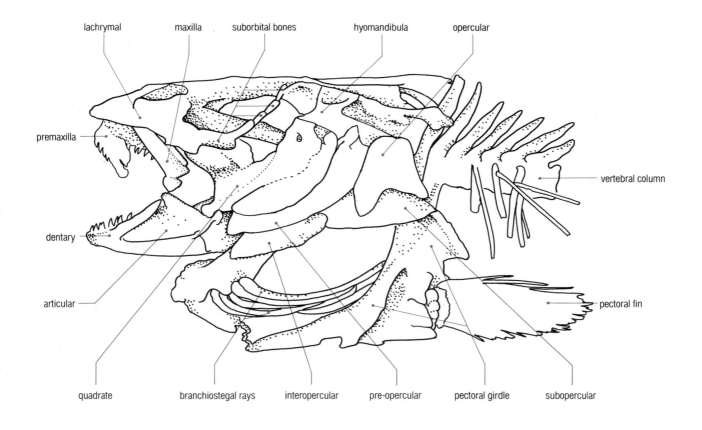

lachrymal   maxilla   suborbital bones   hyomandibula   opercular

premaxilla

vertebral column

dentary

articular

pectoral fin

quadrate   branchiostegal rays   interopercular   pre-opercular   pectoral girdle   subopercular

Fig. 2.22 The codling skull in left lateral view.

The water current is used to suck in food and, as such, a round mouth with a small gape is the most efficient shape for utilising a large suction pressure.

Furthermore, when a mouth with a wide gape closes, water and pieces of food are swept out at the sides. In early ray-finned fishes (fig. 2.23) the mouth opening was not circular, but wide and grinning. The premaxilla and maxilla of the upper jaw were firmly attached to the skull and the jaws would be snapped shut on the prey. This is an adequate mechanism if the prey are large and slow-moving, but it permits little precision when dealing with small food items. In primitive teleosts like the trout, the maxilla has become free and can swing down, closing the side of the mouth with a flap of skin. More advanced teleosts, like the codling, also have a loosely attached premaxilla. Both bones can swing forward as the mouth opens, so the mouth assumes a rounded shape with the sides completely closed. In some fish (for example, the cyprinoids) the premaxilla becomes completely detached from the maxilla and can be protruded forward so that the mouth opening is at the end of a tube pointing forwards. This may be useful in facilitating feeding at the surface; or in closing the mouth faster; or in allowing a greater range of movements when the food is being positioned between the lips.

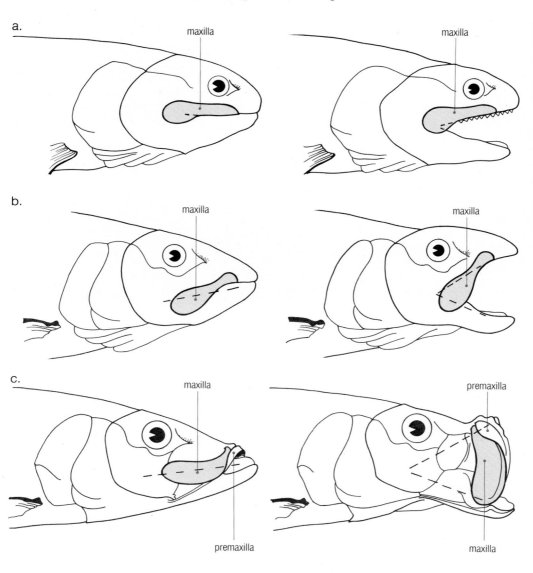

Fig. 2.23 A diagram illustrating the evolution of the maxilla and premaxilla in ray-finned fishes. (a) is an early ray-finned fish with a wide, grinning gape. (b) is a primitive teleost in which the maxilla is free to swing down and close the side of the mouth. (c) is an advanced teleost in which the premaxilla is also free to move and, together with the maxilla, closes the side of the mouth completely, giving the mouth a round gape. The diagrams on the left show the jaws closed and those on the right show them opened.

3 The Frog

Amphibia
Lissamphibia
Anura
Rana temporaria

Introduction

The frog is an amphibian. The early amphibians were the first vertebrates to adopt a terrestrial existence and to assume the tetrapod form. Consequently, we shall be studying the frog as an example of tetrapods in general and the amphibians in particular.

The frog is dissected as an example of an amphibian, but it is important to remember that it does not represent what is considered to be the ancestral amphibian form. Modern amphibians appear to be specialised amphibians; the frog is specialised even further in being adapted to jumping (saltatory locomotion) and swimming.

Modern amphibians are usually classified in three groups: the Anura (frogs and toads); the Urodela (salamanders and newts); and the Apoda (legless forms). Together they comprise the Lissamphibia (or modern Amphibia). There is considerable debate as to whether the Lissamphibia comprise a natural group since the characteristics of the modern forms may have arisen more than once among the early amphibians. Some workers consider that the Lissamphibia form a natural group because of specialised features which the three subgroups have in common.

These features are skin glands, green rods in the retina, a special membrane in the ear (papilla amphibiorum), and teeth in which the crown is separated from the root by a band of fibrous tissue. It is important to note, however, that many of these features are soft parts of the animals and cannot be traced in the fossil record. It is possible that some of these characteristics may have been inherited from a very early common tetrapod ancestor. Alternatively, the specialised characters may have arisen in parallel in the three groups. If either of these were true the Lissamphibia would be an unnatural group. Recently it has been suggested that frogs and salamanders arose from different ancestors as far back as the early Carboniferous, and that features considered typical of the Lissamphibia evolved in parallel in the two groups in the Permian and Triassic. Differences in the pattern of the jaw musculature have been used as evidence for this suggestion. Unfortunately, resolution of the problem of lissamphibian origins must await the discovery of further fossil forms.

Amphibians are thought to have arisen from crossopterygian fish. One extinct group of these fish, the rhipidistians, include the closest known relatives of tetrapods. They show similarities to early amphibians in the pattern of bones in the skull roof, and in the way that the braincase is divided into two halves which are connected by a hinge. An internal nostril is present in rhipidistians, as in amphibians. Furthermore, it is possible that the tetrapod limb arose through a series of modifications of the rhipidistian fin.

It is usually envisaged that such fish, living near the banks of lakes or ponds, evolved certain structures useful to their life in water which also enabled them to survive on land. For example, a muscular fin could be used for supporting the head above water in order to gulp air, or for passage through particularly weedy ponds. Such a fin could also help to support the body on land. A lung would be advantageous to a fish which lived in oxygen-deficient water. Such a structure would also be essential on land where an animal uses gaseous oxygen. These fish might have made excursions onto the land, where initially they would have been very successful because of the wealth of unused habitats and food sources, and the absence of predators and competitors.

The actual pressure which forced tetrapod ancestors onto land has been much debated. Some workers argue that the climate of the time was seasonally arid and that ponds inhabited by rhipidistian fishes would have occasionally dried out, creating a selection pressure favouring those capable of terrestrial existence. Other workers feel that predation on the rhipidistian larvae might have favoured adults which travelled overland to small bodies of water to lay eggs where the larvae might have stood a better chance of surviving. It is impossible to be certain about the particular selection pressures involved.

Life on land presents several problems: the body must be supported in air for locomotion and breathing; temperature is more variable, especially from day to night; and there is a tendency for animals to lose water. However, there are also advantages. Metabolically, it is cheaper to move on land. This is because water is denser than air, and oxygen is more readily available in air than in water. Modern amphibians have adapted to some of the problems of living on land, and they are successful in terms of species diversity. However, they have not become entirely independent of water. Most of them require some body of water in which to lay eggs, even if it is only a water-filled plant.

3.1

Skeleton

The frog skeleton possesses features representative of all land-living vertebrates as well as its specialisations for saltatory locomotion (fig. 3.1).

The spinal column no longer functions merely to resist change in length as it does in fish; it must also bear the weight of the body on land. Consequently, each vertebra has become more firmly attached to its neighbours through the interlocking centra and additional articulations, called zygapophyses, which develop on the neural arch (see fig. 3.2). The centrum is not amphicoelous (see fig. 2.2).

The vertebrae in all tetrapods exhibit considerably more regional variation than those of fish. In fossil amphibians the vertebrae along the thorax and back usually bore stout ribs – these are absent or reduced in most modern amphibians. The ribs functioned as attachment areas for muscles used in respiration and in supporting the body. They also provided some protection for the contents of the abdomen and thorax. In the tail region the anterior vertebrae were sturdily built to form a surface for muscle attachments. Posteriorly, these tail vertebrae gradually became smaller; they did not bear ribs, but they did have haemal arches, which are the remnants of the fish's ventral ribs. Ventral ribs are not found in other tetrapods and it is generally accepted that tetrapods' ribs are homologous with the dorsal ribs of fish (see p. 2.3).

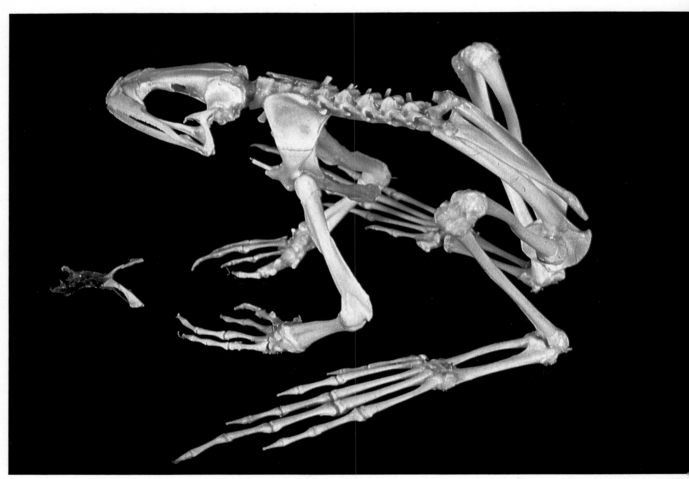

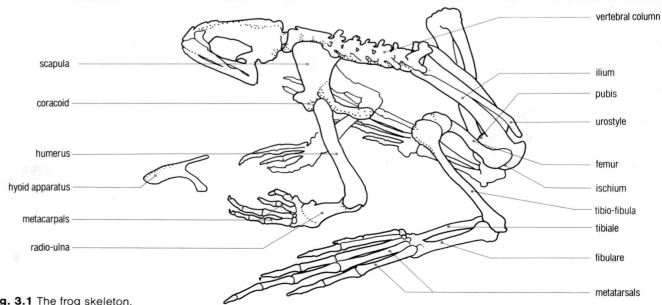

Fig. 3.1 The frog skeleton.

The frog shows many modifications of this basic tetrapod skeletal plan. The vertebral column is very modified; there are usually only nine vertebrae present, one of which abuts against the pelvic girdle. Behind the pelvic girdle, the vertebrae are fused into a rod called the urostyle. The force generated on jumping is transmitted efficiently to the body by this short, rigid vertebral column.

The limb of all tetrapods has a relatively constant configuration (although it undergoes considerable specialisation in some forms). It is called a pentadactyl limb because some of the elements are consistently arranged in groups of five, as shown in fig. 3.3. It is possible to homologise the bones in the tetrapod limb with those in the fin of a crossopterygian fish as shown in fig. 3.4.

The frog's hind legs are long – an adaptation to saltatory locomotion. Long legs can push against the ground for a longer time, so reducing the amount of work done in moving the body at any particular moment. The leg is lengthened due to the elongation of the femur, the fibula and tibia, and two of the ankle bones, the tibiale and fibulare. The ilium, which is a long, slender bone that extends forwards and upwards from the acetabulum, contacts the sacral vertebra in a movable joint and effectively adds another limb segment to the already lengthened back leg. The tibia and fibula, and many of the ankle bones, are fused. This gives them the strength and rigidity necessary to transmit thrust efficiently. Five elongated toes are present in the foot and they provide a wide platform from which to push off on land. Webbing between the toes increases the surface area of the foot when swimming.

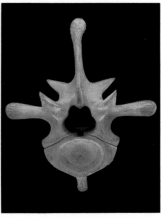
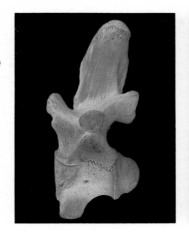
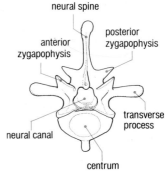
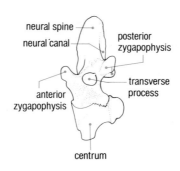

Fig. 3.2 A tetrapod vertebra in left lateral view (left) and anterior view (right). (Note: this vertebra is not from an amphibian).

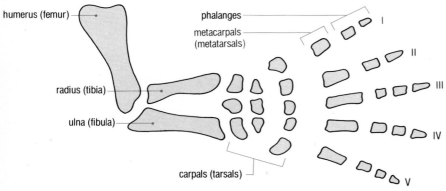

Fig. 3.3 Diagram to show the general pentadactyl pattern of limb construction in early tetrapods. The digits are indicated by Roman numerals and terms in parentheses refer to the hindlimb.

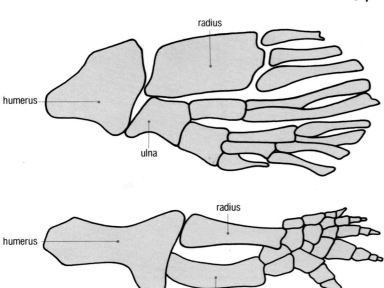

Fig. 3.4 A diagram of the shoulder girdle and front left appendage in a crossopterygian fish (top) and an early tetrapod (bottom), to show the homology which exists between them.

The tetrapod limb is used as a strut to lever the animal's body off the ground. Consequently, there must be a firm attachment of the limbs to the body and this is accomplished by the limb girdles. The pectoral girdle is far more robust than that of a fish. The coracoid plates and the small cartilage bone, the scapula, have increased in size to form a muscle-bearing surface. The scapula and coracoid plates bear the glenoid socket with which the humerus articulates. A single interclavicle, paired cleithra and paired clavicles are also present. The clavicles form a brace between the two halves of the limb girdle so preventing it collapsing when the limb is moved. The complete girdle is connected to the vertebral column by a series of muscles which form a 'sling'.

The pectoral girdle in frogs is adapted to withstanding shock on landing. The forelimb is shorter and more robust than the hindlimb, and the elements of the pectoral girdle tend to undergo fusion to provide a strong brace between the limbs (see fig. 3.5). No interclavicle is present but the clavicle forms a bar connecting scapula and sternum (the breastbone). Although there is no interclavicle ventrally to strengthen the girdle, other bones (such as the coracoid plates which contact each other ventrally) may be modified to give additional strength.

The pelvic girdle is firmly attached to the vertebral column by the bony connection formed by the sacral rib. In fish the pelvic girdle is made of one cartilage bone only; in a tetrapod, however, this bony structure is elaborated, especially ventrally, to provide areas for muscle attachment. The resulting paired bones are termed the ilium, ischium and pubis (see fig. 3.1).

Skin

The skin of modern amphibians contains one of their specialised features, the skin glands (see fig. 3.6). There are three kinds of these: hedonic glands, which are found on the male's body and are thought to produce a secretion which stimulates the female during courtship; mucous glands, which are distributed all over the body of both sexes and secrete mucopolysaccharides which help to keep the skin moist and permeable; and poison glands, which are located on the dorsal surface of the animal. Possession of the latter is often associated with warning coloration and behaviour.

An important aspect of the amphibian skin is its high permeability to water and gases. This is particularly useful since it permits the animals to respire through the skin. Blood is brought to the skin by a special branch of the pulmo-cutaneous arch, the cutaneous artery, and the oxygenated blood returns to the systemic circulation via the cutaneous vein (fig. 3.8). This form of respiration does not rely on muscular contraction and the expenditure of energy, which are necessary in ventilating lungs. In fact, frogs have no ribs for costal muscles to attach to, and some salamanders have even lost their lungs.

Water passage through the skin presents a problem since amphibians out of water will tend to dry out. Consequently, they are confined, on the whole, to damp, cool environments. The skin can actively transport sodium ions and will also retain urea within the body. These substances will tend to raise the osmotic pressure of the body fluid helping terrestrial species to take up water.

Not all respiration is cutaneous. The oxygen supply can be supplemented by buccal ventilation (see. p. 3.8), a process which requires a wide head and nostrils which open internally, as seen in the frog.

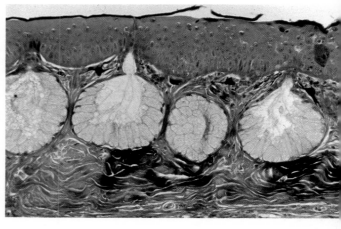

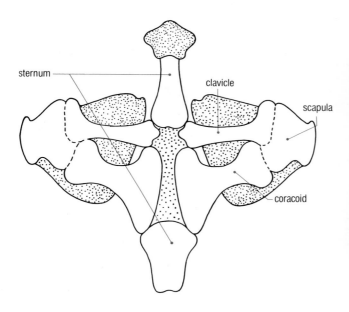

Fig. 3.5 A diagram of the pectoral girdle of a frog showing the coracoid which connects the scapula and sternum. Stippled areas represent cartilage.

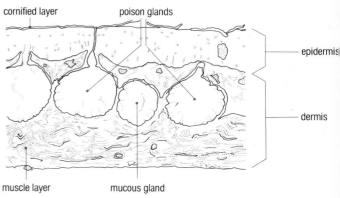

Fig. 3.6 A cross-section of amphibian skin, x 150, showing two types of gland.

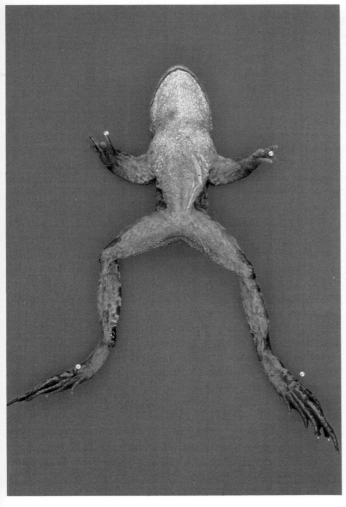

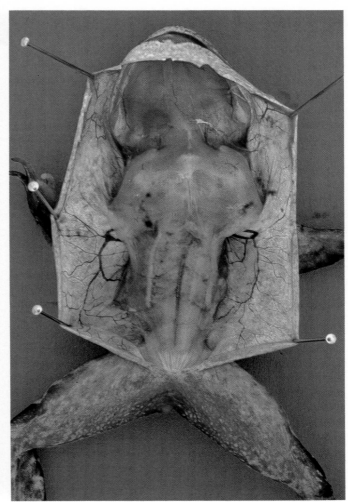

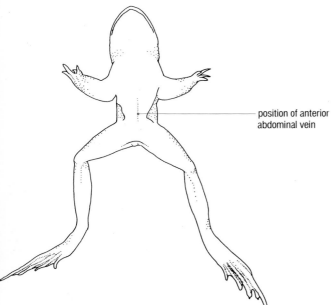

position of anterior
abdominal vein

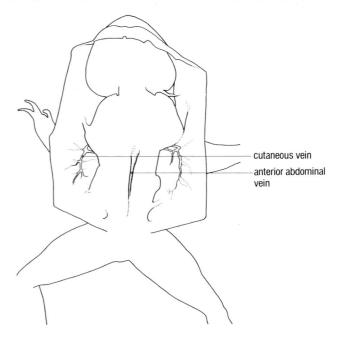

cutaneous vein

anterior abdominal
vein

**Fig. 3.7 Ventral view –
animal prepared for
dissection.**

**Fig. 3.8 Body cavity – 1st
dissection stage.**

● Make a median ventral
incision and deflect the skin
laterally, to show the anterior
abdominal vein running along
the mid-ventral surface of the
abdomen. Take care not to
damage the cutaneous
vessels which join the skin in
the region near the forelimbs.

3.5

Body cavity

The amphibian digestive system (fig. 3.10) does not differ radically from that of fish. The simple tubular intestine (similar to that of teleosts) is fairly unspecialised and perhaps primitive. It is divided into two distinct parts: the small intestine, which has a narrow diameter and is constricted at its lower end by the iliocaecal valve; and the large intestine, or colon. The small intestine is responsible for most of the absorption of digested food. The colon may also absorb food and water, although its main task is to collect matter to form into faeces.

Unlike the digestive system of fish, amphibians possess an oesophagus – a well-defined tube connecting the mouth and stomach. Also, the pharynx is much reduced owing to the loss of gills.

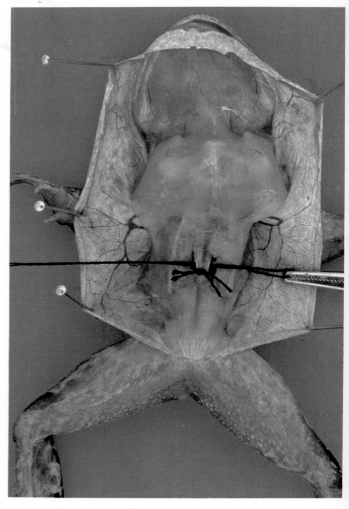

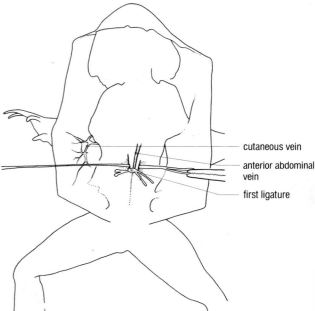

Fig. 3.9 Body cavity – 2nd dissection stage.

● Make a 1cm slit in the ventral abdominal muscle on each side of the anterior abdominal vein. Take care not to damage the underlying structures.

● Make a ligature by pulling a thread under the vein and tying it at the posterior end of the slit. Pull a second thread under the vein and tie it about 1cm in front of the first. Now cut the vein between the two ligatures.

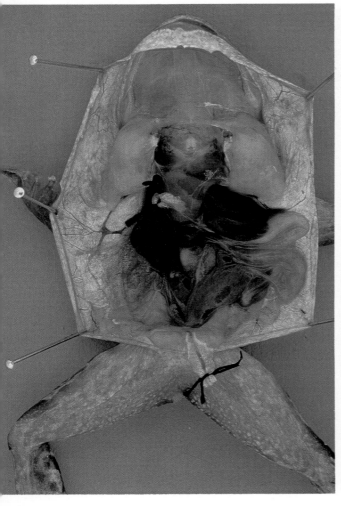

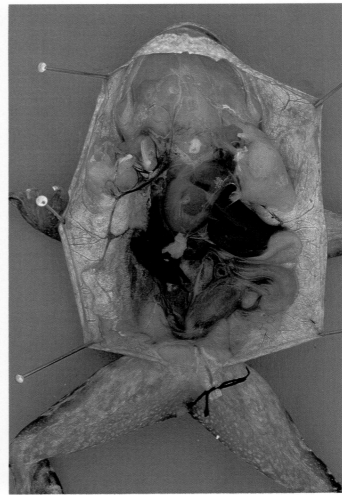

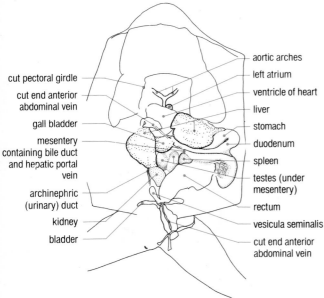

cut pectoral girdle

cut end anterior
abdominal vein

gall bladder

mesentery
containing bile duct
and hepatic portal
vein

archinephric
(urinary) duct

kidney

bladder

aortic arches

left atrium

ventricle of heart

liver

stomach

duodenum

spleen

testes (under
mesentery)

rectum

vesicula seminalis

cut end anterior
abdominal vein

external jugular vein

innominate vein

left part of pectoral
girdle

right atrium

left atrium

pericardium

subclavian vein

testis

Fig. 3.10 Body cavity – 3rd dissection stage.

● Cut along each side of the vein anteriorly and posteriorly to separate it from the abdominal muscle. Take particular care where the vein enters the liver anteriorly and where it divides into the pelvic veins posteriorly.

● Remove the mid-ventral portion of the pectoral girdle by cutting through the coracoid and clavicle bones on each side of the midline. Lift it clear by gently cutting the connective tissue. Keep the scissors horizontal and the pectoral girdle lifted in order to avoid damage to the underlying heart and blood vessels.

● Displace the alimentary canal to the animal's left side to show the mesentery with the hepatic portal vein and bile duct.

Fig. 3.11 Body cavity – 4th dissection stage.

● Lift up the right half of the pectoral girdle and gently free it from the underlying connective tissue, taking care not to damage the underlying veins.

● Cut the pectoral girdle close to its connection with the humerus to allow dissection of the main anterior veins on the right side.

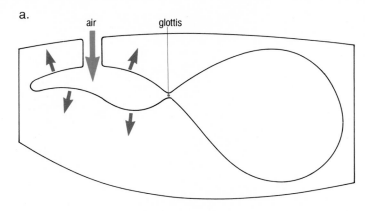

a.

air   glottis

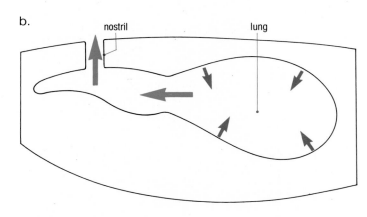

b.

nostril   lung

Buccal cavity

Gills are subject to desiccation on land but the respiratory surface within a lung is protected from water loss. However, the method of ventilation adopted by modern amphibians is very similar to that of fish in that it requires changes in the volume of the buccal cavity. If the pressure is reduced, air can be drawn in from the exterior. The cycle of events is shown in fig. 3.12. A certain amount of used air is mixed with the fresh air and it takes several cycles to dispose of a lungful of used air.

A special branch of the pulmo-cutaneous arch, the cutaneous artery, takes blood to the skin, where it absorbs oxygen. This oxygenated blood returns to the heart in the systemic circulation which also contains deoxygenated blood. This may seem inefficient, but it is extremely useful to an animal which can respire not only in air (using lungs) but also in water (using the skin).

The muscles which cause the volume changes of the buccal cavity are shown in fig. 3.13. Some of the muscles attach to a cartilaginous element, the corpus, which is part of the hyoid (or hyobranchial) skeleton. The hyoid skeleton is derived from some of the fish gill-bar elements in the same way as the stapes (see p. 3.16). The buccal cavity is enlarged by contraction of the sternohyoideus muscles which run from the corpus to the pectoral girdle. The geniohyoideus, intermandibularis and petrohyoideus reduce the volume of the buccal cavity by pulling the corpus upwards and forwards.

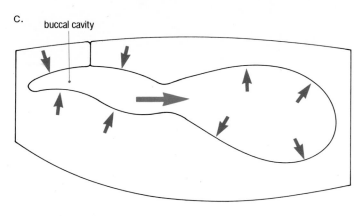

c.

buccal cavity

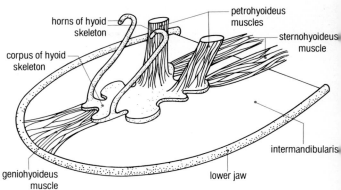

horns of hyoid skeleton   petrohyoideus muscles

corpus of hyoid skeleton   sternohyoideus muscle

geniohyoideus muscle   lower jaw   intermandibularis

Fig. 3.13 A diagram showing the muscles associated with the hyoid skeleton which are responsible for changes in the volume of the buccal cavity in a frog.

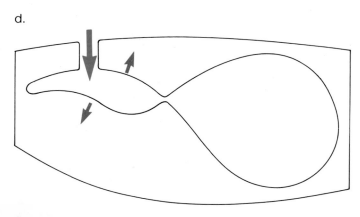

d.

Fig. 3.12 A diagram showing the ventilatory cycle in the frog. In (a) the nostril is open, the glottis is closed and the volume of the buccal cavity increases, drawing in air. On opening the glottis, in (b), air is forced out of the lungs by their elastic recoil. The air passes through the buccal cavity and out of the body. In (c) the nostrils are closed and the volume of the buccal cavity decreases forcing the fresh air in the buccal cavity into the lungs. In (d) the cycle begins again. Red arrows represent changes in volume.

Venous system

Various differences exist between the venous system of the frog (fig. 3.14) and that of a fish. The most important of these differences concerns the posterior cardinal veins. In the teleost these run from the kidney along the dorsal side of the body to the common cardinals and into the sinus venosus. In amphibians the posterior cardinals have fused into one vein in the region of the kidney. A branch of the hepatic vein has developed which runs dorsally to contact this posterior part of the posterior cardinal vein. This produces a shorter route to the heart, and is called the posterior vena cava. The anterior part of each posterior cardinal has degenerated in most amphibians to become the small azygos vein which drains the intercostal muscles.

The anterior cardinal veins are present (fig. 3.15); they are usually called the anterior venae cavae, and it is into these that the veins draining the forelimbs (the subclavians) empty. The veins draining the hindlimb (femoral) enter the abdominal veins, or the renal portal system (fig. 3.16). Both pathways from the hind end of the body to the heart are open, as noted in the codling.

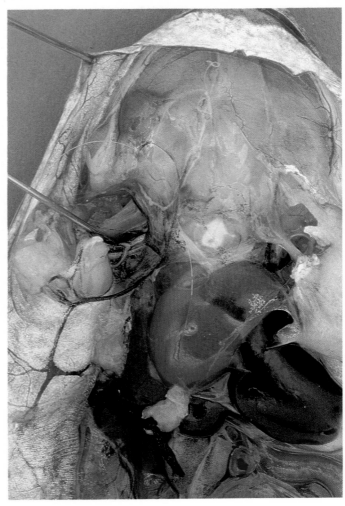

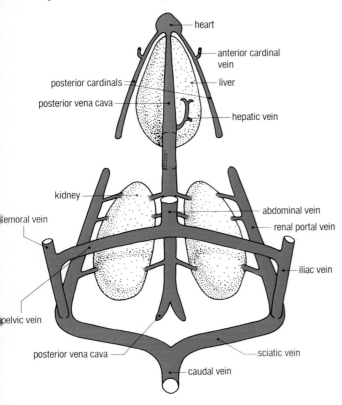

Fig. 3.14 The major veins of an amphibian in ventral view. Note that the left posterior cardinal vein and the caudal vein are lost in frogs.

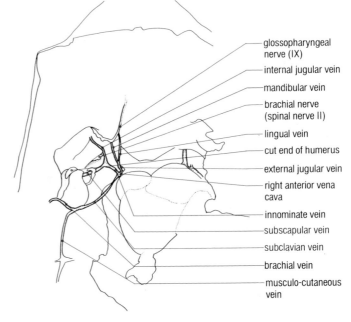

Fig. 3.15 Anterior venous system.

● Clear the tissue from the anterior veins to display this system more clearly.

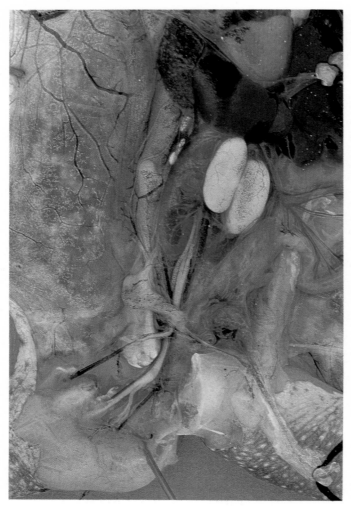

Urinogenital system

The urinogenital system is very similar to that of the dogfish, except that in both the adult male and female the kidney is rather more compact than in fishes (figs. 3.16 and 3.19).

In the male, sperm are transported from the testis to the anterior part of the kidney by the anterior kidney tubules. These tubules perform no excretory function. Sperm travel down the archinephric duct (or Wolffian duct) to the cloaca (fig. 3.17). The archinephric duct also drains the posterior excretory part of the kidney, the opisthonephros. In most amphibians there is a tendency for separate ducts to form to drain the kidney and testis, but this does not happen in the frog. The bladder is a new structure in amphibians; it is not present in fish.

In tadpoles the organisation of the urinogenital system is rather different. In the larval state no gonads are present. In an early embryo, and theoretically in the ancestral vertebrate, kidney tubules would be found in all trunk segments; the most anterior part of this row of tubules is the pronephros. In modern vertebrates this part of the kidney rarely persists in the adult – it is chiefly an embryonic feature. However, some fish and amphibians provide their embryos with little yolk so that the embryo, or larva, must actively seek out its own food. Such a larva must satisfy its excretory needs and,

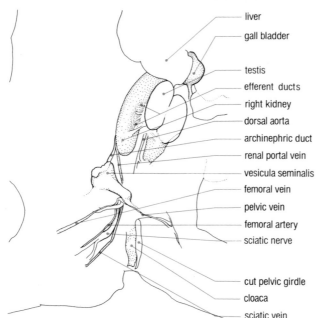

liver
gall bladder
testis
efferent ducts
right kidney
dorsal aorta
archinephric duct
renal portal vein
vesicula seminalis
femoral vein
pelvic vein
femoral artery
sciatic nerve

cut pelvic girdle
cloaca
sciatic vein

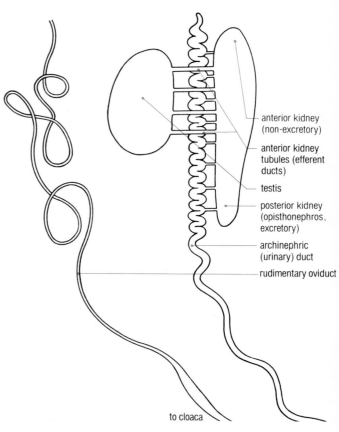

anterior kidney (non-excretory)
anterior kidney tubules (efferent ducts)
testis
posterior kidney (opisthonephros, excretory)
archinephric (urinary) duct
rudimentary oviduct

to cloaca

Fig. 3.16 Posterior venous system and male urinogenital system.

● Skin the ventral surface of the right leg. Dissect away the exposed muscles by cutting their attachments to the pelvis, and find the sciatic, pelvic and femoral veins.

● Remove the peritoneum to display the renal portal vein. Trace its connection with the sciatic vein which runs under the femur and behind the

cloaca. Take care not to damage the archinephric duct, and bladder.

● Dissect away the upper femur. Take care not to damage the sciatic nerve and femoral artery.

● Cut away the muscles from the back of the leg. Cut through the pubic symphysis and remove the right pelvis. Display the testes, kidneys, archinephric duct, vesicula seminalis and bladder.

Fig. 3.17 A diagram of the male amphibian urinogenital system.

herefore, the embryonic kidney, the pronephros, persists. Tadpoles utilise the pronephric kidney for xcretion until metamorphosis, when the adult structures develop.

n the female, the archinephric duct drains only the osterior part of the kidney and the anterior part of both uct and kidney degenerates. Another duct, the oviduct, ansports eggs to the cloaca where the oviduct is istended into a sac which stores eggs (fig. 3.18 and 3.19). rudiment of the oviduct is present in males, reflecting the act that early in development both sets of ducts are resent in both sexes.

ne final excretory product in adult terrestrial amphibians urea. The ammonia which fish excrete must be diluted large quantities of water. On land, water conservation important and the less toxic product, urea, is excreted. he kidney tubules of frogs have a fairly small renal orpuscle so that small quantities of filtrate are roduced. However, amphibians do not conserve water n the same scale as reptiles. There may be two reasons or this. Firstly, amphibians are confined on the whole to oist environments, due to their cutaneous respiration nd aquatic larvae. Secondly, their urinary bladders can ore urine from which water can be taken up by the sorptive walls.

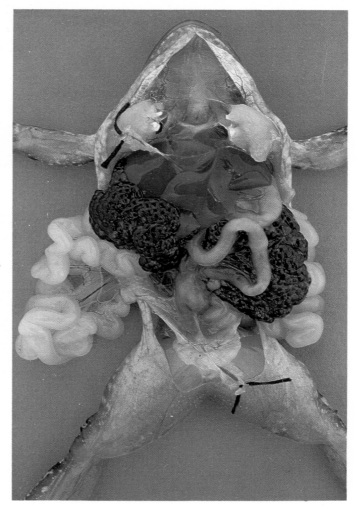

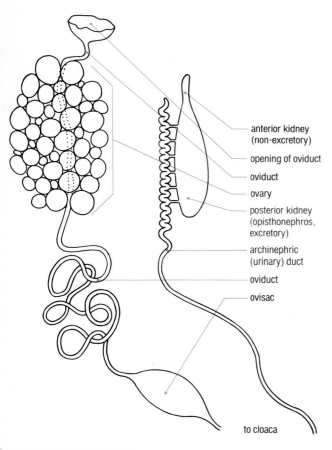

anterior kidney
(non-excretory)

opening of oviduct

oviduct

ovary

posterior kidney
(opisthonephros,
excretory)

archinephric
(urinary) duct

oviduct

ovisac

to cloaca

ig. 3.18 A diagram of the
male amphibian
rinogenital system.

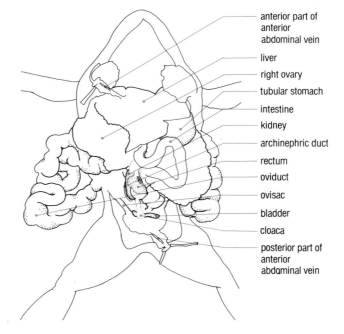

anterior part of
anterior
abdominal vein

liver

right ovary

tubular stomach

intestine

kidney

archinephric duct

rectum

oviduct

ovisac

bladder

cloaca

posterior part of
anterior
abdominal vein

**Fig. 3.19 Female
urinogenital system.**

● Ligature and cut the
anterior abdominal vein as
described for fig. 3.9.

● Remove the mid portion of
the pectoral girdle as
described for fig. 3.10.

● Display the right ovary,
oviduct and ovisac by freeing
the underlying oviduct and
tracing its connection with
the anterior end of the cloaca.

Now display the right kidney,
archinephric duct and bladder.

Heart and aortic arches

Radical differences exist between the arterial system of amphibians (figs. 3.21 and 3.23) and that of fish. In the fish blood flows from the ventral aorta through the gill arches to the dorsal aorta. There are five such gills, or aortic arches, in the dogfish and four in the codling. The arrangement is very different in the frog since the gills are absent (fig. 3.20). Each afferent artery joins with its efferent artery to produce a continuous aortic arch, but not all the arches persist. If the arches in a hypothetical ancestral vertebrate are numbered 1 to 6, from the front of the animal, arches 1 and 2 are always lost early in development. In frogs arch 5 is also lost, but it may remain in salamanders. The part of the dorsal aorta that connects arches 3 and 4 is also lost in adult tetrapods. Arch 3 (carotid arch) supplies the head (via the internal carotid artery) and arch 4 (the systemic arch) supplies the body. There is, therefore, a separation of the two circulations. Arch 6 takes blood to the lung (the pulmo-cutaneous arch).

During larval development when the lungs are not used, blood travels straight to the dorsal aorta, bypassing the lungs. In adult frogs this bypass, the ductus arteriosus, is closed off. The pulmo-cutaneous arch carries deoxygenated (venous) blood. It constitutes a separate channel from the heart, so that the ventral aorta is effectively split into two as it leaves the heart. One branch forms the pulmo-cutaneous arch, while the other forms the carotid and systemic arches.

We have already seen how the simple, one-way circuit of circulation in fish is interrupted in amphibians which use

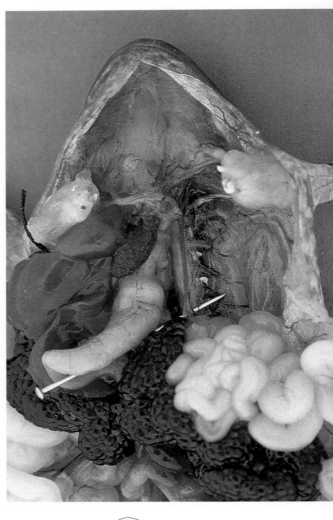

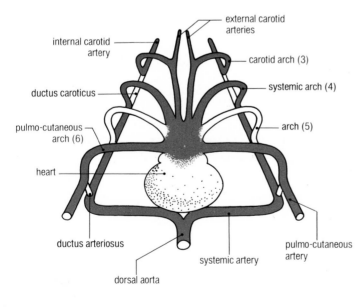

Fig. 3.20 The aortic arches of a frog in ventral view, shown in red. Arch 5 is present in some adult salamanders and the ductus caroticus and ductus arteriosus are present in some adult salamanders and legless amphibians.

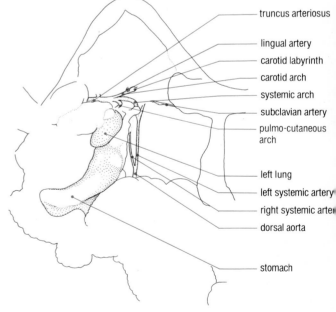

Fig. 3.21 Arterial system – 1st dissection stage.

● Trim back the left half of the pectoral girdle as described in fig. 3.10 in order to expose the venous system.

● Carefully remove the left anterior venous system to expose the underlying arteries. Locate the three main arterial arches – carotid, systemic and pulmo-cutaneous – which arise from the left half of the truncus arteriosus.

● Displace the viscera and the heart to the animal's right side in order to display the course of each of the arterial arches.

● Carefully dissect the pericardium away from the heart.

(The cutaneous artery has been removed to show the course of the systemic arch).

heir lungs. This results in oxygenated and deoxygenated blood mixing and, ideally, these should be kept separate. To do this they must take separate paths through the heart and around the body. Only in mammals and birds is this final solution achieved with the separation of ventricle and atrium into right and left halves. In the amphibians only the atrium is divided (fig. 3.22). All the blood from the body enters the reduced sinus venosus and then flows into the right atrium. Oxygenated blood from the lungs enters the left atrium. At this stage the blood streams are separate but one would expect the streams to mix on passing through the ventricle. However, there is evidence that the muscular construction of the ventricle wall prevents such mixing. Instead, fresh blood tends to pass into the carotid and systemic arches, while deoxygenated blood tends to pass through the pulmonary arch.

It is postulated that the lack of division of the ventricle is a secondary feature in modern amphibians. Since lungs are almost useless for obtaining oxygen under water there is little point in sending blood to the lungs for oxygenation when the frog is submerged. However, this would be inevitable if the circulation were completely divided into pulmonary and systemic circuits. In the system seen in modern amphibians, blood entering the right atrium from the body can be shunted to the skin along the pulmo-cutaneous artery when the animal is submerged. At the skin it can absorb oxygen and return, with the systemic circulation, to the right atrium.

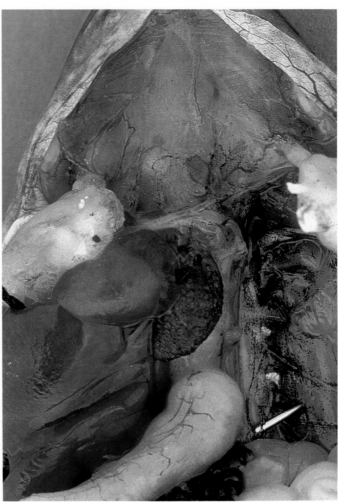

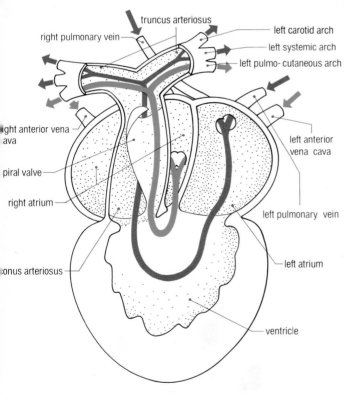

Fig. 3.22 A diagram of the amphibian heart to show the single ventricle, paired atria and direction of blood flow.

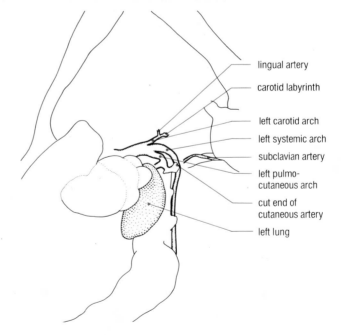

Fig. 3.23 Arterial system – 2nd dissection stage.

● Carefully trace and dissect out the main arteries of the anterior part of the body, which branch off the carotid, systemic and pulmo-cutaneous vessels.

Nervous system

It is thought that two nervous systems, having little connection with one another, may have existed in the ancestors of vertebrates. One system would have received and reacted to external stimuli and would have given rise to the brain and spinal cord. The other system would have been concerned with adjusting the visceral organs in relation to internal stimuli. In modern vertebrates the two systems are connected and the central nervous system has come to dominate the visceral system, but the latter still plays an important part in the animal. Although the two systems are connected, many responses of the visceral system (such as constriction and dilation of blood vessels) are not mediated by the higher centres of the brain.

The visceral nervous system, like the central nervous system, contains afferent and efferent fibres. Afferent visceral sensory fibres monitor the states of the visceral organs. They enter the spinal cord through special visceral trunk nerves, or through the vagus nerve. The efferent fibres mainly innervate smooth muscles and glands and these fibres constitute the autonomic nervous system. This is sometimes called the sympathetic nervous system but it is less confusing to reserve this name for a certain part (the thoracolumbar part) of the autonomic system. Each fibre in the system is a two-neuron pathway in contrast to the usual one-neuron motor efferent pathways.

In mammals the autonomic system is divided into a sympathetic (thoracolumbar) system and a parasympathetic (craniosacral) system. These two differ in the actions they produce and in the places where the efferents leave the spinal cord. The sympathetic system generally increases the activity of an animal, making it ready for 'fight or flight'. The neurotransmitter used is noradrenaline (or adrenaline). The parasympathetic system tends to slow down the animal's activities and its transmitter substance is acetylcholine.

The autonomic system is only well known in mammals, but the description above may fit all tetrapods. The degree to which sympathetic and parasympathetic systems can be distinguished is variable, but the two systems are probably established in the frog (fig. 3.24).

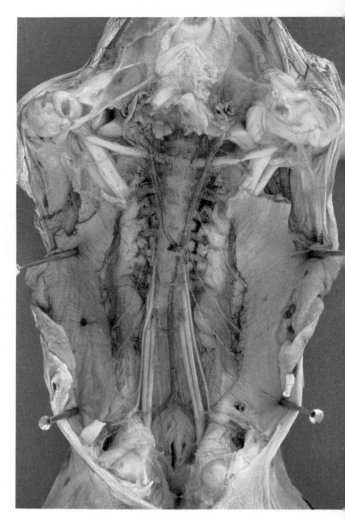

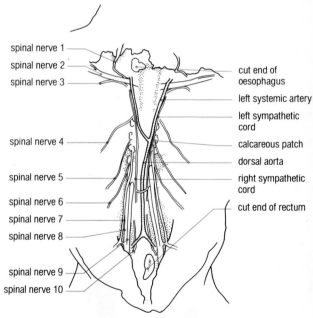

spinal nerve 1
spinal nerve 2
spinal nerve 3 — cut end of oesophagus
— left systemic artery
— left sympathetic cord
spinal nerve 4 — calcareous patch
— dorsal aorta
spinal nerve 5 — right sympathetic cord
spinal nerve 6 — cut end of rectum
spinal nerve 7
spinal nerve 8
spinal nerve 9
spinal nerve 10

Fig. 3.24 Spinal nerves.

● This dissection is best carried out on a specimen which has been opened and preserved in 70% alcohol.

● Cut through the aortic arches, bronchi and oesophagus anteriorly, and the mesentery and rectum posteriorly, in order to remove the viscera.

● Remove the urinogenital system carefully to avoid damaging the aorta, along the sides of which run the sympathetic cords.

● Carefully dissect away the dorsal abdominal peritoneum to display the ventral branches of the spinal nerves which run through the abdominal lymph sacs. Trace the sympathetic cords on either side of the aorta.

Skull

The skull of the frog (fig. 3.26), like the skeleton, is very specialised but it also shows features which one would expect to find in any terrestrial vertebrate. These terrestrial features are most easily understood by considering an early extinct amphibian, such as *Palaeoherpeton*. The most obvious differences between the skull of such an animal and that of a fish are the following: the loss of the gill region; the loss of the connection with the shoulder girdle; and the development of sensory structures appropriate for life on land.

Unlike early amphibians, ossification is much reduced in the skull of modern amphibians. In particular, many of the dermal bones of the skull roof are lost and the braincase becomes broad and flat and poorly ossified (fig. 3.25). In the palate of the frog, large vacuities are present, and the orbits (eye-sockets) are disproportionately large.

The connection between the skull and the shoulder girdle is lost in amphibians. This enables the head and body movements to be independent, and allows the head to be positioned to pick up sensory information from the environment. Mobility of the head is also important for food capture. Land animals cannot rely on sucking in food with a stream of water and must grab or bite at their food source. Several groups of modern amphibians have variously modified tongues for catching food. The tongue is attached to the front of the mouth and folded back on itself when not in use. It is flipped out when prey approaches (all modern adult amphibians are carnivorous), and sticky secretions of the mucous glands ensure that the prey adheres to it. The hyoid apparatus, which anchors some of the respiratory muscles, also supports the tongue and its muscles. Modern amphibians that feed in water employ the same sucking method as fish.

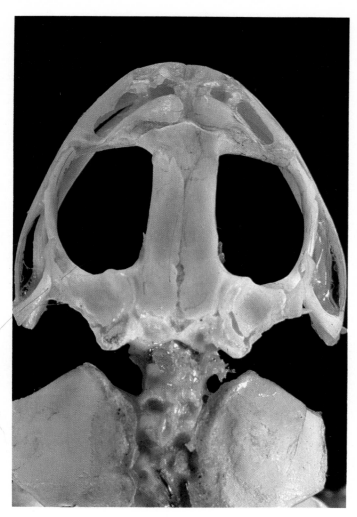

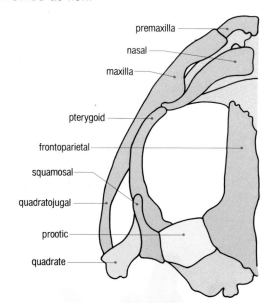

premaxilla
nasal
maxilla
pterygoid
frontoparietal
squamosal
quadratojugal
prootic
quadrate

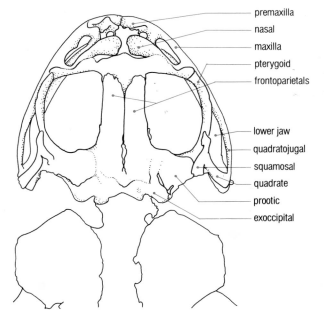

premaxilla
nasal
maxilla
pterygoid
frontoparietals
lower jaw
quadratojugal
squamosal
quadrate
prootic
exoccipital

Fig. 3.25 The skull of the frog showing the principal dermal bones (blue) and cartilage bones derived from both the gill arches (pink) and the braincase (pale pink).

Fig. 3.26 The frog skull in dorsal view.

The gill bars take on a new function in tetrapods. In the fish, the hyomandibula lies just behind the spiracular pouch and helps to brace the upper jaw to the braincase. In land vertebrates, the upper jaw is fused to the braincase so that the hyomandibula is no longer necessary as a brace. Instead, it has become modified to form a sound-conducting structure positioned between the otic (auditory) region of the braincase and the ear-drum. The hyomandibula (or stapes, as it is now called) lies in the middle-ear cavity of the tetrapod (fig. 3.27). This cavity might be homologous with the spiracular pouch of the fish. Similarly, the ear-drum might have arisen from the operculum and from a membrane covering the spiracular pouch. This kind of ear responds to far-field sound waves, unlike the lateral line of fish which responds to near-field sound set up by pressure changes in the water. The lateral line does not function in air and is therefore lost in amniotes. The sensory cells of the inner ear of tetrapods are very like the neuromast cells of the lateral line system, and it is thought that the vertebrate ear may have arisen from a special part of the lateral line which sank below the skin. The nerves for both types of sensory structure are closely related, forming the acoustico-lateralis nerve system.

In modern amphibians the inner ear is concerned with auditory discrimination and maintaining equilibrium. There is also a specialised sensory structure called the papilla amphibiorum which is probably responsible for sound perception in the sacculus. In some modern amphibians the ear may be degenerate. Often the ear-drum and middle ear, and sometimes the stapes, are missing, as in salamanders. Most frogs and toads, however, have a well-developed middle ear, a large ear-drum and a stapes. In amphibians which do not have a middle ear and ear drum, it is possible that sound is picked up from the ground, through the lower jaw or forelimb, and transmitted to the stapes.

The bones of the skull in an early amphibian like *Palaeoherpeton* form a pattern which persists – though with some modification – in all tetrapods. Various series of bones can be distinguished. There are several series of dermal bones making the skull roof. These are the tooth-bearing series, the dorsal midline series, the circumorbital series (around the eye), a temporal series, and a cheek series (see fig. 3.28).

Each side of the palate (the roof of the mouth) is made up of four dermal bones: the vomer, the pterygoid, the palatine, and the ectopterygoid. In addition there are two cartilage bones: the epipterygoid and the quadrate (fig. 3.29). The latter forms the upper part of the jaw-hinge. The palate may contain larger holes, or vacuities. A particularly obvious one is the interpterygoid vacuity. Between the skull roof and the palate is the braincase which consists of the parasphenoid (a dermal bone), and the occipital bones, posteriorly. The prootic and opisthotic bones are found in the otic region of the braincase. In early amphibians the lower jaw was composed of several bones. The largest bone, the dentary, bore the marginal teeth. The articular bone (a cartilage bone) formed the lower part of the jaw-hinge. The lower jaw of frogs contains only two dermal bones and is toothless.

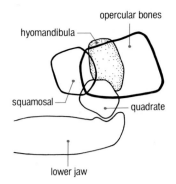

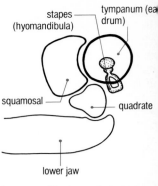

Fig. 3.27 A diagrammatic comparison of the jaw-hinge region in a fish (left) and a tetrapod (right). Note the homology between the hyomandibula and stapes, and the possible homology between the opercular bones and tympanum.

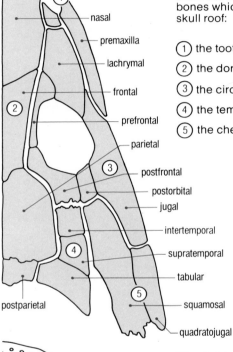

Fig. 3.28 The right half of the skull of an early amphibian to show the five series of dermal bones which make up the skull roof:

① the tooth-bearing series
② the dorsal midline series
③ the circumorbital series
④ the temporal series
⑤ the cheek series

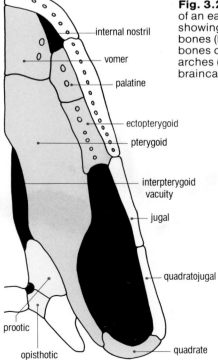

Fig. 3.29 The palatal view of an early tetrapod skull showing the principal dermal bones (blue) and cartilage bones derived from the gill arches (pink) and the braincase (pale pink).

4 The Lizard

Reptilia
Squamata
Lacertilia
Lacerta muralis

Introduction

Lizards are unlike other modern reptiles in that they are not highly specialised. Tortoises are encased in shells, and snakes have lost their limbs, but lizards are quite generalised in their body form. Many are insectivorous, some are carnivorous, and most of the few large forms are herbivorous.

Modern reptiles are characterised by their scaly skin, by laying cleidoic eggs (see below) and by their excretion of uric acid. All of these features are linked to the reptiles' independence of water. Unlike amphibians they do not need to return to water to breed. They have minimised their problems of water loss and can therefore inhabit drier places.

Many reptiles have a capacity for keeping their body temperature fairly constant. They do this behaviourally by basking in the sun, or lying in the shade to cool down; this strategy is called ectothermy. If differs from endothermy which is the mechanism employed by mammals and birds where excess heat from metabolism is used to maintain a constant body temperature.

Lizards and snakes belong to the sub-class Lepidosauria, one of the three sub-classes which contain modern reptiles. The other two sub-classes are the Anapsida (turtles and tortoises) and the Archosauria (crocodiles). All of these sub-classes contain other extinct forms. In addition there are sub-classes of entirely extinct forms, such as the ichthyosaurs and mammal-reptiles. The position and number of fenestrae (large holes) in the skull is one of the features used to distinguish between these sub-classes (p. 4.11).

Reptiles are thought to have evolved from a group of extinct amphibians and probably the most important feature of their evolution was the development of the cleidoic, or amniotic, egg. The advantages of the cleidoic egg are that it protects the embryo and prevents its desiccation; it provides an area for the deposit of waste substances so that these do not need to be reprocessed; and it allows efficient gas exchange even in large eggs where the surface area/volume ratio is small.

Skeleton

The skeleton of the lizard (fig. 4.1) is not as specialised as that of the frog. For example, extensive ribs are attached to the spine, unlike the condition in most of the specialised modern amphibians. So-called abdominal ribs may also be present. These may be of two kinds, one of cartilage bone and the other of dermal bone. The ventral ends of the proper ribs may fuse together in each segment forming a V-shaped chevron which may then lose its connection with the rest of the rib. Such chevrons are cartilage bones (found in lizards) and should not be confused with similar abdominal ribs of crocodiles which are dermal bones and lie under the skin of the abdomen.

The tail is usually long. Haemal arches are present and are fused to small crescents of bone, the intercentra, which are wedged between successive vertebrae. In some reptiles intercentra are also found in the back and neck regions. Intercentra are thought to be remnants of the anterior element in the two-part centrum of crossopterygian fish (see fig. 4.2). Some lizards possess an unusual method of escaping predators. If the tail is grabbed by a predator, it can be shed in order to escape. Later a new tail is regenerated, although not perfectly. Halfway along the centrum of each caudal vertebra there is a zone containing no bone (an unossified zone) which allows the vertebra to snap in two when special muscles pull on it. The breaking process is called autotomy.

The limb girdles are not greatly different from those of a more generalised early amphibian, except that the cleithrum has been lost from the pectoral girdle. In the pelvic girdle (fig. 4.3), the blade of the ilium is extended not only for the attachment of the extra sacral rib, but also for the attachment of the limb musculature. A large fenestra, the thyroid fenestra, is found in the plate formed by the pubis and ischium. The edges of this fenestra are probably more important than the hole itself, since it is thought that an edge gives a better site for muscle attachment than a flat plate. This reasoning has also been applied to the fenestrae of the skull.

Effective locomotion is important unless a very secretive lifestyle is adopted. On the whole, lizards are capable of moving very efficiently around their habitat. They have well-developed legs, the back leg being longer than the front and these can raise the body off the ground and serve in propulsion. They often have a long tail, which is useful as a counterbalance.

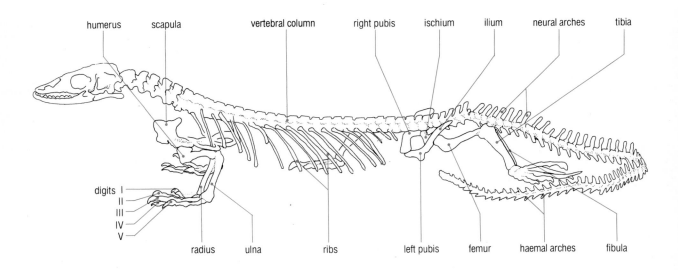

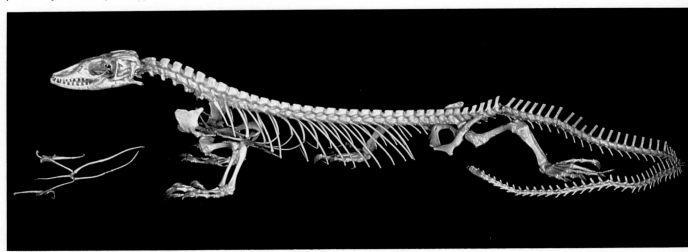

Fig. 4.1 The lizard skeleton in left lateral view.

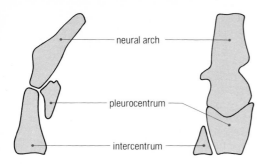

Fig. 4.2 A diagram to compare the structure of the crossopterygian vertebra (left) with that of a reptile (right).

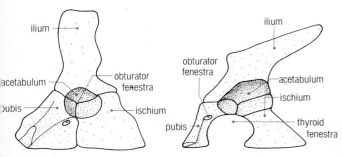

Fig. 4.3 A diagram to compare the pelvic girdle of an early amphibian (left) and that of a reptile (right).

The upper part of the limbs sprawl out at right angles from the body in most lizards. There is little departure from a generalised vertebrate condition except in the wrist and ankle regions, which are variable in all vertebrates. There is some fusion of both carpal and tarsal bones, but five digits are present. The number of bones per digit is relatively constant within the reptiles; starting with the thumb (or big-toe), the number of bones per digit is 2-3-4-5-3. This gives rise to an asymmetrical foot. In an animal with sprawling limbs, as the forefoot (or hindfoot) is put down, it hits the ground at an angle. In order for all the digits to gain a firm footing together, the outer digits must be larger, therefore necessitating an asymmetrical form.

The fifth digit of the hindfoot in lizards is unusual in having a metatarsal which bears a backwardly-pointing hook. This hooked metatarsal plays two roles in the action of the foot. It allows the fifth digit to be opposed to the first, giving a better grip of the ground. It is also the attachment site of muscles which extend the limb during the locomotory stroke, making this action more powerful.

In mammals the legs are more ventrally directed and the problem of lifting the digits off, and putting them onto the ground evenly, is less acute. The mammalian foot (p. 6.2) is primitively much more symmetrical than that of the reptile. It is interesting that there is an adaptation to produce powerful extension, similar to that in the lizard. However, it is not a metatarsal, but a tarsal bone, the calcaneum, which bears a backwardly-pointing projection for muscle attachment.

Skin

One of the most sriking external features of a reptile, compared with other tetrapods, is the scaly skin (fig. 4.4). A fully terrestrial animal such as the lizard must protect itself from desiccation and the scales are important in this respect. They are formed mainly from epidermal tissue (although the dermis may also be involved) and it is the keratin found in the epidermal tissue which gives the scales their water-conserving properties.

The scales are not separate elements but are actually a series of thickenings in the epidermis, between which the skin thins out and may be deeply folded to allow for expansion. This is particularly important in snakes which swallow large prey. Considerable variation in scale form may occur; they may be rough horny scutes as in crocodiles, or they may be moulded into spines or horns. In the lizard specimen used here they are fairly unspecialised.

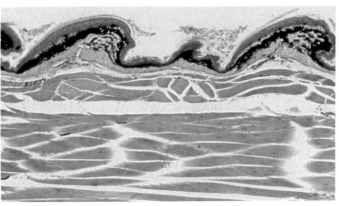

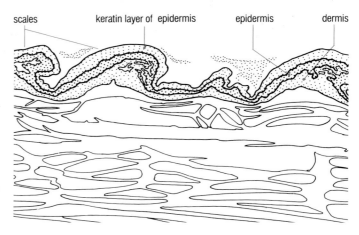

Fig. 4.4 The skin of a reptile in surface view (top) and vertical section (bottom), x 60. Note the thickening in the epidermis, which constitutes scales, and the thinner, folded epidermis between scales.

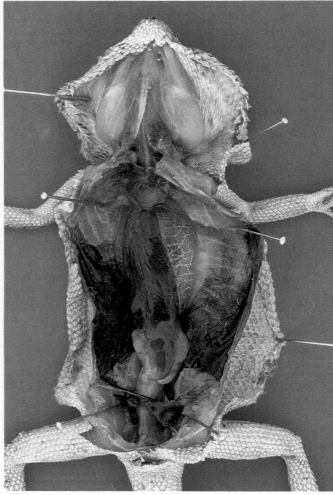

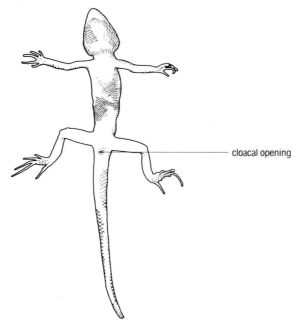

cloacal opening

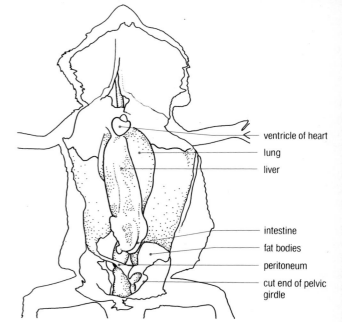

ventricle of heart

lung

liver

intestine

fat bodies

peritoneum

cut end of pelvic
girdle

**Fig. 4.5 Ventral view –
animal prepared for
dissection.**

● Lay the lizard out, ventral
surface uppermost, taking
care not to stretch the legs
out too tightly since this may
damage the delicate blood
vessels.

Fig. 4.6 Body cavity.

● Open the body cavity with
a median ventral incision
through the skin extending
from the pelvic to the
pectoral girdle.

● Make a similar incision
through the muscle of the
body wall and deflect it
laterally to expose the
viscera.

● Now cut carefully along the
mid-line of the pelvic girdle

and leave the ventral surface
of the black peritoneum
uncut immediately under the
girdle.

Male urinogenital system

There is not a great deal of difference between the organ systems of the lizard (fig. 4.6) and the frog (fig. 3.10). However, two important differences exist between the urinogenital system of reptiles and that of amphibians (figs. 4.7 and 3.17). Firstly the excretory part of the kidney in the reptile is confined to the posterior embryonic region – it is a metanephric kidney. Secondly, a new duct, the ureter, forms to drain the kidney. Embryologically this duct is an outgrowth of the archinephric duct itself. In the male, the archinephric duct (vas deferens) is concerned solely with the transport of sperm from the testis to the hemipenes (fig. 4.8).

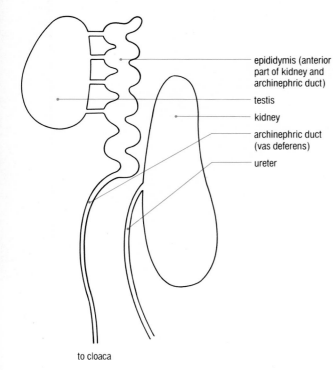

to cloaca

Fig. 4.7 A diagram of the male reptilian urinogenital system.

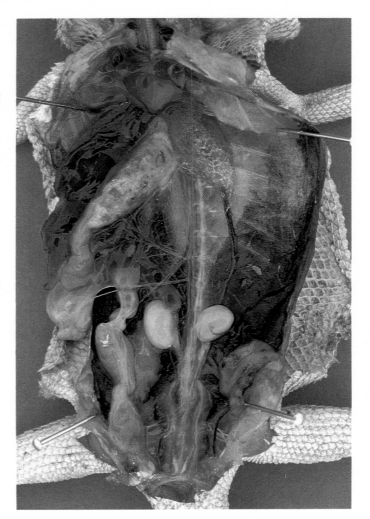

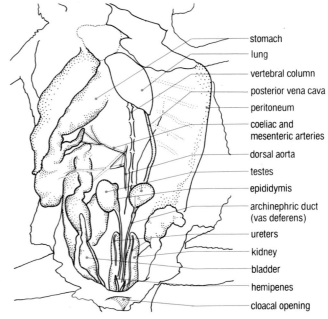

Fig. 4.8 Male urinogenital system.

● Displace the intestine carefully to the animal's right side in order to expose the contents of the abdominal cavity.

● Follow the rectum back to the cloaca and identify the bladder lying on the ventral surface of the rectum. Carefully dissect the peritoneum away from the kidneys and cloaca to show the testes, archinephric ducts (vasa deferentia), kidneys and ureters.

Female urinogenital system

The female lizard, like the male, possesses a metanephric kidney and a new duct, the ureter, which drains the kidney (figs. 4.9 and 4.11). However, unlike that of the male, the archinephric duct in the female is found as the rudimentary epididymis (coiled upper part of the duct).

The cleidoic egg (fig. 4.10) was mentioned in the introduction as probably the most important feature of the evolution of reptiles. The shell and the three membranes (chorion, amnion and allantois) within the egg provide a fluid-filled chamber which protects the embryo from violent movements and also from desiccation. The chorion and the allantois fuse to form the chorio-allantois, a richly vascularised membrane which acts as a lung allowing efficient exchange of gases through the porous shell. The cavity of the allantois stores uric acid, the nitrogenous waste product. These features allow reptiles to lay eggs on dry land thus emphasising their independence of water.

Not all lizards lay eggs, some are ovoviviparous. They protect the eggs by retaining them within the body, and the young feed off the yolk supply. Some lizards are viviparous. They retain the foetus within the oviduct, and nourish it directly in a similar, but less sophisticated, way to that found in mammals.

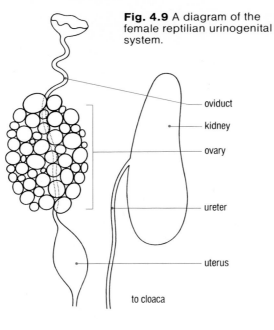

Fig. 4.9 A diagram of the female reptilian urinogenital system.

- oviduct
- kidney
- ovary
- ureter
- uterus

to cloaca

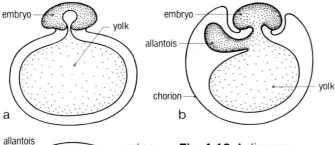

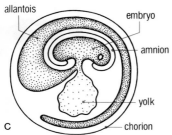

embryo
yolk

embryo
allantois
chorion
yolk

a

b

allantois
embryo
amnion
yolk
chorion

c

Fig. 4.10 A diagram illustrating the development of the cleidoic egg. (a) shows the early embryo and its yolk sac. At a later stage, the chorion and allantois grow, as seen in (b), and the chorion eventually fuses with itself to form an enclosed, fluid-filled chamber, (c).

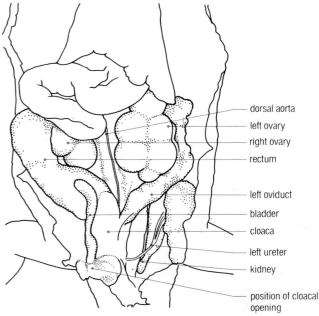

- dorsal aorta
- left ovary
- right ovary
- rectum
- left oviduct
- bladder
- cloaca
- left ureter
- kidney
- position of cloacal opening

Fig. 4.11 Female urinogenital system.

● Open the body cavity as described in fig. 4.6.

● Displace the intestine carefully over to the animal's right side in order to expose the contents of the abdominal cavity.

● Follow the rectum back to the cloaca and identify the bladder lying on the ventral surface of the rectum.

Carefully dissect the peritoneum away from the kidneys and cloaca to display the left ovary, oviduct, kidney and ureter.

4.6

Cardiovascular system

Three aortic arches leave the heart (fig. 4.12): the pulmonary arch, the left systemic arch and the right systemic arch which supplies the head and front legs. This arrangement can be seen in the three dissection stages (figs. 4.14, 4.15, 4.16) and can be compared with that of the frog (figs. 3.21 and 3.23) where only two vessels leave the heart.

The venous system (fig. 4.13) of the lizard is very similar to that of the frog, but two differences are worth noting. The cutaneous veins are small in the lizard due to the absence of cutaneous respiration. Also, the renal portal vein is much smaller in lizards.

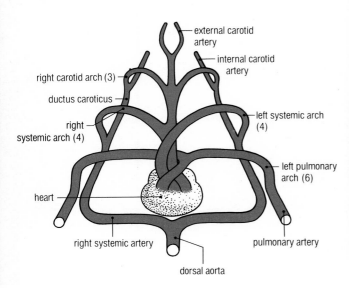

Fig. 4.12 The aortic arches of a lizard in ventral view.

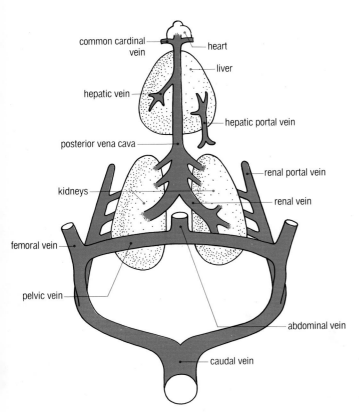

Fig. 4.13 The major veins of a lizard in ventral view.

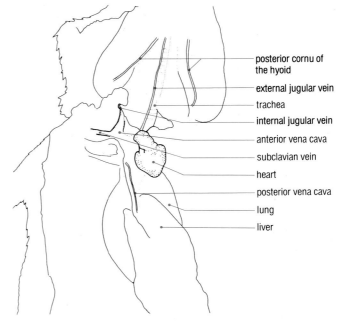

Fig. 4.14 Arterial system – 1st dissection stage.

● Carefully trim back the pectoral girdle on each side to show the heart and the main blood vessels lying underneath.

● Clear the pericardium from the heart and display the main veins.

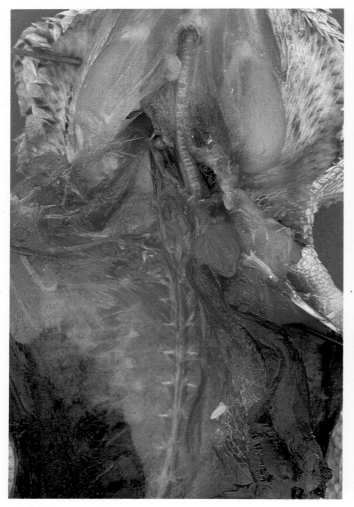

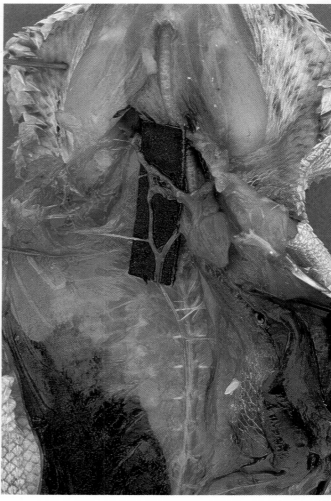

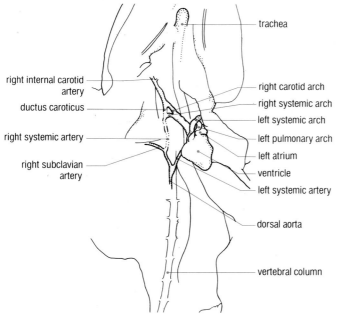

right internal carotid artery — ductus caroticus — right systemic artery — right subclavian artery

trachea — right carotid arch — right systemic arch — left systemic arch — left pulmonary arch — left atrium — ventricle — left systemic artery — dorsal aorta — vertebral column

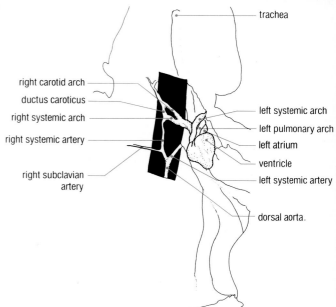

right carotid arch — ductus caroticus — right systemic arch — right systemic artery — right subclavian artery

trachea — left systemic arch — left pulmonary arch — left atrium — ventricle — left systemic artery — dorsal aorta.

Fig. 4.15 Arterial system – 2nd dissection stage.

● Remove the right atrium, anterior vena cava and posterior vena cava to show the carotid, systemic and pulmonary arterial arches.

● Deflect the heart to the animal's left side to show the fusion of the systemic arches into the dorsal aorta. Display the right ductus caroticus joining the carotid and systemic arches.

Fig. 4.16 Arterial system – 3rd dissection stage.

● Display the main arteries by placing a piece of black card underneath them.

The heart has an incompletely divided ventricle, and therefore a separated, double circulation is not present (fig. 4.17). The pulmonary and left systemic arch open from the right ventricle, and the right systemic arch from the left ventricle. Blood from the body enters the right atrium and is carried to the lungs in the pulmonary arch. It would be expected that some blood would also go back around the body in the left systemic arch, or even through the right systemic arch. Blood from the lungs enters the left atrium, and again, because of the incompletely divided ventricle, might be expected to exit through the right or left systemic arches, or even go back through the pulmonary arch. But the latter does not seem to happen. The complicated arrangement of incomplete partitions within the heart ensures that only deoxygenated blood goes through the pulmonary arch, and only oxygenated or partly oxygenated blood goes through the systemic arches in normal conditions.

Why, then, is the heart not completely divided? Reptiles which dive (turtles, some lizards, and crocodiles), experience periods when the lungs cannot provide oxygen in the normal way; in snakes the efficiency of the lung is reduced when swallowing large prey. In a completely divided heart deoxygenated blood is forced to travel round the pulmonary circuit even if there is little oxygen in the lungs to be picked up. However, in the incompletely divided heart of reptiles, during periods of oxygen starvation, the pulmonary arch may be constricted and deoxygenated blood forced through the left systemic arch instead of going to the lungs (fig. 4.17). This might help to make the oxygen store last longer by reducing the blood flow to the lungs where oxygen may be lost. Also, there is the advantage that the pressure of the blood will not be reduced by passing through the capillaries of the lung. Blood, therefore, can be 'shunted' through those aortic arches most appropriate for the animal's situation. Another example is seen in the lizard when it is basking in the sun to warm its body. The blood vessels supplying the skin dilate to allow a greater volume of blood to pass near the skin and transfer heat into the body core. In this situation a greater volume of blood is required in the systemic circulation relative to the pulmonary circulation, so most of the venous blood returning to the heart is shunted into the systemic circulation, bypassing the pulmonary circuit. This shunting is not possible in mammals.

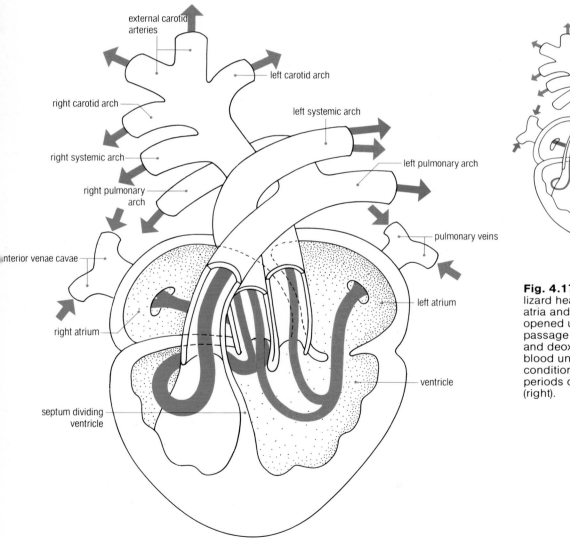

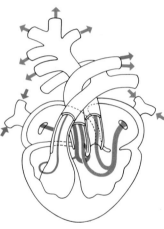

Fig. 4.17 A diagram of the lizard heart with the ventricle, atria and arterial trunk opened up to show the passage of oxygenated (red) and deoxygenated (blue) blood under normal conditions (left) and during periods of oxygen starvation (right).

Skull

We shall study the reptilian skull by comparing it with the skull of an early amphibian, since the frog skull is too specialised to afford a good comparison.

The reptilian skull tends to be higher and narrower than that of the amphibian. This is correlated, to some extent, with the way the muscles are attached to the jaw (fig. 4.18). Muscles pull most efficiently if they are attached at right angles to the element that they are pulling. In early amphibians the jaw muscles were at a right angle to the jaw when it was open. Consequently, they pulled most efficiently when the jaw was open, producing a snapping movement. In reptiles, the muscles are positioned so that they are at a right angle to the jaw when it is closed, and contraction of these muscles produces a squeezing action, like tongs. This reflects the different feeding patterns of the two groups. Amphibians tend to snap the jaws shut on prey, relying on the impetus of the jaws closing to immobilise the prey. Reptiles tend to rely on the squeezing action produced when the jaws are closed to immobilise and break up the prey. A high skull is needed in reptiles to allow muscles of sufficient length to attach straight up on the skull. In early amphibians, the muscles could achieve the desired length because they ran forwards along the skull.

A bifid (forked) tongue may be present in the mouth. Many lizards, like snakes, flick the tongue in and out of the mouth. The tongue picks up particles from the air and deposits them inside the mouth near to the opening of a sensory structure called the organ of Jacobson. This originates in embryology as a pocket of the nasal sac and is supplied with nerves from the olfactory portion of the brain. It is probably responsible for detecting chemical stimuli in a similar way to the nose.

Lizard teeth are usually simple conical structures. They are present on the margins of the jaws and sometimes on the bones of the roof of the mouth. They are attached along the biting edge of the jaw and have no sockets. This is called pleurodont attachment (fig. 4.19) as opposed to thecodont attachment (some examples are found in a few snakes, most mammals and most carnivores other than fish) and acrodont attachment (some examples are found in various reptiles and most teleosts).

Early amphibians had an otic notch which supported the tympanum at the back of the skull. This is lost in early reptiles, and the skull is consolidated by fusing the cheek region to the skull roof. In doing this the intertemporal, supratemporal and tabular bones are reduced. Lizards redevelop an 'otic notch' behind the quadrate (fig. 4.20) for supporting the conspicuous tympanum. Air-borne vibrations are picked up by this membrane and transmitted via the stapes to the inner ear.

In early reptiles the back of the skull was complete, as it is (though in a modified form) in tortoises and turtles. Most reptile lines developed fenestrae in the skull, possibly to aid jaw muscle attachment in the same way as mentioned earlier in connection with the pelvis. In early lizard-like forms there are two complete fenestrae. However, the lower bar of the lower fenestra has been lost in modern lizards, leaving no firm connection for the quadrate bone (see fig. 4.21). As a result the quadrate can move backwards and forwards, a condition known as streptostyly. It is thought that a quadrate which is free to swing backwards and forwards effectively adds another segment to the lower jaw thus increasing the gape produced when the jaw is lowered. Recently it has been suggested that a more important use of streptostyly is to allow one of the jaw-closing muscles, the pterygoideus, to act at a greater mechanical advantage than it would do otherwise, and to enable it to make a major contribution to the bite force.

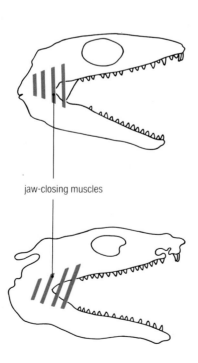

jaw-closing muscles

Fig. 4.18 A diagrammatic comparison of the skull of an early reptile (top) and an early amphibian (bottom) to show the change in orientation of the jaw-closing muscles.

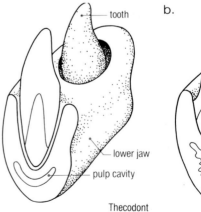

a.

tooth

lower jaw

pulp cavity

Thecodont

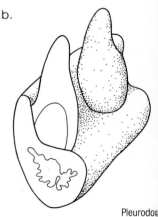

b.

Pleurodont

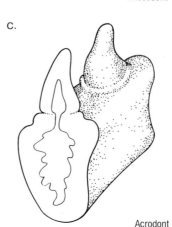

c.

Acrodont

Fig. 4.19 Sections through reptilian lower jaws showing various methods of tooth attachment.

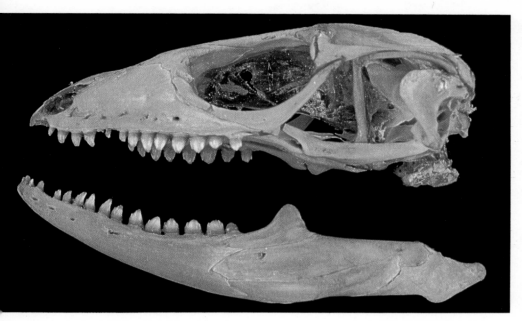

Fig. 4.20 The lizard skull in left lateral view.

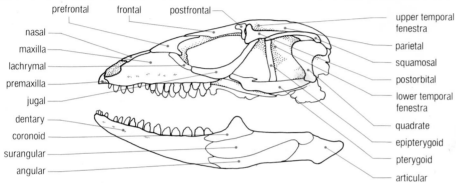

prefrontal · frontal · postfrontal · upper temporal fenestra
nasal · parietal
maxilla · squamosal
lachrymal · postorbital
premaxilla · lower temporal fenestra
jugal
dentary · quadrate
coronoid · epipterygoid
surangular · pterygoid
angular · articular

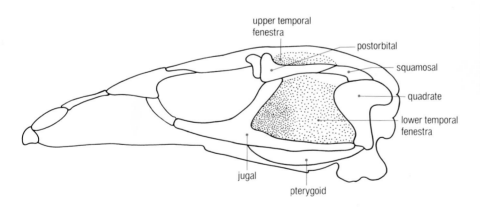

upper temporal fenestra · postorbital
squamosal
quadrate
lower temporal fenestra
jugal · pterygoid

Fig. 4.21 A diagram illustrating the diapsid or two-arched condition of the skull (top). The lower temporal bar, formed mainly by the jugal, is not present in modern lizards (bottom), but was present in their ancestors.

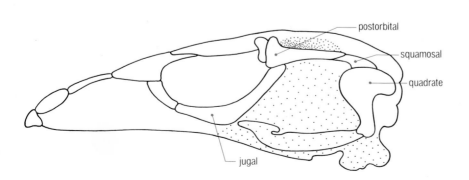

postorbital
squamosal
quadrate
jugal

A streptostylic quadrate is also a prerequisite for cranial kinesis – the relative movement of bones of the skull. Kinesis demands that certain bones of the skull have loose articulations. There is a flexible region in the palate, and a hinge joint across the skull roof between the frontal and parietal bones. If the palate is pulled forwards, the snout automatically tips upwards because of the movable chain of bones (fig. 4.22). Kinetic movements have been thought to be useful in containing struggling prey within the mouth and in shifting prey further into the mouth. Excessive forward movement is prevented by large flanges on the palatal surface of the skull which are braced against the lower jaw.

The braincase is usually well ossified in reptiles in contrast to the condition in modern amphibians (see fig. 3.26).

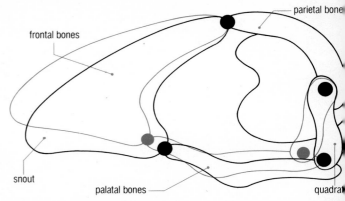

Fig. 4.22 A diagrammatic view of the lizard skull illustrating its kinetism. On opening the jaw, the quadrate is pulled forwards, pushing forwards the palatal bones which in turn push the snout forwards and upwards.

5 The Pigeon

Aves
Neornithes
Columbiformes
Columba livia

Introduction

Birds differ from other vertebrates by their adaptations to flight. These adaptations have probably limited further structural variation so that although over 8,600 species of birds are known, structural differences between the groups are small.

The modern orders of birds may be divided into two groups which are distinguished by the structure of the palate. The palaeognathous type is found in the flightless birds (ratites), such as the ostrich and emu; almost all other birds, including the pigeon, belong to the neognathous group. Orders within this group tend to be classified according to characteristics such as plumage and beak features and aspects of behaviour.

The pigeon belongs to the family Columbidae of the order Columbiformes. Columbids usually live in wooded country and feed on the ground. They can also perch well, aided by their claws and curled digits, and may take berries and other fruit from trees and shrubs. The young are fed on milky fluid secreted by the parent's crop.

Birds are thought to have evolved from the archosaur reptiles. This is the group containing crocodiles and dinosaurs, amongst other forms. It is hotly debated as to which group of archosaurs birds are most closely related to, most of the archosaur groups have been favoured at one time or another. The fossil record is of little help since birds are lightly built and are not often preserved as fossils. However, one fossil bird, *Archaeopteryx*, is known from late Jurassic times (about 150 million years ago). It was found in extremely fine-grained sediments which preserved an impression of feathers; without its feathers *Archaeopteryx* might be mistaken for one of the small dinosaurs which it resembles closely. The ancestors of modern bird orders are found reasonably soon after the appearance of *Archaeopteryx*, and for this reason certain workers feel that *Archaeopteryx* is too recent to be the direct ancestor of all later birds. It is, nevertheless, a very important (and beautiful) fossil.

5.1

Skeleton

The bird skeleton (fig. 5.1) is modified from the basic tetrapod pattern, as found in the lizard, by its adaptation to flight, the most obvious adaptation being the modified forelimb, the wing.

The bones of the front limb are variously elongated, fused or reduced to form the wing. The humerus, radius and ulna are all lengthened bones. The radius and ulna are jointed in such a way that they always remain parallel to one another, and cannot twist when the wing

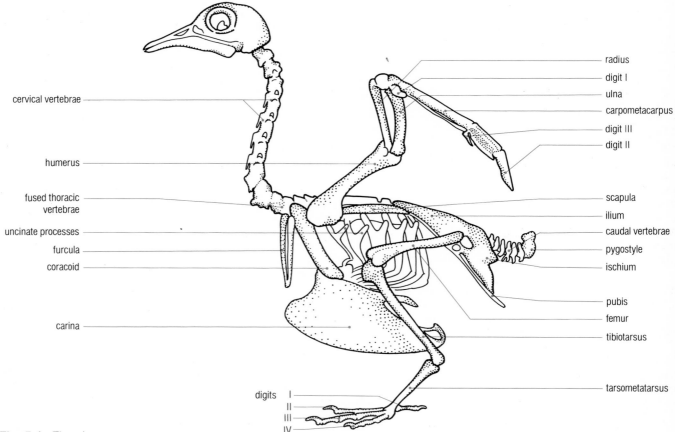

Fig. 5.1. The pigeon skeleton in left lateral view.

s in use. The wrist and elbow joints are built so that when the elbow is bent the wrist bends automatically. This cuts down the number of muscles required to fold the wing (as described later, fig. 5.24). The wrist and hand are very modified; several carpals and metacarpals fuse into a rod-like structure, the carpometacarpus. The phalanges are reduced or absent, and only remnants of digits I, II and III are present.

A great deal of muscle power is required for flight. Consequently, the wing must be connected securely to the body at the shoulder girdle to withstand the strain. The coracoids, clavicles and interclavicle act to brace the wing so that it does not collapse inwards during the powerstroke. The clavicles are fused together into a structure called the furcula (wishbone) for greater strength. The main flight muscles, which are accommodated on the shoulder girdle, are attached to the enlarged part of the sternum called the carina. Muscles also attach on the dorsal part of the shoulder girdle, the scapula, and on the thoracic ribs. These ribs carry posteriorly-directed uncinate processes for the muscles supporting the girdle.

The vertebral column is divided into distinct cervical, thoracic, sacral and caudal regions. The cervical (neck) region has a variable number of vertebrae, and may be elongate. It is flexible, allowing a good deal of mobility of the head. In the pigeon, some of the vertebrae of the thoracic region are fused together to create a firm base against which the wings are braced. Some of the thoracic vertebrae are fused with the neighbouring lumbar, sacral and some of the caudal vertebrae into a structure called the synsacrum. The synsacrum supports the pelvic girdle through which the entire weight of the bird is transmitted to the ground. The tail is very short and the last vertebrae are fused into a pygostyle which supports the tail feathers.

The pelvic girdle is interesting because the pubis has been rotated downwards and backwards. This

condition is also found in some dinosaurs, although it does not necessarily mean that birds and dinosaurs are closely related; it may be an example of convergent evolution. In the dinosaurs, a large anterior process of the pelvis develops, perhaps in order to support the abdominal contents. In birds the enlarged sternum covers so much of the abdomen that an anterior process of the pubis is unnecessary. There is often no ventral symphysis of the pubes or ischia, presumably to allow the bird to lay relatively large eggs. The elongate ilium facilitates attachment of the girdle to the synsacrum. This region needs to be particularly strong to withstand the shock of landing.

Since birds are bipedal the hind limbs must take the full weight when the bird is on the ground. Often, bipedal animals use a tail as a counter-balance, but birds have very short tails due to their aerodynamic adaptation. A short tail results in the centre of gravity lying in front of the hips. In order to place the feet directly below the centre of gravity, the femur is almost horizontal and the knees project forwards; the foot is placed on the ground vertically below the knee joint. This arrangement, together with the bird's relatively large feet, gives a good degree of stability. Four digits are present in the foot and digit I is reversed so that it points backwards, again helping to confer stability.

The hindlimb is a consolidated strut, built to withstand considerable force; the femur is a substantial bone, and the tibia and fibula are often completely or partly fused. As in the wrist, some of the tarsals and metatarsals fuse, forming a tarsometatarsus. The remaining tarsals fuse with the tibia forming a tibiotarsus.

The internal structure of the bones is different from that of most vertebrates. Gravity must be opposed when a bird flies, and weight reduction becomes very important: The long bones (such as the humerus, femur, tibia, and fibula) are basically hollow but contain slender internal struts for strengthening (fig. 5.2).

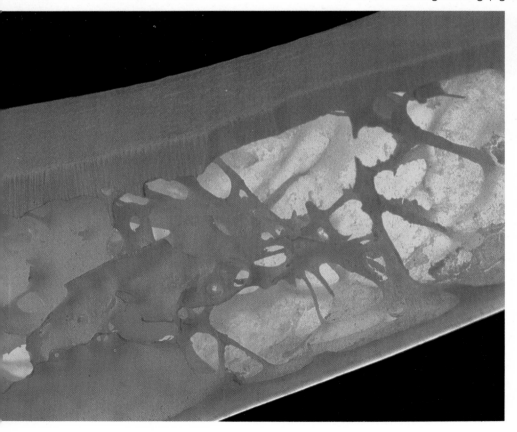

Fig. 5.2 A longitudinal cross-section of the bird femur showing the internal struts which strengthen the hollow bone.

Feathers

The most striking external features of a bird are its feathers (fig. 5.3). They are essential for flight and for heat insulation. Both of these functions are considered so important that there is fierce debate as to which represents the original function of feathers in bird evolution.

Feathers are thought to have arisen from reptilian scales, but the first fossil feathers known, those of *Archaeopteryx*, are as complex as modern-day examples and, therefore, shed no light on the evolution of feathers. Like scales, they are keratinous structures derived from the epidermis.

Various kinds of feathers with different functions are known. Contour feathers are found on the body surface, wings and tail. Down feathers are found in chicks and beneath the contour feathers of the adult, forming the main insulating layer. Filoplumes are small, hair-like feathers which are thought to be sensory. There are free nerve endings in the follicles of filoplumes, and the nerves are thought to connect to pressure and vibration receptors. The filoplumes might transmit slight movements of the contour feathers to these receptors, so that the feathers can be properly adjusted for flight and insulation. The main flight feathers are called primaries and secondaries. The primaries are attached along the posterior edges of the hand bones and the secondaries along the posterior edge of the ulna (fig. 5.4). On digit I a group of small feathers is found, called the alula or bastard wing. In many birds the distal parts of the primaries and secondaries taper abruptly, so that when the wing is spread the feathers are separated by conspicuous slots. These slots help to reduce drag by maintaining a smooth flow of air over the wing. During landing and take-off, the alula also helps to reduce drag, and to prevent stalling.

Contour feathers are the most common type of feather and they have the most complex structure (fig. 5.5). The feather consists of the hollow quill (which is sunk into

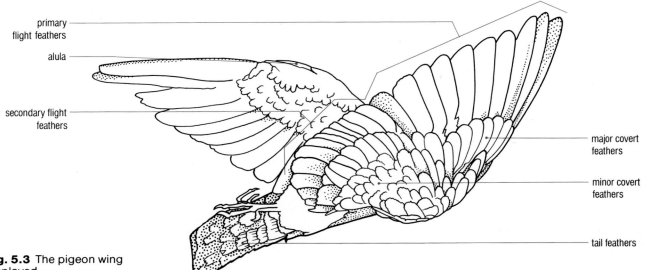

primary flight feathers

alula

secondary flight feathers

major covert feathers

minor covert feathers

tail feathers

Fig. 5.3 The pigeon wing displayed.

he bird's skin) and the feather vane. The vane is made up of a solid shaft, or rachis, from which barbs extend on either side. Tiny barbules arise either side of each barb. The barbules on one side of the barb bear hooks which catch the barbules of the next barb along, so that the feather surface remains smooth and unbroken. If this locking device does become disturbed, the bird rearranges the feather when preening, but any lasting damage can only be made good when the feather is moulted. Feathers are moulted a few at a time in order not to disturb their aerodynamic arrangement.

When the flight feathers are spread out, they are free to twist to control aerodynamic forces acting on them. This becomes useful when a bird is hovering in still air and the body and wing surfaces are more or less vertical. In this situation the wing has a very high angle of attack, and a very high wing speed is necessary in order to prevent stalling. However, the feathers can function as separate aerofoils by individually assuming lower angles of attack, thus reducing the wing speed

necessary to prevent stalling.

Feathers provide insulation by trapping a layer of air next to the bird's body. They also repel water and are often coated by a waxy secretion from a gland at the base of the tail, or glands on the body surface. The barbs themselves also prevent water penetration because they are evenly spaced and water droplets cannot break through.

Pigments within the feathers are in part responsible for a bird's plumage colouration. Some colours are produced by structural phenomena – interference and scattering of light. Scattering produces only blue colouring, whereas interference produces irridescent colours by reflecting and refracting light from the feather barbules. Short wavelengths of light are scattered by particles within the feather that are smaller than the wavelength of the light.

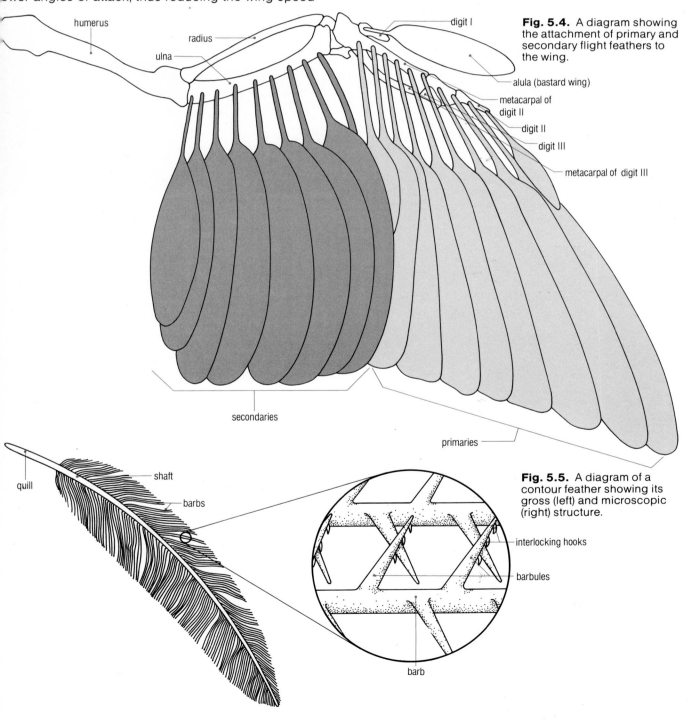

Fig. 5.4. A diagram showing the attachment of primary and secondary flight feathers to the wing.

humerus
radius
ulna
digit I
alula (bastard wing)
metacarpal of digit II
digit II
digit III
metacarpal of digit III
secondaries
primaries

quill
shaft
barbs

Fig. 5.5. A diagram of a contour feather showing its gross (left) and microscopic (right) structure.

interlocking hooks
barbules
barb

Air sacs

The air sacs are part of the respiratory system (fig. 5.6). They were once thought to be important in reducing the weight of the bird's body, but this is probably of secondary importance. Each air sac is a thin-walled bag which can distend considerably (figs. 5.8 and 5.9), but has a poor blood supply. The bird's respiratory system is quite complex. It consists of a number of air sacs which we can put into two groups, the anterior air sacs and the posterior air sacs.

The trachea is the pathway to the exterior, as in other tetrapods, and it forks into two bronchi. Each bronchus then subdivides to produce a number of parallel tubes, the parabronchi. It is here that respiratory exchange takes place. The path that air takes through the system has been investigated using anemometers (flow meters) inserted into the parabronchi. When the bird breathes in, air is drawn from the outside down into the bronchi and straight into the posterior air sacs. When the bird breathes out, air from the posterior air sacs travels through the parabronchi, and air in the anterior sacs travels through the bronchus to the outside.

This system is quite unlike that of any other land vertebrate and is a particularly efficient system since it produces a one-way passage of air through the lungs. This allows a counter-current system between incoming air and the blood supply which removes oxygen from the air. Efficiency is important since flight is metabolically very costly and requires a high and constant supply of oxygen. Another way of increasing the oxygen supply is to increase the area of the respiratory exchange surface. However, this would lead to an increase in the bird's body weight and volume – a disadvantage in an animal built to aerodynamic requirements.

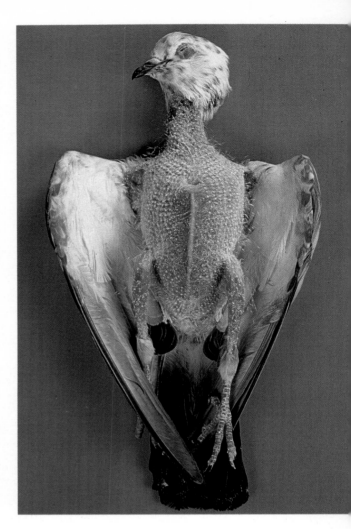

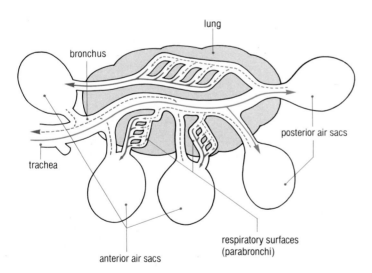

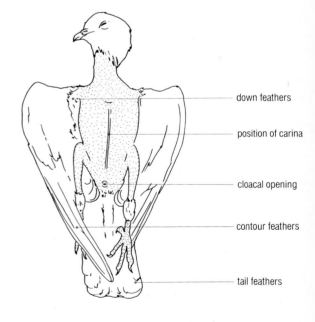

Fig. 5.6. A diagram of the avian respiratory system (in left lateral view) to show the path of air flow. On inhalation fresh air (solid blue line) passes to the posterior air sacs and used air from the lung (solid red line) passes to the anterior air sacs. On exhalation the fresh air in the posterior air sacs (blue dotted line) passes to the lung and the used air in the anterior air sacs (red dotted line) passes out through the trachea. In this way, a unidirectional flow of air through the lung is achieved.

Fig. 5.7. Ventral view – animal prepared for dissection.

● Carefully pluck the feathers from the ventral surface of the legs and the neck. Take care to avoid tearing the skin in the neck region where it is very delicate.

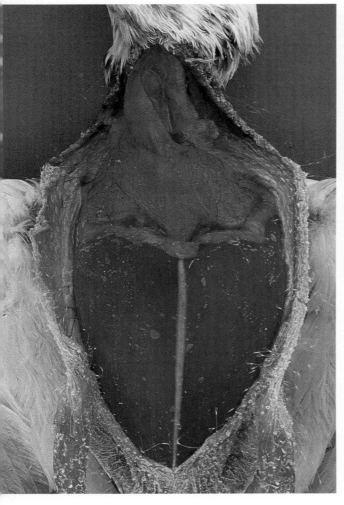

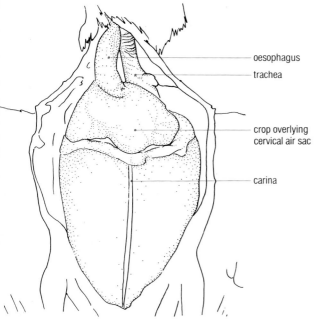

oesophagus
trachea

crop overlying
cervical air sac

carina

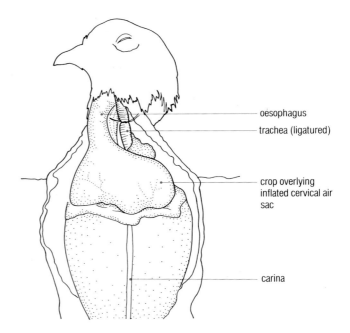

oesophagus
trachea (ligatured)

crop overlying
inflated cervical air
sac

carina

Fig. 5.8. Cervical air sac and crop.

● Make a median incision along the mid-ventral line to remove the skin, and lay it back on each side of the bird. Take care to avoid rupturing the crop and the cervical air sac, which adhere closely to the skin of the neck.

Fig. 5.9. Cervical air sac inflated.

● Expose the trachea and separate a small portion from the surrounding tissues.

● Arrange a thread loosely round the trachea to act as a ligature. Make a small incision in the trachea anterior to the thread; insert a blowpipe into the trachea and inflate the air sacs by blowing gently down the pipe. Tighten the ligature thread while the air sacs are under pressure.

Body cavity

A distinct neck is present in birds and, consequently, an oesophagus is present to take food from the mouth to the stomach. Grain and other foods are stored in a distensible sac, the crop (fig. 5.10); this is found part of the way down the oesophagus and secretes a milky material which is fed to the chicks.

The stomach can be divided into two sections. Nearest the oesophagus is the proventriculus (fig. 5.12) which contains the fundic epithelium where enzymes and hydrochloric acid are secreted. Nearer the intestine the stomach gives rise to the muscular gizzard. In grain-eating birds, small stones are allowed to collect in the gizzard forming a mill which takes over the function of the teeth. It has been assumed that loss of teeth and reduction of jaw muscles are weight-reducing adaptations. However, this explanation is too simple because gizzard stones, and the muscular gizzard itself, probably weigh more than teeth and jaw muscles. The answer probably lies in the bird's need to keep its body stable; it is necessary to have heavy organs situated as close to the centre of gravity as possible and the gizzard is closer to this point than the mouth. Birds have a high metabolic rate and loss of teeth has been associated with the need for speed in ingesting and digesting food. A muscular gizzard enables food to be ingested quickly without preliminary chewing; it can then be finely divided so that digestion can take place efficiently. This system requires a storage place, such as the crop.

The small intestine is highly convoluted and very long compared to that of most vertebrates. Again this is probably correlated with the high metabolic rate which flight demands. The large intestine is quite short and empties, with the ureters, into the cloaca. Urine and faeces are mixed before being voided to the exterior.

The syrinx, or vocal organ, is found at the junction of the trachea and bronchi where the last few bony supporting rings of the trachea and the first ring of each bronchus are modified to form a chamber containing a membrane, the tympanum. In order to produce sounds, this membrane is made to vibrate using special musculature.

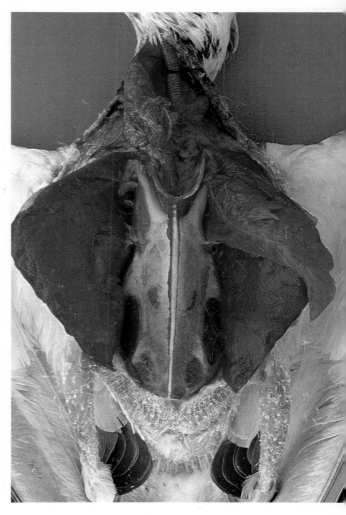

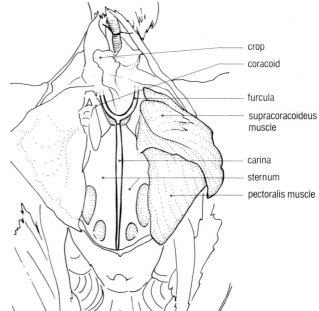

crop
coracoid
furcula
supracoracoideus muscle
carina
sternum
pectoralis muscle

Fig. 5.10. Body cavity – 1st dissection stage.

● (If the same specimen is to be used for dissecting both the body cavity and the wing musculature, figs. 5.21, 5.23 and 5.25 should be referred to next). Separate the supracoracoideus and pectoralis muscles from the left side of the sternum and coracoid to reveal the ventrolateral surface of these bones. Ligature the pectoral artery and vein as shown in fig. 5.21.

● Deflect the pectoralis and supracoracoideus muscles laterally from the bones on the right side.

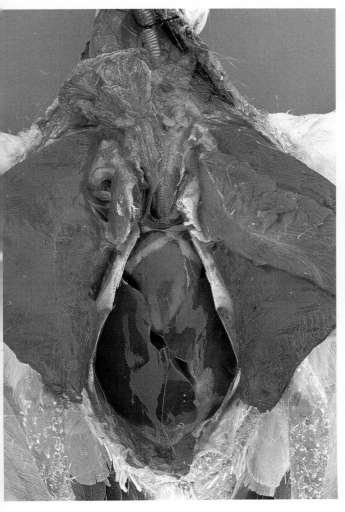

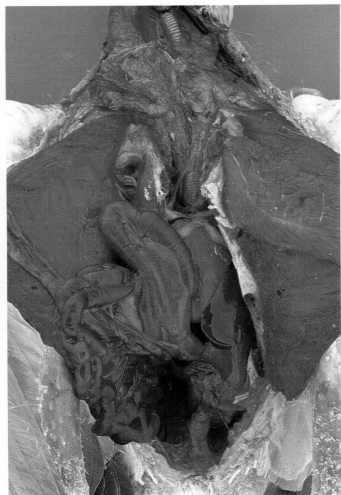

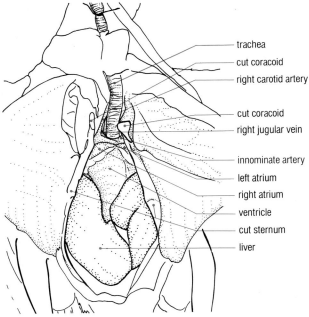

trachea
cut coracoid
right carotid artery

cut coracoid
right jugular vein

innominate artery
left atrium
right atrium
ventricle
cut sternum
liver

oesophagus

proventriculus
trachea
right carotid artery
duodenum

ventricle
small intestine
left lobe of liver
gizzard

large intestine

region of cloaca

**Fig. 5.11. Body cavity –
2nd dissection stage.**

● Remove the furcula and lift
the median sternum clear by
making lateral cuts along its
edge and through the ventral
ends of the coracoids. Take
care not to damage the
underlying liver and heart.

**Fig. 5.12. Body cavity –
3rd dissection stage.**

● Deflect the gut to the
animal's right to show the
mesenteries and the
organisation of the alimentary
canal.

Urinogenital system

The bird kidney develops in the embryo from the most posterior trunk segment; it is, therefore, a metanephric kidney. However, the tubules proliferate so that the adult kidney is a very large, lobed structure (fig. 5.14); there may be twice as many tubules in the bird's kidney as in that of a mammal of similar size. Regulation of the body fluid contents becomes very important when metabolic turnover is rapid, as in flight, and the kidney of the adult bird must carry out glomerular ultrafiltration efficiently. This requires a high blood pressure and we shall consider how this is produced a little later.

The kidney performs two important operations. First, blood is filtered through the glomerulus so that blood cells and plasma proteins are retained in the general circulation but other constituents pass into Bowman's capsule. From here they enter the tubule where the second operation takes place: useful substances such as water and glucose are picked up by the venous network around the tubule, to be returned to the general circulation. Waste and harmful substances continue through the tubule, eventually to be collected in the ureter and passed to the cloaca. In birds, as in lizards, the endpoint of nitrogenous metabolism is uric acid, a highly insoluble compound which can be excreted with minimum water expenditure. This property is extremely important to the developing embryo enclosed in a shelled egg (fig. 4.10). Waste can be deposited without the necessity of transforming it metabolically, and without using up large quantities of water.

The urinogenital system of the pigeon is very similar to that of the lizard in that the ureter drains the kidney and is separate from the archinephric duct which transports only sperm in the male, and degenerates in the female (fig. 5.13).

The testes are paired, but only the left ovary and its duct, the oviduct, are present in the female. The oviduct can be divided into two sections: the uterus, and the uterine tube, a broad muscular cylinder leading from the ovarian funnel into the uterus. The distinction between these two structures would be visible in fig. 5.15 if the bird had been in breeding condition, since the uterus expands greatly at this time. The uterine tube secretes albumen (egg-white) and the uterus forms the shell.

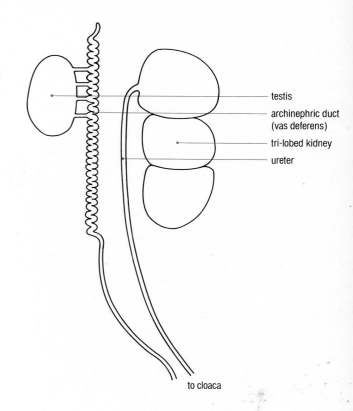

testis
archinephric duct (vas deferens)
tri-lobed kidney
ureter

to cloaca

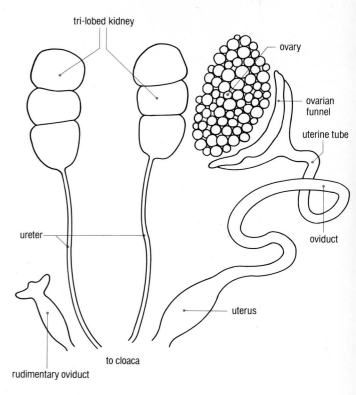

tri-lobed kidney
ovary
ovarian funnel
uterine tube
ureter
oviduct
uterus
rudimentary oviduct
to cloaca

Fig. 5.13. A diagram of the avian urinogenital system in the male (top) and female (bottom).

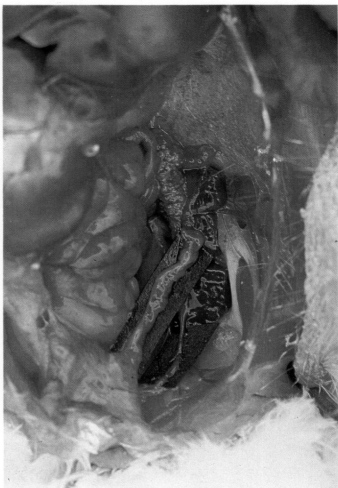

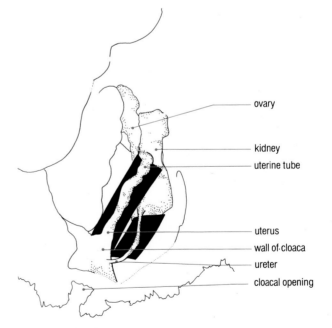

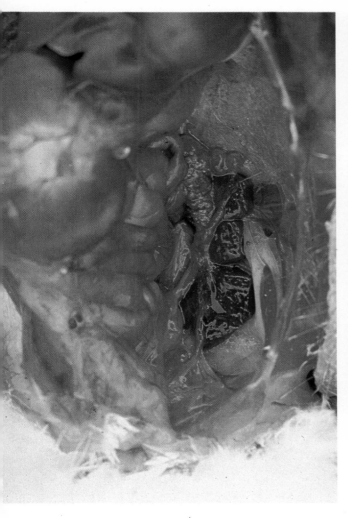

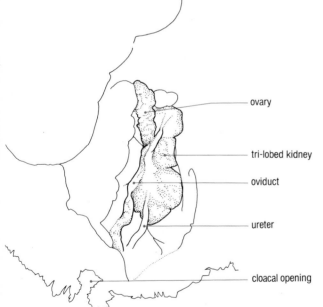

Labels for Fig. 5.14:
- ovary
- tri-lobed kidney
- oviduct
- ureter
- cloacal opening

Labels for Fig. 5.15:
- ovary
- kidney
- uterine tube
- uterus
- wall of cloaca
- ureter
- cloacal opening

Fig. 5.14. Female urino-genital system – 1st dissection stage.

● Displace the large intestine to the animal's right side to expose the kidneys and ovary lying against the left abdominal wall.

● Trace the oviduct from the ovary and the ureter from the kidney to their points of entry into the cloaca.

Fig. 5.15. Female urino-genital system – 2nd dissection stage.

● Black paper has been inserted under the oviduct and ureter.

Cardiovascular system

In contrast to the hearts of the vertebrates that we have seen so far, that of the pigeon is completely divided and provides a double circulation (figs. 5.16 and 5.17). Deoxygenated blood from the body enters the right atrium and is propelled by the right ventricle to the lungs. Oxygenated blood returning from the lungs enters the left atrium and is forced out through the left ventricle to begin its path around the body. Right and left sides of the heart are quite separate so that oxygenated and deoxygenated blood cannot mix and the systemic circulation is always supplied with oxygenated blood, never mixed blood. An additional advantage of the divided circulation is that it is possible to maintain a higher blood pressure in the systemic circulation than in the pulmonary circulation. This high blood pressure is essential for an animal with a high metabolic rate.

A completely divided heart has the possible disadvantage that blood cannot be shunted from one circulation to another, as in amphibians and reptiles. However, the high metabolic rate of birds probably demands an efficient supply of oxygenated blood at all times, so the versatility of the amphibian or reptilian heart is unnecessary.

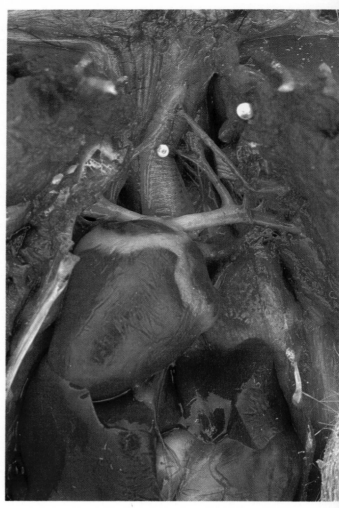

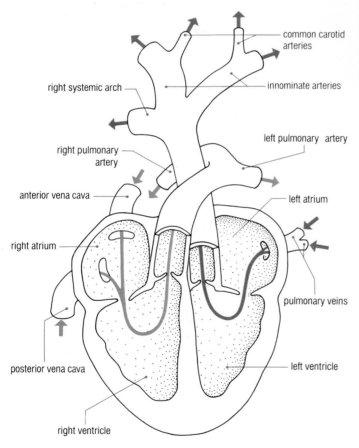

Fig. 5.16. A diagram of the pigeon heart in ventral view showing the path of oxygenated (red) and deoxygenated (blue) blood.

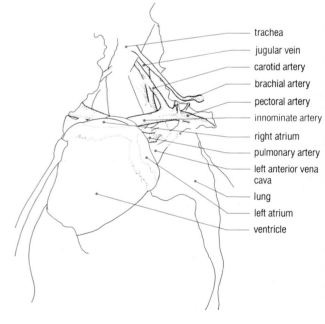

Fig. 5.17 The heart and aortic arches

● Carefully clear the pericardium and connective tissue in the region of the heart and trachea to reveal the main arterial blood supply to the neck and forelimbs.

● Cut back the coracoids dorsally, and clear the systemic arch with its main branches; take care not to damage the underlying main veins.

In the lizard, three vessels open from the heart: the pulmonary arch, the left systemic arch and the right systemic arch. In birds the left systemic arch has been eliminated (figs. 5.18 and 5.19). The right systemic arch, or aorta, is the only vessel leaving the heart which carries oxygenated blood, and the pressure within this vessel is, therefore, relatively high. The right systemic arch supplies the head (through the carotid arteries), and the rest of the body.

Certain differences exist between the venous system of reptiles and that of birds (fig. 5.20). In the other vertebrates that we have discussed, the anterior part of the head and the brain are drained by the lateral head vein which enters the anterior cardinal vein. In birds, venous sinuses develop within the cranial cavity and are drained by internal jugular veins. As these approach the heart, they are joined by the external jugulars, forming the common jugulars. Eventually these empty into the anterior venae cavae – the anterior cardinals of reptiles.

The renal portal veins are well-developed in birds, and the kidney has both afferent and efferent venous systems. The renal veins constitute the efferent venous system, the renal portal the afferent system. Blood from the hind limb approaches the kidney in the external iliac vein. In the kidney the iliac vein branches to form the common iliac veins (which empty into the vena cava) and the renal portal vein. Blood from the hindlimb either goes straight to the vena cava, via the common iliac vein, or it goes through the renal portal vein and capillaries first, and eventually enters the renal veins and passes into the vena cava. The route taken is decided by the renal portal valve, a muscular sphincter found near the junction of the renal and common iliac veins. If the valve is contracted, blood is prevented from flowing directly into the vena cava, and is shunted through the renal portal system instead. Shutting down the portal flow may be a physiological response, mediated through neurohumoral effects. In an emergency, it could be used to provide a temporary supply of extra blood in the general circulation.

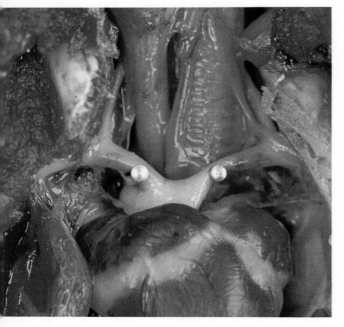

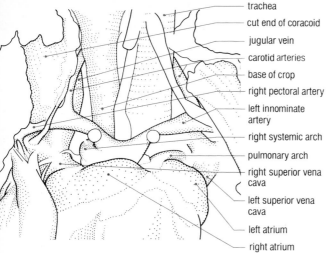

trachea
cut end of coracoid
jugular vein
carotid arteries
base of crop
right pectoral artery
left innominate artery
right systemic arch
pulmonary arch
right superior vena cava
left superior vena cava
left atrium
right atrium

Fig. 5.18 The origins of the systemic and pulmonary arches are shown here in detail (see fig. 5.17)

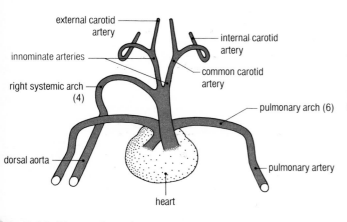

external carotid artery
innominate arteries
right systemic arch (4)
dorsal aorta
internal carotid artery
common carotid artery
pulmonary arch (6)
pulmonary artery
heart

Fig. 5.19 The aortic arches of the pigeon in ventral view.

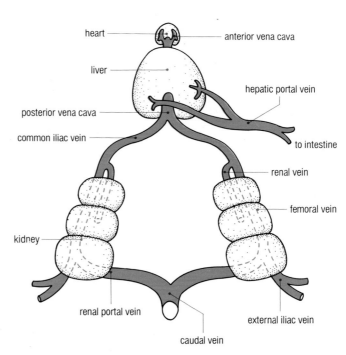

heart
liver
posterior vena cava
common iliac vein
kidney
anterior vena cava
hepatic portal vein
to intestine
renal vein
femoral vein
renal portal vein
external iliac vein
caudal vein

Fig. 5.20 The major veins of a bird in ventral view.

Wing musculature

In order to fly, a bird must generate a lift force to overcome gravity. If an asymmetrical object moves in a fluid (a liquid or gas, like air) a lift force acts on it at right angles to its movement; this will tend to suspend the object in the fluid. However, another force also acts on the object; this is drag and it represents resistance to the object's movement, slowing it down and reducing the lift. Ideally, we would want to maximise lift and minimise drag in order to keep an object suspended in a fluid most efficiently. The shape of the object affects the lift/drag ratio; it has been found that the aerofoil section, as seen in bird wings, is the best shape for maximising this ratio.

The wing-beating is the source of the bird's forward movement. Contrary to popular opinion, the wing beat does not thrust the bird up in the air; it is the aerodynamic lift force that causes the bird to rise. This is obvious when one considers a bird flying in a horizontal path – it still beats its wings, even though it is not rising in the air.

The muscles mainly responsible for moving the wings are the pectoralis and supracoracoideus (fig. 5.21). The pectoralis attaches to the sternum and produces the down-and-back stroke, the power stroke, and is necessarily very large. The supracoracoideus muscle produces the up-and-forward recovery stroke and is also attached to the sternum. Both muscles are attached to the same bones and yet they produce different movements; this is due to the way the supracoracoideus muscle is inserted on the humerus. In order to reach the humerus, the tendon of the supracoracoideus must pass up and over a process on the coracoid bone of the shoulder girdle. In fact, the tendon passes through a foramen, the foramen triosseum at the point where scapula, coracoid and clavicle bones meet (figs. 5.22 and 5.23). In this way, the tendon is running over a pulley (the coracoid process) which changes the direction of the pull of the muscle, making the wing move upwards and forwards.

It might seem simpler to use a dorsal muscle to produce the recovery stroke. However, the weight of large muscle blocks, like the wing-movers, can be used to increase the stability of the bird by lowering the centre of gravity. This can be done by placing them as ventrally as possible and may be the reason for not elaborating the dorsal muscles.

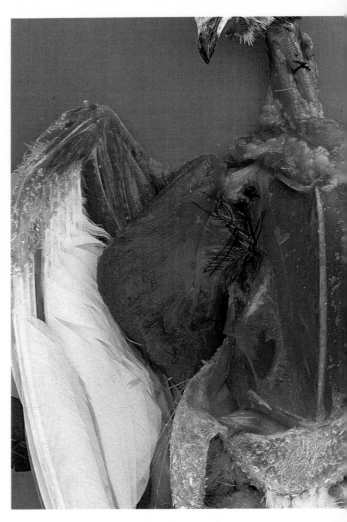

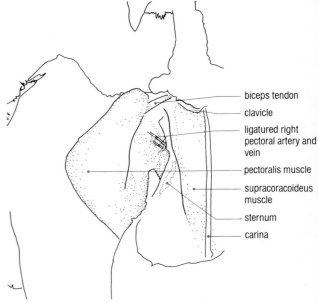

- biceps tendon
- clavicle
- ligatured right pectoral artery and vein
- pectoralis muscle
- supracoracoideus muscle
- sternum
- carina

Fig. 5.21. Wing musculature – 1st dissection stage.

● A different bird has been used for the dissection of the flight muscles, but the complete dissection can be done using one specimen.

● Remove the skin from the breast, back and dorsal and ventral surfaces of the right wing. Be careful not to damage the patagial tendon which runs along the anterior edge of the wing. Clear the muscles of fat and connective tissue.

● Separate and displace the crop from the pectoralis muscles and cut this muscle away from the carina and clavicle to reveal the supracoracoideus muscle. An air sac and the pectoral vein and artery will be visible between the two muscles.

● Ligature and cut the vein and artery and continue to free the pectoralis muscle from the lateral border of the sternum.

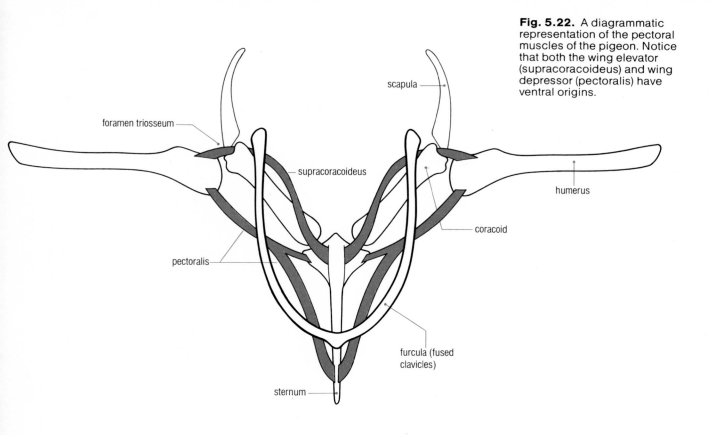

Fig. 5.22. A diagrammatic representation of the pectoral muscles of the pigeon. Notice that both the wing elevator (supracoracoideus) and wing depressor (pectoralis) have ventral origins.

foramen triosseum

scapula

supracoracoideus

humerus

coracoid

pectoralis

furcula (fused clavicles)

sternum

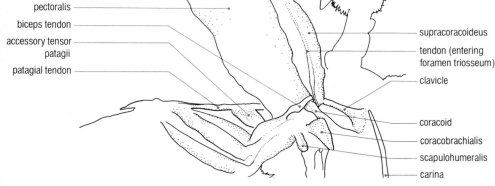

pectoralis

biceps tendon

accessory tensor patagii

patagial tendon

supracoracoideus

tendon (entering foramen triosseum)

clavicle

coracoid

coracobrachialis

scapulohumeralis

carina

Fig. 5.23. Wing musculature – 2nd dissection stage.

● Detach the supracoracoideus from the surface and keel of the sternum and free it at its anterior edge leaving its tendon in place. Reflect the muscle forwards to reveal the scapulohumeralis and coracobrachialis muscles.

● Examine the wing and find the biceps and triceps muscles and the accessory tensor patagii inserting into the patagial tendon. On either side of the radio-ulna there are extensors, flexors and rotators of the wrist, as well as short flexors and rotators of the elbow joint.

It is very simplistic to treat the wing as being moved by a single pair of muscles. In reality various muscles work together, each performing a slightly different task in order to produce the overall movement that is desired. For example, the coracobrachialis muscle aids the pectoralis; it runs from the coracoid to the humerus, and pulls the humerus backwards.

The wing must also be folded and unfolded. The biceps contributes to wing-folding by pulling in the radius and ulna. The triceps unfolds the wing; it runs from the scapula to the ulna and extends the elbow joint. The patagial tendon runs from the shoulder to the wrist; when the elbow joint extends, the tendon is stretched automatically extending the wrist, thus economising on muscular effort (fig. 5.24).

The muscles that we have discussed so far are those with ventral attachments but some muscles attach dorsally (fig. 5.25). None of these muscles are involved in the power-stroke but are important in other ways, some of which are described below.

The scapulohumeralis and latissimus dorsi help in wing folding; the latissimus raises the humerus, and they both pull it backwards. The deltoideus is a large and important muscle, divided into several parts, one being the tensor patagii which pulls the humerus forwards and, because it is inserted into the patagial tendon, it also flexes the wrist. The deltoideus major inserts on the humerus which it raises and pulls forwards. The deltoids are of use, therefore, in the recovery stroke and wing unfolding. There are additional muscles which attach the shoulder girdle firmly to the vertebral column. They are responsible for support and posture of the wing. The main muscles in this category are the rhomboideus, and the serratus series. Active muscle, like pigeon flight muscle, demands an adequate supply of oxygen and nutrients. The large vessels supplying the wing muscles have already been seen in fig. 5.21.

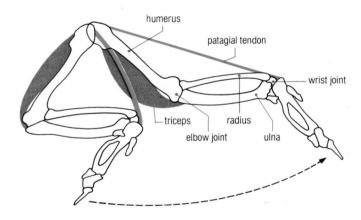

Fig. 5.24. A diagram showing the action of the patagial tendon and triceps muscle. When the wing is folded the triceps is relaxed and the tendon loose. To unfold the wing the triceps contracts and extends the elbow. This pulls the tendon taut and extends the wrist automatically.

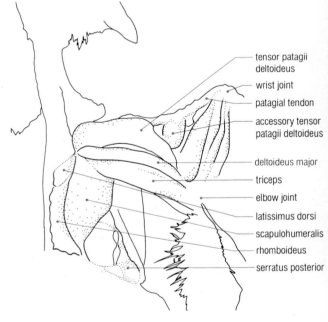

Fig. 5.25. Wing musculature – 3rd dissection stage.

● Place the pigeon facedown and note the dorsal muscles: scapulohumeralis, deltoideus, latissimus dorsi and rhomboideus.

● Carefully separate out the deltoideus minor, tensor patagii and triceps.

● Look for the serratus posterior which arises from the ribs and inserts on the inner surface of the scapula.

Skull

The distinguishing features of the skull are the large, rounded braincase, the large orbits and the long pointed beak (fig. 5.26). Most of the bones of the cranium are firmly attached to each other and sutures are difficult to find in adult birds.

The upper half of the beak is composed of the premaxilla, whilst the lower half is composed of the angular, dentary, splenial, surangular and articular bones. No teeth are present, as noted before, but the beak bones are covered in tough horn.

The snout region forms a relatively small proportion of the skull and very little space is available for nasal structures. Birds have a limited sense of smell and this is reflected in the small olfactory centres in the brain. Vision is well-developed and this is illustrated by the large orbits. Birds are capable of a high degree of binocular vision – an essential pre-requisite for an animal that flies. The development of large optic centres and a large cerebellum (which coordinates locomotion) accounts for the large, rounded cranium.

One of the most distinguishing functional aspects of the skull is its kinetism – the ability of certain bones to move with respect to others (fig. 4.22). In the bird there are movable or flexible joints between the palatines and pterygoids, the quadrate and cranium, the quadrate and palate, and between the quadrate and jugal. Flexible regions also exist between the top of the beak and the cranium, and the base of the beak and the jugal (fig. 5.27). If the palate and jugal are pushed forwards the upper jaw also tilts upwards. When the lower jaw is opened a ligament running up to the cranium is tightened. This pulls up the back end of the lower jaw which in turn pushes the quadrate forwards and raises the upper jaw. This means that opening the lower jaw pushes up the upper jaw at the same time. This certainly allows a wider gape to be achieved, but, as seen in the lizard skull, the purpose of the kinetic skull is far from clear.

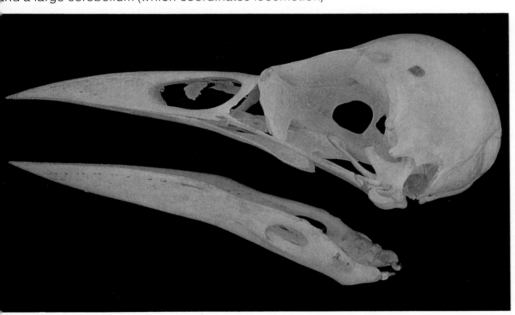

Fig. 5.26. The skull of the pigeon in left lateral view.

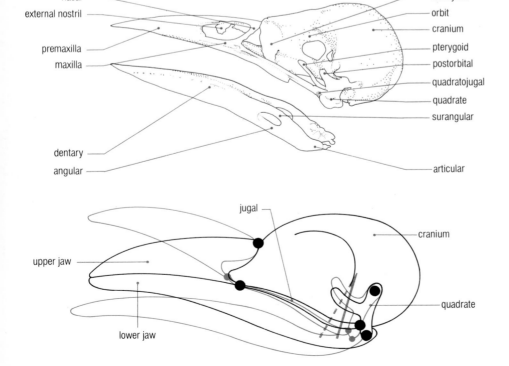

Fig. 5.27. A diagram of the bird skull illustrating its kinetism. On opening the jaw, the quadrate is pulled forwards tilting the upper jaw upwards. The ligament is represented by a red line.

6 The Rat

Mammalia
Rodentia
Myomorpha
Rattus rattus

The rat belongs to the order Rodentia which contains, amongst others, mice, squirrels, porcupines and guinea pigs. All of these animals are equipped with continually-growing, self-sharpening incisors used for gnawing. Like all rodents the rat can deal with tough food and will feed on almost anything. However, its natural diet is largely seeds and nuts. The Rodentia is one of many orders belonging to the Eutheria (placental mammals). Examples of some of the other orders are the Insectivora (hedgehogs, shrews, moles, etc.), the Carnivora (dogs, cats, bears, weasels, etc.) and the Chiroptera (bats). For convenience, mammals can be divided into the Prototheria and the Theria. The former group contains the monotremes, echidna and platypus, and certain extinct forms. The latter group is broken down into the Metatheria (the pouched mammals or marsupials) and the Eutheria.

Mammals are usually defined as warm-blooded animals which are covered in fur, bear live young and suckle the young on milk produced by mammary glands. There are problems with this definition since the egg-laying echidna and platypus are fur-covered and generally regarded as mammals. In addition, this definition, is not directly applicable to fossil forms, since soft features like hair rarely fossilise. So a palaeontological definition of mammals might include the following features: only one bone, the dentary, in the lower jaw; the other lower jaw bones are reduced and have been freed from the dentary

to become the middle ear bones; teeth are replaced as a set only once during the animal's life, in contrast to the continuous replacement of teeth in reptiles; in the postcranial skeleton, the pubis is reduced and backwardly pointing, and the ilium is expanded dorsally and anteriorly; usually there is no interclavicle in the shoulder girdle and the scapula is divided into two areas by a sharp crest.

There is dispute about when exactly such a character suite may have arisen in the evolution of the ancestral mammal. However, this set of characters provides useful guidelines for the recognition of fossils as mammalian. Almost all workers agree that mammals arose from one or more of the extinct group of reptiles called cynodonts. These animals belonged to the mammal-like reptiles (Synapsida), so called because during their evolutionary history they gradually evolved the characters which later came to typify mammals. Several groups of the synapsids seemed to have evolved some of these characters in parallel, but one line, that of the cynodonts, gave rise to the mammals as we know them today.

The very first mammals arose in the Triassic and were small, insectivorous animals. They were probably nocturnal to avoid competition with the reptiles of the time. Pouched mammals and placental mammals (including some of the modern orders) had arisen by the end of the Cretaceous.

6.1

Skeleton

The rat has a fairly generalised mammalian skeleton (fig. 6.1); it lacks any special adaptations to digging, swimming or fast running. It was once thought that mammals were characterised by upright limbs such as those found in horses and deer. However, this upright stance seems to be a specialisation of fast-running or heavy animals, not of mammals in general.

The vertebral column is clearly divisible into several regions, which are characterised mainly by the presence or absence of ribs. The neck usually consists of seven vertebrae in which the heads of each double-headed rib are fused to the transverse process and centrum of the vertebra. The first two neck vertebrae, the atlas and axis, are modified to permit rotation of the head. The atlas is a bony ring with wide, wing-like transverse processes; the axis has a process formed by the fusion of the axis centrum and the atlas centrum. This process fits into the atlas ring like a peg into a socket (see fig. 6.2).

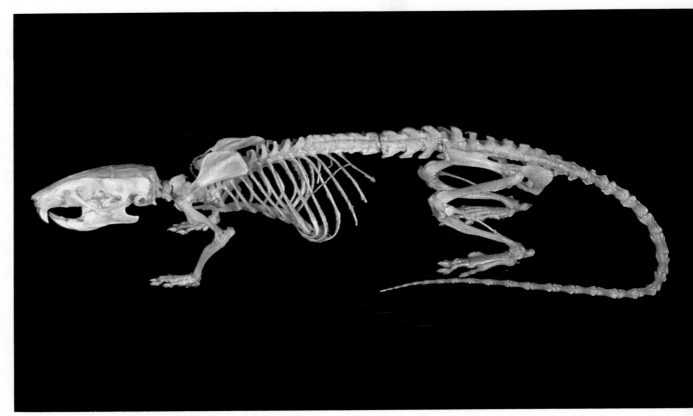

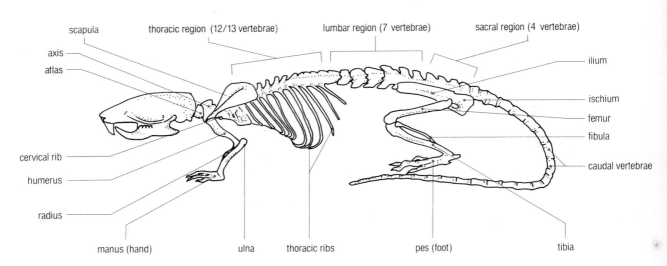

Fig. 6.1. The rat skeleton in left lateral view.

The trunk vertebrae can be divided into two regions: the thoracic region bears ribs, of which the anterior ones connect ventrally with the sternum; the lumbar region is ribless. The head and neck musculature is attached to the long neural spines of the thoracic vertebrae. These point backwards in the anterior region, unlike the short, forward-pointing neural spines of the lumbar vertebrae. These two regions also differ in the size of their centra; those of the lumbar vertebrae are much larger and carry robust transverse processes. However, the lumbar and posterior thoracic vertebrae resemble one another in being able to move in the vertical plane only. This, when translated into the animal's gait, is a bounding movement. In a fast-moving mammal such movements are used to increase the length of the stride.

In a land mammal like the rat, the vertebral column, together with its associated muscles and ligaments, acts as a beam to support the total weight of the body off the ground (fig. 6.3), but between the legs the body will tend to sag. This leads to compression forces on the dorsal side of the vertebral column, and tension forces on the ventral side. The compression forces are resisted by the centra of the vertebrae, while the tension forces are counteracted by ligaments and muscles running between the vertebrae and the ribs. The vertebral column is arched gently upwards which helps effective weight-bearing.

Both pelvic and pectoral girdles of the rat are different from those of the reptile and reflect the fact that the legs have lost the primitive sprawling posture and are turned in under the body (fig. 6.4). Reorientation of the limb necessitates reorientation of the muscles moving the limb, which in turn requires reorientation of the muscle attachment areas. For example, in the shoulder girdle, the muscles mainly responsible for pulling the limb forwards (the recovery stroke) are the spinatus muscles, derivatives of the reptilian supracoracoideus muscle which prevented the limb sagging. The scapula is expanded substantially to accommodate the spinatus muscle in mammals. In the pelvic girdle the gluteal muscles are the power-stroke muscles which pull the limb backwards, and they are derivatives of the reptilian iliofemoralis muscle which raised the leg. The recovery stroke muscles (the iliacus and psoas) are derived from the reptilian

muscles which pulled the leg forwards and downwards. To accommodate these muscles, the ilium has expanded dorsally and anteriorly. The pubis and ischium, however, have become reduced in size, since they were the site of attachment of the postural muscles – muscles which prevented the collapse of the body and the sprawling limb. These muscles are not so important in a mammal since the limbs are not sprawling but are directed underneath the body and consequently there is little tendency for the body to collapse.

a.

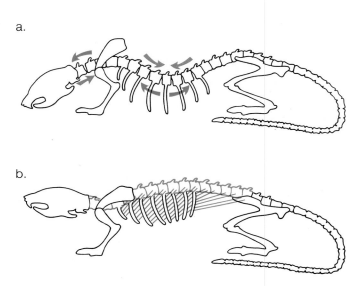

b.

Fig. 6.3. A diagram to show how the vertebral column supports the weight of the head and body.
(a) illustrates the forces of compression (red) and tension (blue) which act on the vertebral column.
(b) illustrates how these forces are counteracted. The compression forces are resisted by the thickest part of the vertebra, the centrum (red), and the tension forces are counteracted by tendons and muscle (blue) ventral to the vertebral column in the thorax, and dorsal in the neck.

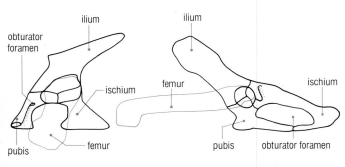

Fig. 6.4. The pelvic girdles of the lizard (left) and rat (right) in left lateral view to compare the orientation of the femur and the configuration of the ilium and pubis. These reflect the difference in posture, and muscle attachment, in the two animals.

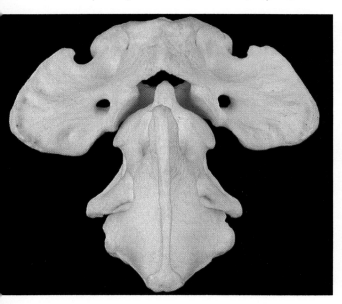

Fig. 6.2. The mammalian atlas and axis vertebrae in dorsal view. Note the peg-like odontoid process of the axis (bottom) which fits into the ring-shaped atlas vertebra (top).

External features

The external views of the male and female rat (figs. 6.6 and 6.7) illustrate several general mammalian features: the vibrissae (whiskers) on the snout, which are tactile organs; the covering of fur; the separate reproductive and excretory openings; the reduced, slender tail; the mammary glands (in the female); and the scrotal sac containing the testes (in the male).

In most adult male mammals the testes descend to a position outside the body cavity and it is thought that this happens because the body temperature of a mammal is too high for sperm development.

The mammary glands are arranged in two lines either side of the ventral surface extending from the neck to the lower abdomen (fig. 6.8). They are prominent in the lactating female and their nipples can be seen quite clearly. Each female can suckle several young and litters of up to 10 are common.

Mammalian skin (fig. 6.5) differs from that of a lizard (fig. 4.4) by the presence of hair and certain glands unique to mammals, and by the absence of epidermal scales. It is composed of a dermis and a two-layered epidermis. Cells of the deeper epidermal layer (stratum germinativum) grow, divide and move towards the exterior, gradually becoming flattened plates of keratin forming the stratum corneum. The underlying dermis contains collagen and elastic fibres as well as nerves and blood vessels.

Hair is an epidermal structure and grows from deep invaginations of the stratum germinativum (hair follicles). Hair exists in a variety of forms, such as vibrissae (fig. 6.6), quills, fur and wool. The unique mammalian glands are also epidermal structures.

The impervious nature of the stratum corneum and the oily secretions from sebaceous glands repel water and are important in preventing water loss. The skin also plays an important part in thermoregulation; the dermis and hair layer serve as insulation and heat is lost through water evaporation from sweat glands. In addition, these glands are responsible for excreting urea, salt and other waste products. The skin also serves as a sense organ; sensory endings receptive to pain, pressure and temperature change are found in the dermis.

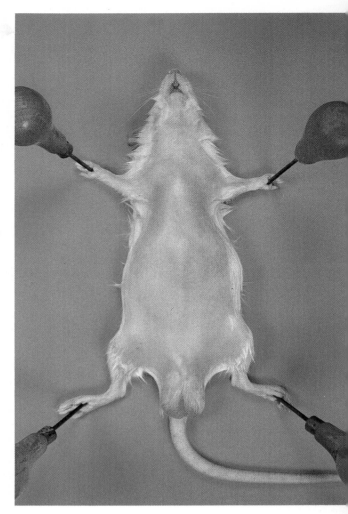

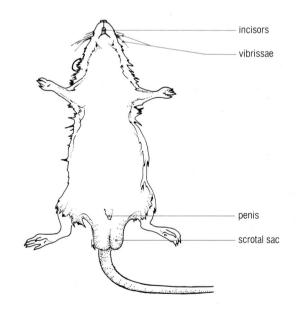

incisors
vibrissae
penis
scrotal sac

Fig. 6.6 External features of the male rat

● Pin the rat out with wooden-handled awls.

● You can use a proprietary hair remover cream or razor to clear the hair from the ventral surface of the neck, thorax and abdomen.

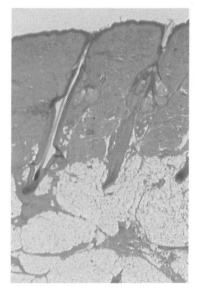

epidermis   sebaceous gland

hair root   hair shaft   dermis

Fig. 6.5 A transverse section through mammalian skin, × 10.

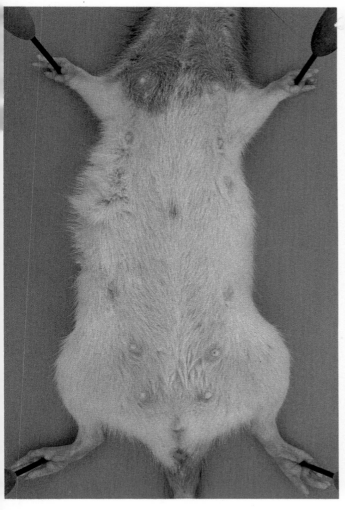

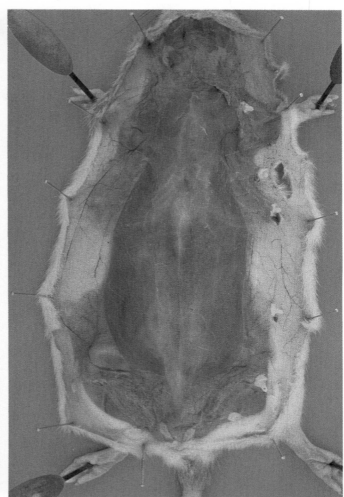

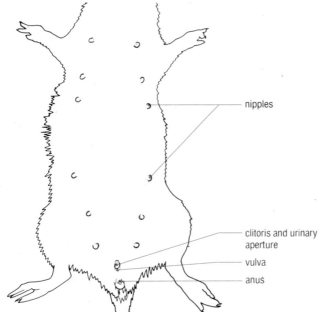

nipples

clitoris and urinary
aperture

vulva

anus

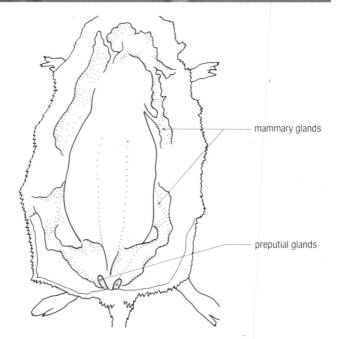

mammary glands

preputial glands

Fig. 6.7 External features of a lactating female rat

● Pin the rat out with wooden-handled awls.

Fig. 6.8 Mammary glands dissected

● Make a median incision through the skin from the urinary aperture to the throat.

● Carefully free the skin from the underlying muscles of the thorax and abdomen and deflect laterally to show the anterior and posterior mammary glands.

(The full dissection of the female urinogenital system can be carried out next, by following figs. 6.21, 6.22 and 6.23).

Abdominal cavity

When the rat has been skinned the divisions of the body can be seen (fig. 6.9). Posterior to the throat the pectoral muscles overly the ribs. The lower ends of the ribs demarcate the thorax which is a cavity closed at its lower end by the muscular diaphragm. It contains part of the digestive system, the heart and the lungs. Volume changes of the thoracic cavity, (produced either by the ribs and intercostal muscles or by the diaphragm), induce pressure changes in the lungs responsible for inhalation and exhalation.

The abdomen has no external bony protection comparable to the ribs of the thorax. The abdominal contents are supported by the body wall muscles and held in position by connective tissue mesenteries.

The liver is the most prominent organ of the abdominal cavity (fig. 6.10). It performs a similar role to that of birds and lizards in detoxification and regulation of nutrients in the blood.

As in other vertebrates the stomach is used as a place for storage, for mechanical digestion and for initiating enzymatic digestion. Various regions of the stomach contain different cell-linings (epithelia). The oesophageal end of the stomach has a non-glandular lining, like that of the oesophagus. The cardiac region is peculiar to mammals and contains tubular mucus-secreting glands. The fundic region contains chief cells responsible for producing digestive enzymes and parietal cells which secrete hydrochloric acid. The pyloric region contains tubular glands rather like those of the cardiac region.

The inner surface of the mammalian intestine is greatly increased in area in a number of ways. Small finger-like projections, villi, of microscopic size, are found on the gut wall. These should not be confused with microvilli, which are invaginations of individual cells of the intestine, and therefore much smaller. Furthermore the surface of the intestine may be thrown into larger folds, such as the folds of Kerkring. Lastly, the whole intestine is elongated and coiled up on itself (fig. 6.11). This large surface area is essential in animals which either have a high metabolic rate, or are large, or both, since a high metabolic rate requires rapid breakdown of a large quantity of food. A large animal faces problems concerning its surface area/volume ratio. As the animal's length increases, its volume (the amount of tissue to be nourished) increases by the length cubed. The amount of surface area of the intestine available to absorb food only increases by area, the length squared. Therefore, in a large animal there must be a disproportionate increase in intestinal surface area to cope with increased body size.

Mammals do not produce an enzyme to break down the cellulose found in plant material. At the junction of the large and small intestines, a pouch, the caecum, is found. This contains a flora of symbiotic bacteria which produce the necessary enzyme, cellulase. In herbivorous mammals, like the rabbit, the caecum can be very large. In the rat, where seeds and nuts form a large part of the natural diet, the caecum is also relatively large. In man it is reduced to the vermiform appendix. Animals with a small caecum may still feed on plant matter. They pierce the cellulose cell-walls with their teeth to extract the nutrients inside. The cell-wall itself is not metabolised, but simply egested, and a large quantity of potential nutrients is lost.

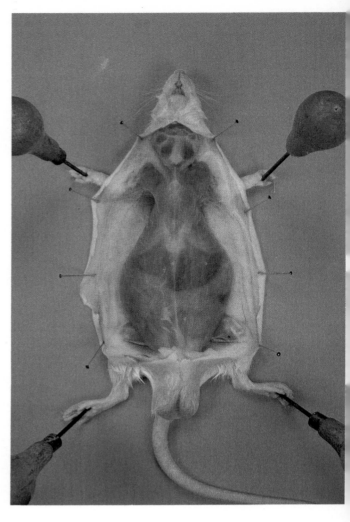

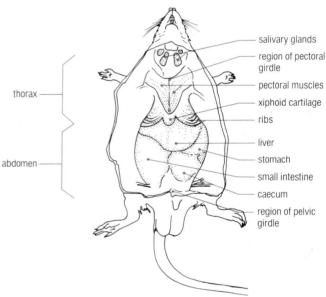

Fig. 6.9 Abdominal cavity – 1st dissection stage

(This dissection stage follows that shown in fig. 6.6)

● Cut through the skin by a median ventral incision from the lower abdomen to the neck, and deflect the skin laterally, as seen already in fig. 6.8.

● Take care not to damage blood vessels to the skin from the region of the pectoral and pelvic girdles.

● Some animals may contain an excessive amount of fat which obscures the body organs. If such fat reserves are present, they should be removed by using blunt forceps.

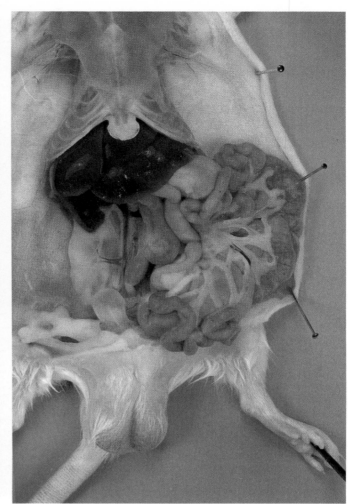

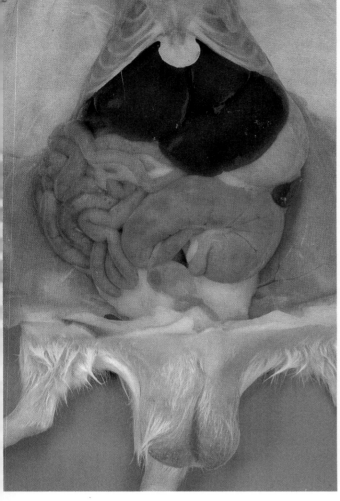

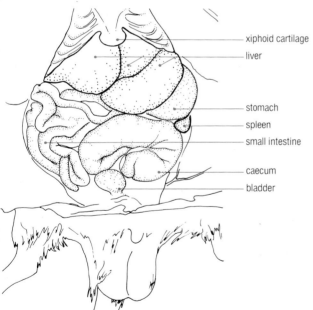

xiphoid cartilage
liver

stomach
spleen
small intestine

caecum
bladder

stomach
posterior vena cava
small intestine
left renal vein
kidney
mesentery
branches of hepatic portal vein
pancreas
caecum
duodenum
rectum
large intestine
bladder

Fig. 6.10 Abdominal cavity – 2nd dissection stage

● Make a median incision in the abdominal muscle from the lower abdomen to the xiphoid cartilage at the base of the rib cage.

● Make lateral cuts anteriorly and posteriorly to deflect the abdominal wall and expose the viscera.

● Take care not to damage the underlying structures, especially the liver, which will bleed copiously if cut.

Fig. 6.11 Abdominal cavity – 3rd dissection stage

● Move the gut over to the animal's left side and unravel it as far as possible, without cutting any of the mesentery.

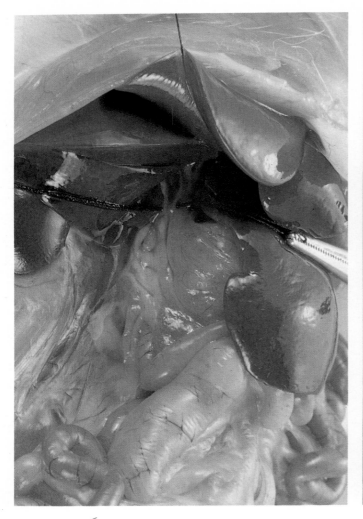

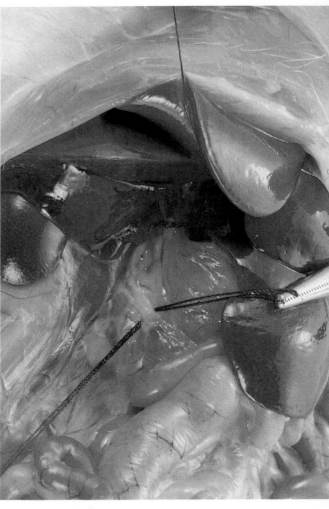

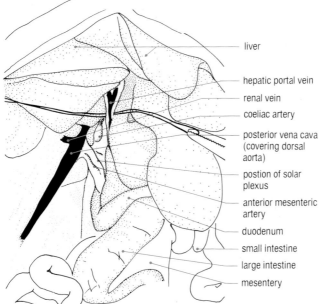

liver
hepatic portal vein
renal vein
coeliac artery
posterior vena cava (covering dorsal aorta)
postion of solar plexus
anterior mesenteric artery
duodenum
small intestine
large intestine
mesentery

hepatic portal vein
first ligature
renal vein
coeliac artery
anterior mesenteric artery
posterior vena cava

Fig. 6.12 Abdominal cavity – 4th dissection stage

● Remove the gut as follows:

● Displace the alimentary canal to reveal the hepatic portal vein and the coeliac and anterior mesenteric arteries. The solar plexus can be seen lying between the two arteries.

● Gently draw a thread under the hepatic portal vein close to this vessel's entry into the liver.

Fig. 6.13 Abdominal cavity – 5th dissection stage

● Knot the thread round the hepatic portal vein and cut it short.

● Make a small incision between the coeliac and anterior mesenteric arteries and gently pull a second thread under the anterior mesenteric.

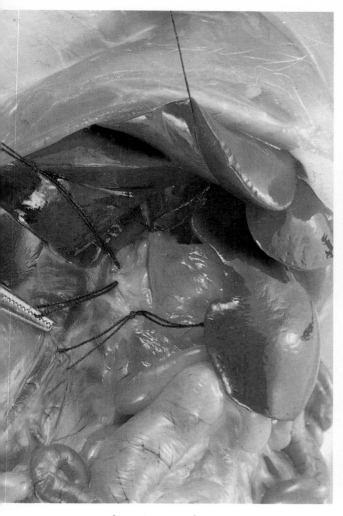

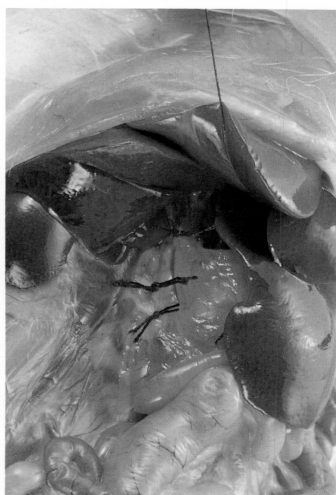

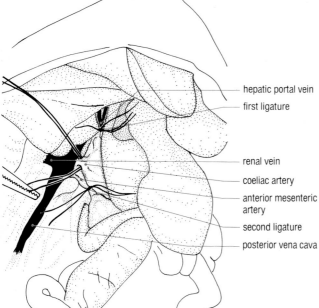

hepatic portal vein
first ligature

renal vein
coeliac artery

anterior mesenteric
artery

second ligature
posterior vena cava

hepatic portal vein
first ligature
renal vein
coeliac artery
third ligature
anterior mesenteric
artery
second ligature
posterior vena cava

**Fig. 6.14 Abdominal cavity
– 6th dissection stage**

● Knot and cut this second
thread.

● Gently draw a third thread
through this incision so that it
lies under the coeliac artery.

**Fig. 6.15 Abdominal cavity
– 7th dissection stage**

● Knot and cut the third
thread, leaving all three
vessels ligatured in
preparation for the removal of
the alimentary canal.

Male urinogenital system

The male urinogenital system of mammals (fig. 6.16) resembles that of reptiles in that the sperm and urine travel separately to the exterior. Urine passes from the kidney to the bladder via the ureter which is a new duct not derived directly from the archinephric duct. Sperm are transported in the vasa efferentia to the epididymis which is a long, coiled tube leading to the vas deferens. The vas deferens, as in male reptiles, is derived from the archinephric duct.

In fish and amphibians, the testis was situated in the abdominal cavity, near the kidney. In mammals, reptiles and birds there is no need for the two organs to be in close proximity since they do not share any ducts connecting them to the exterior, apart from the urethra in mammals. Therefore, the testis is free to migrate. It is thought that the temperature of the mammalian body is too high for sperm development, hence the cooler location of the testis in most mammals, below the abdomen and just under the skin. The spermatic cord connects the testis to the abdomen and contains the spermatic artery and vein running to the dorsal aorta and vena cava respectively (fig. 6.17).

The kidney is metanephric, that is, the kidney tubules develop from the more posterior segments of the embryo. The number of tubules is greatly increased over the ancestral number of one per segment. The renal corpuscle is moderately sized and quite considerable quantities of water pass into the tubule. However, a mammalian and avian innovation, the loop of Henle, which is a new section of kidney tubule, ensures that much of this water (as well as useful substances such as glucose) is reabsorbed. The end-point of nitrogenous metabolism is urea.

Several glands are associated with the male reproductive system (fig. 6.19). The vesicula seminalis is a long pouch which opens into the lower end of the vas deferens; it secretes a thick liquid which is part of the seminal fluid. The prostate gland produces a thinner fluid and, like the Cowper's gland, opens into the urethra. Seminal fluid is thought to contain substances which activate and nourish the sperm for their passage through the female reproductive tract.

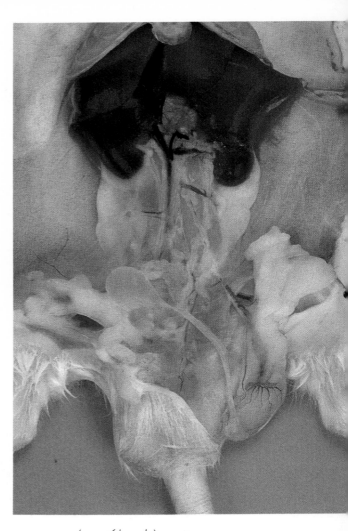

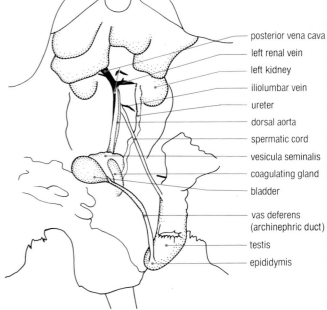

- posterior vena cava
- left renal vein
- left kidney
- iliolumbar vein
- ureter
- dorsal aorta
- spermatic cord
- vesicula seminalis
- coagulating gland
- bladder
- vas deferens (archinephric duct)
- testis
- epididymis

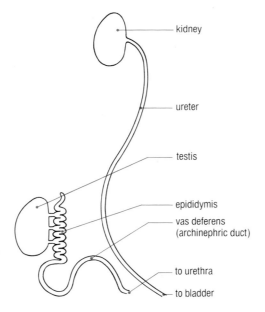

- kidney
- ureter
- testis
- epididymis
- vas deferens (archinephric duct)
- to urethra
- to bladder

Fig. 6.16. The male mammalian urinogenital system.

Fig. 6.17 Male urinogenital system – 1st dissection stage

● Cut the gut just above the entry of the oesophagus into the stomach, and across the lower rectum.

● Free the gut by cutting away the mesentry, starting at the rectum. The spleen and pancreas can be removed at the same time. Removal of the gut reveals the urinogenital system.

● Open the left half of the scrotal sac. Notice how the testis is connected to the abdominal cavity by the spermatic cord, which is composed of the spermatic artery and vein, and the vas deferens. Keep this part of the dissection moist; if the connective tissue dries out, it will be very difficult to find and dissect out the ureter.

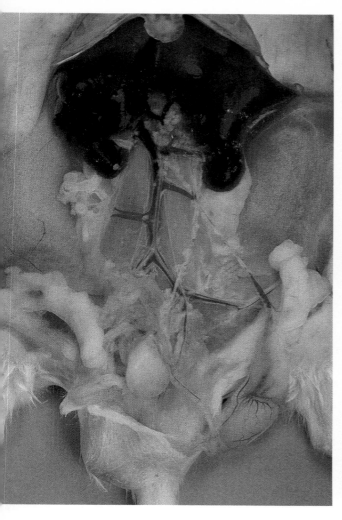

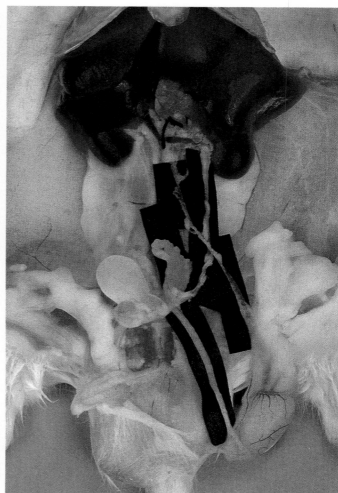

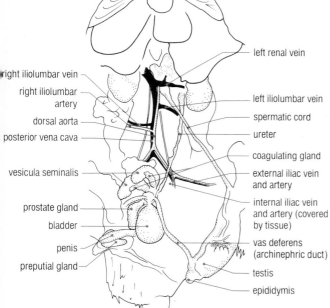

right iliolumbar vein
right iliolumbar artery
dorsal aorta
posterior vena cava
vesicula seminalis
prostate gland
bladder
penis
preputial gland

left renal vein
left iliolumbar vein
spermatic cord
ureter
coagulating gland
external iliac vein and artery
internal iliac vein and artery (covered by tissue)
vas deferens (archinephric duct)
testis
epididymis

ureter
vesicula seminalis
coagulating gland
bladder
spermatic cord
prostate gland
cut edges of pubis
vas deferens (archinephric duct)
Cowper's gland
urethra
penis
testis
epididymis

Fig. 6.18 Male urinogenital system – 2nd dissection stage

Carefully dissect away the thin layer of connective tissue covering the dorsal aorta and posterior vena cava so as to expose these vessels and the arteries and veins serving the abdomen.

Find the ureter and remove the surrounding connective tissue.

● Clear and display the spermatic cord, vas deferens and accessory structures.

Fig. 6.19 Male urinogenital system – 3rd dissection stage

● Remove the muscle on the ventral surface of the pubis. Then using a pair of large scissors, cut through the pubis and ischium on either side a short distance away from the midline, taking care not to damage underlying structures or the prostate gland anteriorly. Now remove the mid-ventral portion of the pelvic girdle.

● Once the ventral portion of the pelvic girdle is free, it can be dissected clear to expose the underlying urethra, Cowper's gland and rectum.

● Black paper has been inserted underneath the ureter, spermatic cord and vas deferens to show these structures more clearly.

Female urinogenital system

Certain similarities exist between the male and female urinogenital systems; the kidney of both sexes is similar and the ureter is quite separate from the archinephric duct. However, in the female, the oviduct is also quite distinct from the archinephric duct (fig. 6.20) and the latter degenerates completely during development.

The ovary is situated in the abdominal cavity (fig. 6.21) and during development it makes a short migration ventrally and posteriorly. Eggs pass from the ovaries into the Fallopian tubes (the upper sections of the oviducts). Here they are fertilised and travel to the uterus to implant. Rats are spontaneous ovulators which means that ovulation occurs regularly (every 4-5 days in practice) regardless of whether copulation occurs.

Placental mammals retain the young within the body to develop and the lower part of the oviduct is modified into a muscular tube, the uterus, where the embryos are nourished. The uterine epithelium, or endometrium, is richly vascularised and unites with the outer membranes of the embryo to form the placenta. The uterus may have various shapes in mammals. The primitive condition is probably that which we see in the rat where there are two completely separate branches which unite only at the vagina, the duplex condition, fig. 6.23. In most mammals the distal parts of the two branches fuse together (bicornute or bipartite) and in higher primates the fusion is complete, producing the simplex condition.

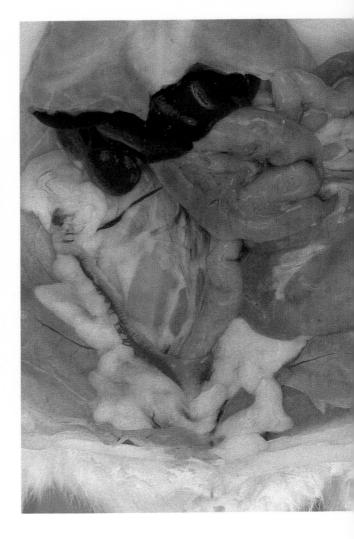

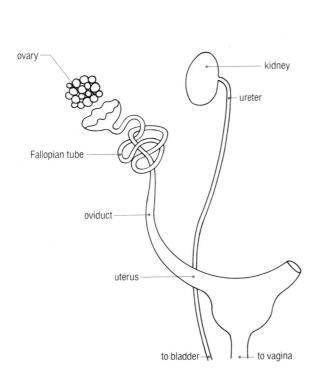

Fig. 6.20. The female mammalian urinogenital system.

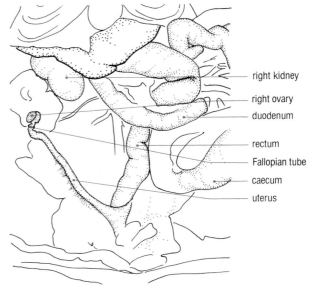

Fig. 6.21 Female urino-genital system – 1st dissection stage

● (This dissection stage can follow fig. 6.8 if necessary).

● Cut and deflect the skin and abdominal wall as described in figs. 6.9 and 6.10. Displace the gut to the animal's left side to reveal the right side of the reproductive system lying in place.

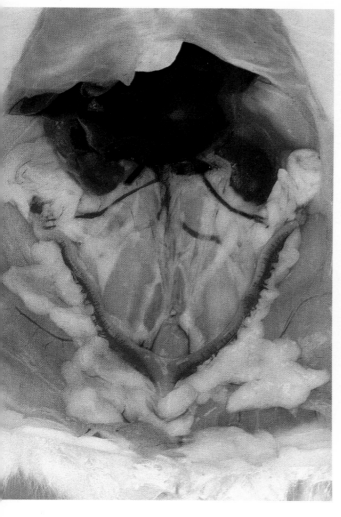

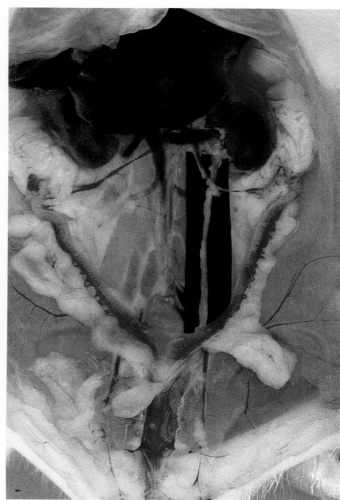

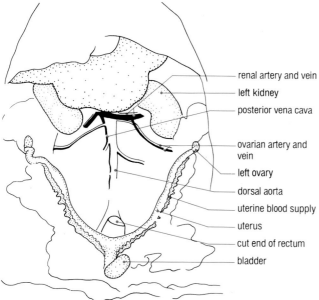

renal artery and vein
left kidney
posterior vena cava
ovarian artery and vein
left ovary
dorsal aorta
uterine blood supply
uterus
cut end of rectum
bladder

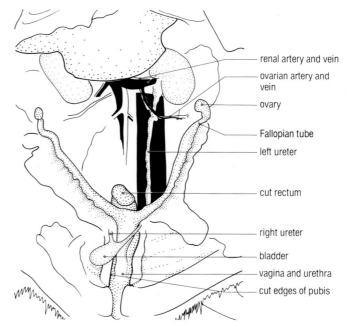

renal artery and vein
ovarian artery and vein
ovary
Fallopian tube
left ureter
cut rectum
right ureter
bladder
vagina and urethra
cut edges of pubis

Fig. 6.22 Female urino-genital system – 2nd dissection stage

Remove the gut using the same procedure as in the male rat (figs. 6.12 – 6.17), to reveal the urinogenital system and the main abdominal blood vessels ing in place.

Fig. 6.23 Female urino-genital system – 3rd dissection stage

● Clear the connective tissue surrounding the main blood vessels and dissect the whole length of the ureter free of other tissues.

● Clear and display the left ovary and its blood supply.

● Remove the muscle on the ventral surface of the pubis. Then, using a pair of large

scissors, cut through the pubis and ischium on either side a short distance away from the midline, taking care not to damage underlying structures. Now remove the mid-ventral portion of the pelvic girdle.

● Once the central portion of the pelvic girdle is free, it can be dissected clear to expose the urethra, vagina and rectum lying underneath.

Venous system

In the anterior venous system, the posterior cardinals of mammals, like those of amphibians and reptiles, are taken over by the hepatic vein, and the common cardinals are incorporated with the anterior cardinals into the anterior venae cavae (fig. 6.24). Further changes in the anterior veins take place in mammals and birds; the lateral head vein is replaced, as the vessel draining the cranium, by the internal jugulars. These meet the external jugulars to form the common jugulars, which join the subclavian veins and empty into the anterior venae cavae (figs. 6.26 and 6.27).

Various differences exist between the venous system of mammals and that of reptiles. We noted in amphibians that a branch of the hepatic vein had developed which runs dorsally and contacts the fused posterior cardinals, so forming a shortened route to the heart called the posterior vena cava. In the lizard we saw that the renal portal system was reduced, rendering the route to the heart via the renal portal and posterior cardinal less important. In mammals the renal portal system and the abdominal vein system are abandoned altogether (figs. 6.24 and 6.25). The only route to the heart is now along the posterior cardinals and posterior vena cava. This route is simply called the posterior vena cava, but this term hides the fact that the mammalian posterior vena cava is a composite of other venous systems: cardinals, renal portals and hepatic veins.

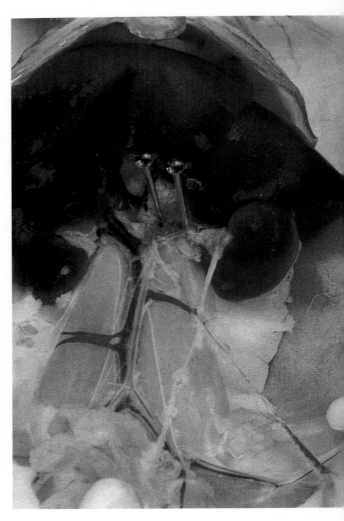

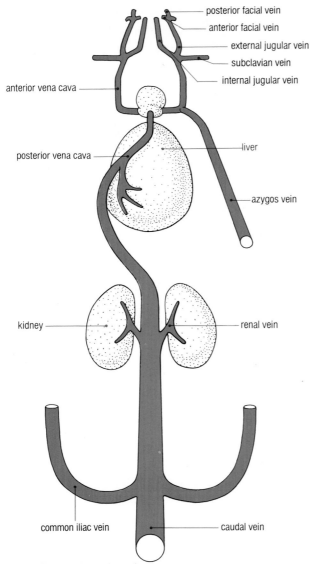

Fig. 6.24. The major veins of a mammal in ventral view.

Labels: posterior facial vein, anterior facial vein, external jugular vein, subclavian vein, internal jugular vein, anterior vena cava, liver, posterior vena cava, azygos vein, kidney, renal vein, common iliac vein, caudal vein

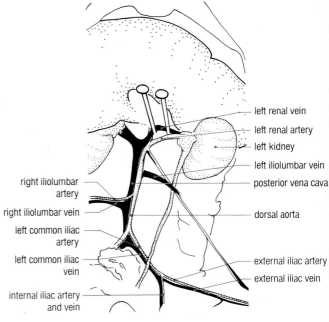

Labels: left renal vein, left renal artery, left kidney, left iliolumbar vein, posterior vena cava, dorsal aorta, external iliac artery, external iliac vein, right iliolumbar artery, right iliolumbar vein, left common iliac artery, left common iliac vein, internal iliac artery and vein

Fig. 6.25 Abdominal veins

● Dissect the main blood vessels free from one another to show the separate courses of the posterior vena cava and dorsal aorta. This dissection has been carried out in a male rat but applies equally to the female.

● Carefully dissect the left renal vein from the underlying left renal artery.

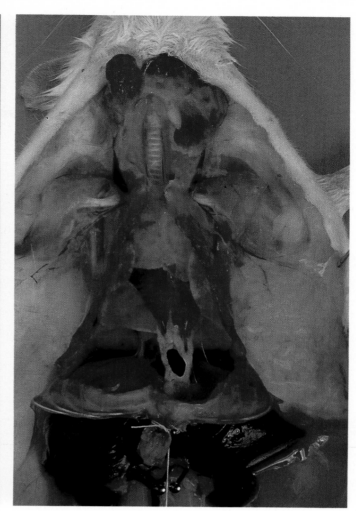

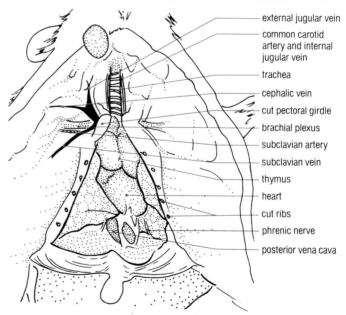

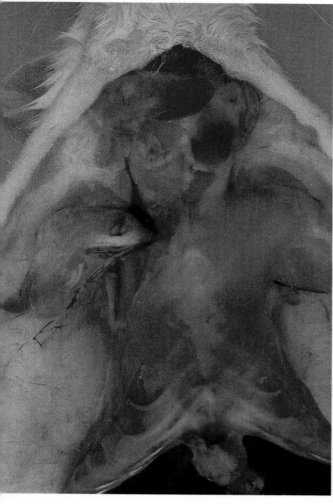

anterior facial vein
posterior facial vein
external jugular vein
cephalic vein

brachial plexus
subclavian artery
subclavian vein

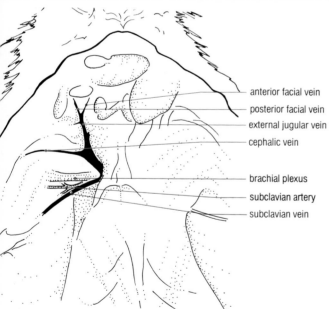

external jugular vein
common carotid artery and internal jugular vein
trachea
cephalic vein
cut pectoral girdle
brachial plexus
subclavian artery
subclavian vein
thymus
heart
cut ribs
phrenic nerve
posterior vena cava

Fig. 6.26 Anterior veins – 1st dissection stage

Deflect the skin of the neck laterally and locate the right external jugular vein.

Clear this forwards to reveal the anterior and posterior facial veins.

Trace the external jugular vein back to the exit of the anterior vena cava from the thorax to show the cephalic and subclavian veins.

● Carefully remove the muscle at the top of the forelimb to reveal the brachial nerve plexus and the subclavian artery.

Fig. 6.27 Anterior veins – 2nd dissection stage

● Make a median cut through the pectoral muscle and deflect laterally. Take care not to damage the anterior venae cavae where they emerge anteriorly.

● Lift up the xiphoid cartilage and carefully cut through the posterior wall of the thorax.

● Tie a piece of thread around the xiphoid cartilage and hook the other end around the tail. Cuts can now be made along each side of the thorax and across the ventral surface between ribs 1 and 2 to remove the rib cage.

● Expose the trachea by making a median cut through the manubrium at the anterior end of the rib cage, and carrying this cut forward up into the muscle of the neck.

Heart and aortic arches

The heart is completely divided, like that in birds, producing separate systemic and pulmonary circulations (figs. 6.28 and 6.29). Consequently blood pressure is kept at a relatively high level which is not only necessary for the efficient supply of nutrients to all tissues, but also essential for the functioning of the ultrafiltration system of the kidney.

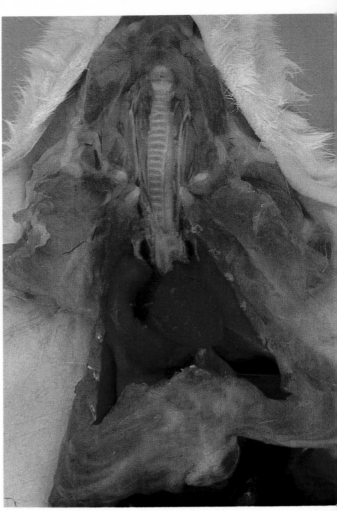

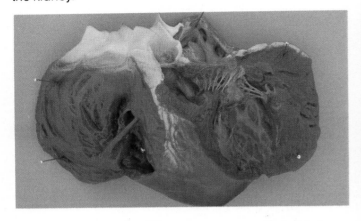

- systemic arch
- left atrium
- semilunar valve
- bicuspid valve
- interventricular septum
- left ventricle
- right ventricle

Fig. 6.28 A sheep's heart opened ventrally by a median incision through each ventricle. The left and right sides of the heart have been deflected laterally to show the mitral (bicuspid) valve on the right side and semilunar valves of the pulmonary arch on the left side.

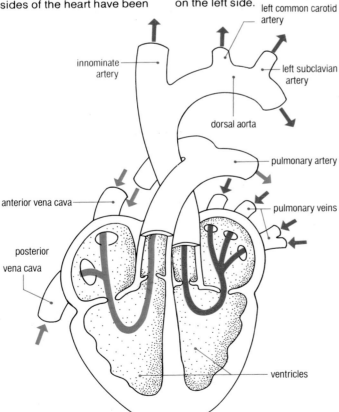

- innominate artery
- left common carotid artery
- left subclavian artery
- dorsal aorta
- pulmonary artery
- anterior vena cava
- pulmonary veins
- posterior vena cava
- ventricles

Fig. 6.29 A diagram of the mammalian heart cut open to show the separate paths of oxygenated (red) and deoxygenated (blue) blood.

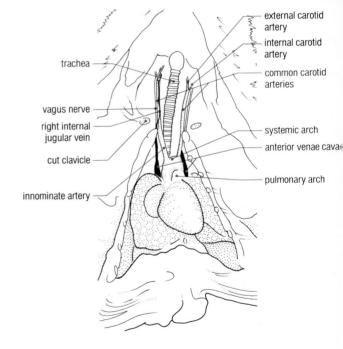

- external carotid artery
- internal carotid artery
- common carotid arteries
- trachea
- vagus nerve
- right internal jugular vein
- cut clavicle
- innominate artery
- systemic arch
- anterior venae cavae
- pulmonary arch

Fig. 6.30 Aortic arches – 1st dissection stage

● Gently dissect away the thymus gland to reveal the systemic arch and the anterior venae cavae.

● Trim the cut ends of the first pair of ribs, taking care not to leave any sharp ends and clean the neck region to show the innominate and carotid arteries.

6.16

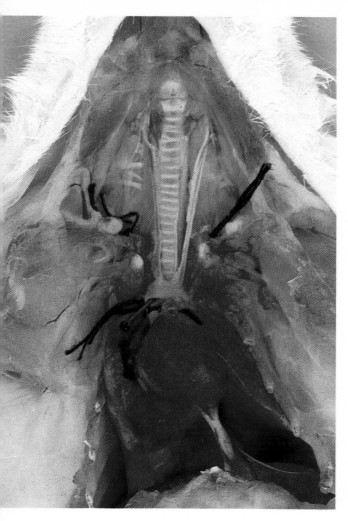

In birds there are only three of the six aortic arches present in fish: the sixth, or pulmonary arch, taking blood to the lungs; the fourth, or systemic arch, supplying the body and leading to the third, or carotid arch, supplying the head. Furthermore we saw that the fourth arch was not paired, the left branch having been eliminated. In mammals, the situation is almost identical, except that it is the right systemic arch that is eliminated, leaving the left arch to supply the body as the dorsal aorta (figs. 6.30, 6.31 and 6.32).

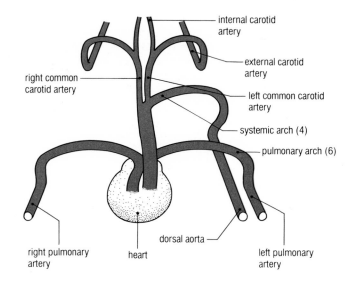

Fig. 6.32 The aortic arches of a mammal in ventral view.

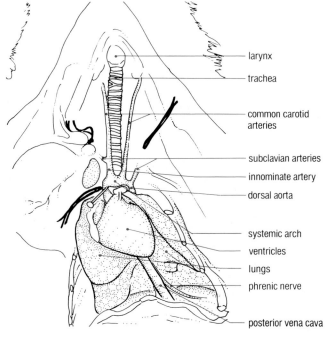

Fig. 6.31 Aortic arches – 2nd dissection stage

● Ligature the anterior venae cavae on each side by double ligature and cut them.

● Deflect the cut ends of these vessels laterally to reveal the anatomy of the systemic arch and the main arteries arising from it. Deflect the heart and oesophagus to show the left phrenic nerve serving the diaphragm.

Skull

Certain characteristics of the mammalian skull have already been mentioned in the introduction: a single bone in the lower jaw, the dentary; the reduction of the other bones in the lower jaw to become the middle ear bones; the replacement of teeth as a set only once during the animal's lifetime. In the rat skull (fig. 6.33) it is possible to see the single bone in the lower jaw, the dentary, but one cannot see the middle ear bones because they are covered over by a bony dome, the bulla.

One should note the large fenestra for attachment of the jaw musculature, and the crest along the braincase which marks the limit of muscle attachment. The single fenestra in the skull is evidence that mammals arose from the synapsid reptiles, as stated earlier, since those reptiles also had only one fenestra on each side of the skull. In early synapsids, and reptiles in general, the main jaw-closing muscles formed an undifferentiated mass inserting on the lower jaw. However, in mammals, the muscle mass is differentiated into a forwardly-directed component, the masseter, and a posteriorly-directed component, the temporalis (fig. 6.34), which enable the lower jaw to move backwards and forwards relative to the upper jaw.

A slip of the masseter jaw muscle runs through a special canal under the eye to insert on the snout. This is a peculiarity of the rat-like rodents. Together with the other parts of the masseter, it produces a very strong anterior pull on the lower jaw, increasing the effectiveness of gnawing and grinding. The incomplete zygomatic arch is another distinguishing rodent feature.

In rodents, the jaw hinge permits anterior and posterior sliding of the lower jaw in order to bring either the

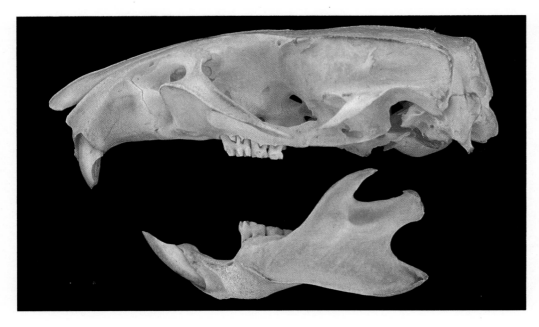

Fig. 6.33. The skull of the rat in left lateral view.

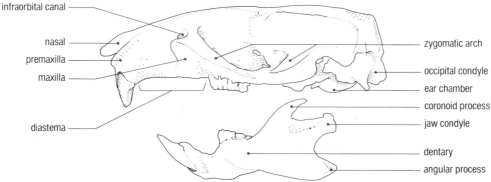

incisors or the cheek teeth into contact. Grinding is produced by a backwards and forwards motion of the lower molars across the upper molars. Notice the gap (diastema), between the two kinds of teeth. In life a fleshy cheek covers this gap at the side. The cheek can be drawn into the back of the diastema to close off the back of the mouth. In this way hard materials like nutshells and wood can be gnawed at without fragments passing into the throat. The rat has upper and lower jaws of equal width so that, in theory, the molars of both sides could be used at the same time. In practice, however, only one side of the jaw is used at a time.

The roof of the mouth shows a feature which is only well-developed in mammals, some synapsids, crocodiles and some dinosaurs. This is the secondary palate, (fig. 6.35). It is the bony shelf separating the mouth and nasal cavity. Air travels to the trachea through the nostrils which open far back in the mouth; this allows the animal to chew continually without interrupting its breathing. This is very important in an animal with a high metabolic rate which requires an adequate supply of both nutrients and oxygen.

In the nasal cavity there are thin, scroll-like bones, called turbinals, which support the elaborate nasal membranes. Their large surface area may enhance olfactory sensitivity. They may also assist in temperature regulation by warming air passing into the lungs and cooling air passing out of the lungs.

The occipital surface of the skull shows the large foramen magnum where the nerve cord passes through to the brain, and the double occipital condyle which articulates with the atlas vertebra.

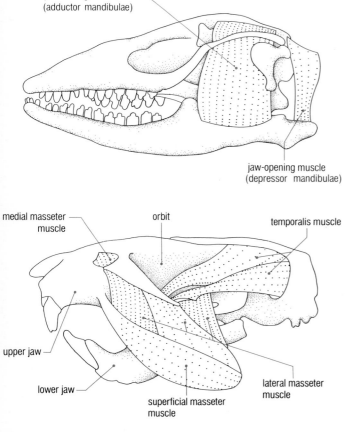

Fig. 6.34. A comparison of the jaw musculature of the lizard (above) and the rat (below). Note the undifferentiated jaw adductor muscle in the lizard, and the temporalis and masseter muscles in the rat.

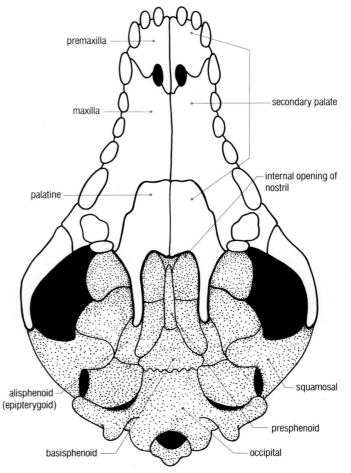

Fig. 6.35. A diagram of the mammalian palate.

7 The Vertebrate Brain

Introduction

It is possible that the early vertebrate brain was no more than a slight enlargement of the spinal cord in the head region where sensory stimuli were picked up and transmitted to the body, and where neuronal pathways would be found which permitted local reflexes in the head and throat. Apart from these interactions, the body would not have come under the influence of the 'brain'.

The trend in evolution is for the brain to increase its control of the body and consequently the size and complexity of the brain also increases. There is a tendency for nerve cells concerned with specific functions to gather in ganglia, or nuclei, which are connected by bundles of fibres, or tracts, but originally the interconnections may have been just a loose network of fibres. The brain of living vertebrates is composed of two symmetrical halves and there are connections called commissures between the same regions in each half.

The main regions of the brain and their development in ontogeny were described briefly on p. 1.31. The following survey illustrates some of the variation in brain structure found in the vertebrates.

7.1

The dogfish

In primitive vertebrates the main centres of nervous activity develop from the anterior part of the brain stem. One such centre, important in the dogfish, is a thickening of the dorsal wall of the optic lobe called the tectum; a section of the brain would show that the tectum is superficial to the optic lobe. The tectum coordinates motor activity, receives sensory stimuli and sends out motor stimuli; it is the major coordinating centre of the dogfish brain. The optic lobes receive stimuli from the eyes and are usually less developed than those of bony fish.

The cerebral hemispheres are not elaborated apart from the large olfactory lobes. The brain of a bony fish closely resembles that of a cartilaginous one in most respects but the cerebral hemispheres are different in that the grey matter (nerve cell bodies which originally surround the spinal canal) forms a massive thickening which displaces the ventricle (the cavity in the middle of the brain) from below. In all fish, the cerebral hemispheres are concerned chiefly with receiving olfactory stimuli.

The hypothalamus is large and bears a vascular sac (found only in fish, both bony and cartilaginous) which may register internal and external fluid pressure. The hypothalamus is the major integrative centre for visceral activities.

The cerebellum is large in active species of

elasmobranchs, as expected, since it is responsible for motor coordination and posture regulation. It accumulates and synthesises information about the position and locomotor activity of the body and relays this information to higher brain centres such as the tectum and cerebral hemispheres. The thalamus (not visible in a surface view) contains both sensory and motor coordination areas and it is not particularly well-developed in elasmobranchs. The motor coordination centres relay information to the brain stem, whereas the sensory areas pass on their information to the cerebral hemispheres.

The frog

The brain of an amphibian resembles that of an elasmobranch very closely; processing of olfactory stimuli is still the main function of the cerebral hemispheres. However, the amphibian brain differs from that of an elasmobranch in that the two cerebral hemispheres are quite far apart and the optic lobes are only moderately developed. The most striking aspect is the rudimentary nature of the cerebellum.

The reptilian brain differs quite considerably from that of the amphibian in possessing larger, more complex cerebral hemispheres. Some of the grey matter of the cerebrum has spread outwards towards the surface to form the cortex, or pallium. Although still concerned with olfactory stimuli, the cerebrum has further correlation functions and competes with the tectum for dominance of brain functions. Some reptiles also develop a new

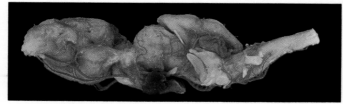

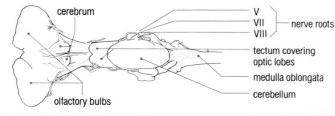

cerebrum

V
VII } nerve roots
VIII

tectum covering optic lobes

medulla oblongata

cerebellum

olfactory bulbs

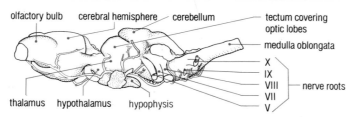

olfactory bulb   cerebral hemisphere   cerebellum

tectum covering optic lobes

medulla oblongata

X
IX
VIII } nerve roots
VII
V

thalamus   hypothalamus   hypophysis

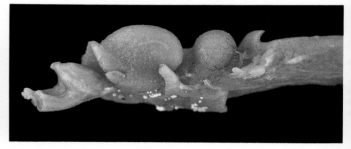

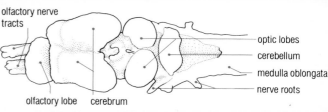

olfactory nerve tracts

optic lobes

cerebellum

medulla oblongata

nerve roots

olfactory lobe   cerebrum

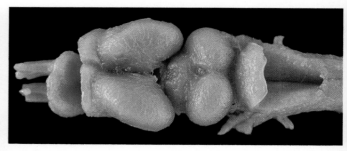

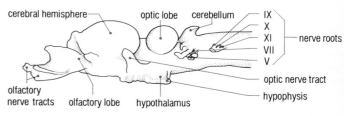

cerebral hemisphere   optic lobe   cerebellum

IX
X
XI } nerve roots
VII
V

optic nerve tract

hypophysis

olfactory nerve tracts   olfactory lobe   hypothalamus

Fig. 7.1 The dogfish brain in dorsal view (top) and left lateral view (bottom). Note the latex-injected blood vessels.

Fig. 7.2 The frog brain in dorsal view (top) and left lateral view (bottom).

region of the cortex called the neocortex (neopallium); this is not visible in a surface view. This is an association centre relaying various sensory stimuli from the brain stem to the medulla. In the floor of the cerebral hemispheres the basal nuclei are large and act as a relay centre to the thalamus and brainstem.

Further differences between the reptilian and amphibian brains are seen in the relative sizes of the olfactory and optic lobes; the olfactory lobes of the reptile are smaller, whereas the optic lobes are larger, reflecting the well developed vision of reptiles.

The pigeon
The cerebral hemispheres of birds are even larger than those in reptiles, but no elaboration of the cortex has taken place. This may be because smell is not important in most birds; the olfactory lobes are usually small. However, the optic lobes are very large (birds have very acute vision) and the basal nuclei are expanded and may be the place where the stereotyped avian behaviour patterns reside. The tectum is still important as a coordinating centre.

The cerebellum is large and convoluted and bears a particularly large area, the neocerebellum, which is concerned with flight. The elaboration of the cerebellum and the cerebrum requires the development of a new structure, the pons, which is a mass of fibres connecting these two areas (only visible in a section). The greater coordinating function of the cerebrum has resulted in the

nuclei of the thalamus taking on the funtion of relaying information and, consequently, the dorsal part of the thalamus is well developed.

The rat
The cerebral hemispheres are again greatly enlarged, this time by the development of the neocortex. The hemispheres are convoluted to increase the surface area in large mammals but remain simple in the rat. They have taken over the functions of the basal nuclei, some brainstem centres and the tectum, and are involved in newer and higher levels of activity – correlation, association and learning. This increased control of coordination by the cerebrum has resulted in a further elaboration of the thalamus as a relay centre. The cerebellum is also large and convoluted and a distinct pons connects it with the cerebral hemispheres.

The hypothalamus is highly differentiated; it is concerned with maintaining homeostasis by the regulation of temperature, blood pressure, and respiration.

The optic lobes are smaller because the role of the tectum in integration has been taken over by the cerebral hemispheres, and the tectum is now a reflex centre. The olfactory lobes are often well-developed, reflecting the importance of the sense of smell.

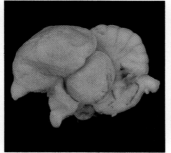
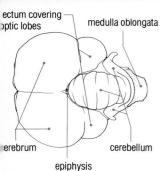
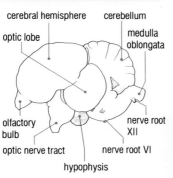
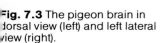

olfactory bulb — cerebral hemisphere — cerebellum
tectum covering optic lobes — medulla oblongata
optic lobe — medulla oblongata
cerebrum — cerebellum — epiphysis
olfactory bulb — optic nerve tract — hypophysis — nerve root XII — nerve root VI

Fig. 7.3 The pigeon brain in dorsal view (left) and left lateral view (right).

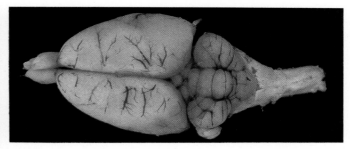

olfactory bulb — cerebellum
— central vermis
— flocculo-nodular zone
neocortex of cerebrum — medulla oblongata
— lateral hemispheres
— epiphysis

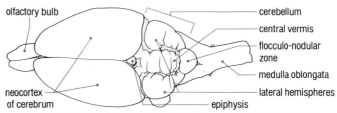
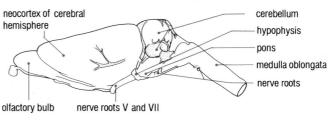

neocortex of cerebral hemisphere — cerebellum
— hypophysis
— pons
— medulla oblongata
— nerve roots
olfactory bulb — nerve roots V and VII

Fig. 7.4 The rat brain in dorsal view (top) and left lateral view (bottom).

7.3

Index

The numbers in **Bold** refer to figures.